Relocating Germanness

Discursive Disunity in Unified Germany

Edited by

Patrick Stevenson
Reader in Modern Languages
University of Southampton

and

John Theobald
Associate Professor in Modern Languages
Southampton Institute

First published in Great Britain 2000 by
MACMILLAN PRESS LTD
Houndmills, Basingstoke, Hampshire RG21 6XS and London
Companies and representatives throughout the world

A catalogue record for this book is available from the British Library.

ISBN 0–333–79462–1

 First published in the United States of America 2000 by
ST. MARTIN'S PRESS, INC.,
Scholarly and Reference Division,
175 Fifth Avenue, New York, N.Y. 10010

ISBN 0–312–23043–5

Library of Congress Cataloging-in-Publication Data
Relocating Germanness : discursive disunity in unified Germany / edited by
Patrick Stevenson and John Theobald.
p.   cm.
Includes bibliographical references and index.
ISBN 0–312–23043–5
1. Germany—Politics and government—1990– 2. Germany—Social conditions—
1990– 3. National characteristics, German. 4. Germany—Intellectual life—20th
century. 5. Political culture—Germany. I. Stevenson, Patrick II. Theobald, John,
1946–
DD290.29 .R46   1999
943.087'9—dc21

99–049748

This book is printed on paper suitable for recycling and made from fully managed and sustained
forest sources.

10   9   8   7   6   5   4   3   2   1
09   08   07   06   05   04   03   02   01   00

Printed and bound in Great Britain by
Antony Rowe Ltd, Chippenham, Wiltshire

Contents

List of Tables

List of Figures

Acknowledgements

We are very grateful to the British Academy, the Arts Faculty School of Research and Graduate Studies at the University of Southampton, and Southampton Institute for providing financial support for the conference on which this book is based. We would also like to express our gratitude to colleagues and students in Southampton who contributed in various ways to the organization of the conference, especially Alan Bance, Karine Brissy, Jane Copeland, Frances Nyland and Jean Watts. Finally, special thanks are due to Mike Weaver, who conceived the idea of the conference with us and helped to organize it.

PATRICK STEVENSON
JOHN THEOBALD

Preface

This book is the concrete outcome of a conference held in Southampton in April 1998 under the title *Dis-unification: Competing Constructions of Contemporary Germany*. The principal aim of the conference was to bring together people working in different academic disciplines (sociolinguistics, discourse analysis, economics, politics, oral history, literature and cabaret, among others), but who shared a common interest in contemporary Germany and whose research was based on the analysis of texts in the broadest sense of the term. Its motivation was the widespread recognition amongst observers that, almost 10 years after the fall of the Berlin Wall, the politically and economically unified Germany was characterized by continuing social and cultural disunity, by diverging discourses and multiple identities. Starting from the premise that 'the Germans' were still attempting to relocate themselves amidst the complex realities of the post-unification world, participants in the conference were invited to make a contribution to the discursive mapping of contemporary Germany, from which new constructions of Germanness might emerge.

Individual papers dealt with a very wide range of topics within this general theme, and so for the purposes of this book it was necessary to concentrate on exploring one aspect of it. For reasons that we hope are made clear in our opening chapter, we chose to focus on issues relating to the particular question of the continuing east-west division of Germany. However, we would like to take this opportunity to acknowledge the many stimulating papers that were given at the conference but which fell outside this more narrowly circumscribed topic. We also look forward to the completion of work still in progress by younger researchers such as Joannah Caborn (Duisburg), Stefanie Lotz (Lancaster), Julie Maxwell (Leicester), Mechthild Matheja-Theaker (Bristol), Alissa Shethar (Berkeley), Mike Weaver (Southampton) and Ulrike Zitzlsperger (Exeter).

We hope that the book will appeal to a broad readership, and we believe that it has things to say both to those interested in German studies and to non-German-speakers working in the fields of discourse and communication. For the benefit of this latter constituency, we have translated all German material (individual words, quotations, and transcripts of speech) into English, but it may also be worth pointing out for them two particular points of usage that might otherwise be confusing. First, most of the chapters refer at some point to the *Wende*, a term meaning 'radical change of direction' or 'turning point', and which has been used in connection with various significant moments in post-war German history. In the recent past, however, it has been used almost universally to designate the period of upheaval in late 1989 which heralded the demise of the GDR. More broadly, it is used as a shorthand means of marking contrasts between the periods before and after unification: 'before/after the *Wende*'. Second, although the book deals with contemporary Germany, the authors inevitably refer also to the past, and in line with common practice elsewhere we have tried to differentiate between references to the past (by using the terms East and West) and references to the present (by using east and west, or eastern and western). There are undoubtedly some grey areas, but we have tried to be consistent in this practice, and we hope that readers will find it helpful.

Southampton

PATRICK STEVENSON
JOHN THEOBALD

Notes on the Contributors

Peter Auer is Professor of German Linguistics at the University of Freiburg, Germany. He has done extensive research on bilingualism, phonology, dialectology, prosody, and syntactic aspects of spoken language. His many publications include: *Bilingual Conversation* (John Benjamins, 1984), *Phonologie der Alltagssprache* (de Gruyter, 1990), and (with Elizabeth Couper-Kuhlen and Frank Müller) *Language in Time* (Oxford University Press, 1999); and, as editor, *Code-switching in Conversation* (Routledge, 1998), and three books co-edited with Aldo di Luzio: *Interpretive Sociolinguistics* (Narr, 1982), *Variation and Convergence* (de Gruyter, 1988), and *The Contextualization of Language* (John Benjamins, 1992).

Birgit Barden has been working since 1996 on a research project on properties of spoken German (Eigenschaften gesprochener Sprache) at the Institut für Deutsche Sprache, Mannheim, Germany. Her main research interests are sociolinguistics, German dialectology, conversation analysis, and structures of spoken German. She recently published (with Beate Großkopf) *Sprachliche Akkommodation und soziale Integration. Sächsische Übersiedler und Übersiedlerinnen im rhein-/moselfränkischen und alemannischen Sprachraum* (Niemeyer, 1998), and (with Peter Auer and Beate Großkopf) 'Subjective and objective parameters determining "salience" in long-term dialect accommodation' in *Journal of Sociolinguistics* (1998).

Jennifer Dailey-O'Cain is Assistant Professor of Germanic Linguistics at the University of Alberta in Canada. Her main areas of research are sociolinguistic variation and language attitudes. Recent publications include: 'Canadian raising in a midwestern U.S. city' in *Language Variation and Change* (1997), 'The perception of post-unification German regional speech' in Dennis Preston (ed.) *Handbook of Perceptual Dialectology*, vol. 1 (John Benjamins, 1999), and (with Meghan McKinnie) 'A perceptual dialectology of anglophone Canada from the perception of young Albertans and Ontarians', to appear in *Handbook of Perceptual Dialectology*, vol. 2.

Stephan Elspaß is a Lecturer in Linguistics at the Westfälische Wilhelms-Universität Münster, Germany. His main research interests are in language and politics, sociolinguistics, phraseology, the history of New High German (especially nineteenth century), and German as a Foreign Language. His recent publications include: *Phraseologie in der politischen Rede. Untersuchungen zur Verwendung von Phraseologismen in ausgewählten Bundestagsdebatten* (Westdeutscher Verlag, 1998), and 'Phraseologie im deutschen Parlamentarismus. Zu historischen Entwicklungen im Sprachverhalten politischer Redner', in Armin Burkhardt and Kornelia Pape (eds) *Sprache des deutschen Parlamentarismus* (Westdeutscher Verlag, forthcoming).

Kathrin Hörschelmann is completing her PhD on 'Placing "The East" in The German Nation: Representations of Otherness in German National and Regional Television' at the University of Bristol, UK. Her main research interests are in the field of socio-cultural and feminist geography, media studies, and the impact of globalized media on youth identity. She has written several articles relating to her current research, including 'Watching the East: constructions of "otherness" in TV representations of East Germany' (*Applied Geography*, 1999).

Helen Kelly-Holmes is a Lecturer in German in the School of Languages and European Studies, Aston University, Birmingham, UK. Her main research interests include intercultural aspects of marketing and media discourses (in particular advertising) and how these relate to identities and perceptions of identities. Her recent publications include the following edited volumes: (with Sue Wright) *Languages in Contact and Conflict* (Multilingual Matters, 1994), (with Christina Schäffner) *Discourse and Ideologies* (Multilingual Matters, 1996), and (with Nigel Reeves) *The European Business Environment: Germany* (International Thompson Press, 1997).

Grit Liebscher studied at the University of Leipzig, Germany, and is currently completing her PhD at the University of Texas at Austin, USA. Her main research interests are conversation analysis, ethnography of communication, media interaction, deixis, and language and identity. Her recent publications include: (with M. Egbert and A. Vlatten) *Aktuelle Videos für Wirtschaftsdeutsch* (American Association of Teachers of German, 1995), 'Unified Germany(?): Processes of identifying, redefining and negotiating in interactions between east and west Germans' in A. Chy *et al.* (eds) *Proceedings of the Fourth Annual Symposium about Language and Society Austin* (University of Texas at Austin, 1997), and, as editor (with M. Brody and H. Ogren) *Proceedings* *of the Sixth Annual Symposium about Language and Society Austin* (forthcoming).

Beth Linklater is a Lecturer in German at the University of Wales, Swansea. Her research interests are in GDR literature and sexual identities. Her book *'Und immer zügelloser wird die Lust'. Constructions of Sexuality in East German Literature* was published by Peter Lang in 1998. She has also written widely on the work of Irmtraud Morgner and Gabriele Stötzer Kachold.

Joanne McNally is currently working as a guest researcher for a project on East German cabaret at the Zentrum für Zeithistorische Forschung Potsdam, Germany. Before this she worked for eight years as lecturer and senior lecturer in German at the University of Brighton, UK. Her research interests focus on German cabaret, and also on irony and satire in the language classroom. Her PhD (King's College London), entitled '"Creative Misbehaviour": The Use of German *Kabarett* within Advanced Foreign Language Learning Classrooms', combined the cultural and linguistic operational levels of cabaret with pedagogical concerns. Forthcoming publications include 'The changing discourses of German cabaret in response to National Socialism between 1929 and 1935' in The Twentieth Amherst Colloquium on German Literature, Amherst Colloquia Series.

Ulrike Hanna Meinhof is Professor of Cultural Studies at the University of Bradford, UK. In collaboration with Dariusz Galasinski she is currently investigating identity discourses of three-generation families on the former German-German and the German-Polish borders. Recent publications include: *Language Learning in the Age of Satellite Television* (OUP, 1998) and (with Kay Richardson) *Worlds in Common? Television in a Changing Europe* (Routledge, 1999); and the edited volumes: (with Kay Richardson) *Text, Discourse and Context: Representations of Poverty in Britain* (Longman, 1994), (with Sally Johnson) *Masculinity and Language* (Blackwell, 1997) and (with Jonathan Smith) *Intertextuality and the Media: from Genre to Everyday Life* (Manchester University Press, in press).

Gerd Thomas Reifarth studied at the Friedrich-Schiller-Universität Jena, Germany and spent five years as a Lektor at the National University of Ireland, Galway. He is currently completing his PhD and working on a book about distorted depictions of the negative side of GDR reality.

Susanne Schrabback is working on her PhD on German media in east and west since unification at the University of Strathclyde, UK. Her main research interests are in ideology and the media, and in first language acquisition. Recent publications include: (with K. Meng) 'Interjektionen im Erwachsenen-Kind-Diskurs' in G. Brünner and G. Gräfen (eds) *Texte und Diskurse* (Westdeutscher Verlag, 1994), and (with K. Meng) 'Discourse markers in adult–child discourse' in *Journal of Pragmatics* (in press).

Patrick Stevenson is Reader in German at the University of Southampton, UK. His main research interests are in German sociolinguistics, language and politics, and language and ethnicity. His recent publications include: *The German-Speaking World* (Routledge, 1997), (with Stephen Barbour) *Variation im Deutschen: soziolinguistische Perspektiven* (de Gruyter, 1998); and, as editor, *The German Language and the Real World* (Clarendon Press, 1995/1997).

John Theobald is Associate Professor in Modern Languages at Southampton Institute, UK, where he teaches German language, media and film studies. His current research and recent publications are in the fields of comparative critical discourse analysis of media output on contemporary Germany, and of the history of radical mass media criticism. His book *The Paper Ghetto: Karl Kraus and Anti-Semitism* was published by Lang in 1996.

List of Abbreviations

CDA   Critical Discourse Analysis
CDU   Christlich-Demokratische Union (political party)
CSU   Christlich-Soziale Union (political party)
END   European Nuclear Disarmament
EOS   Erweiterte Oberschule (sixth form)
FDJ   Freie Deutsche Jugend (East German youth movement)
FDP   Freie Demokratische Partei (political party)
IGBE   Industriegewerkschaft Bergbau und Energie (miners' and energy workers' union)
IM   Inoffizieller Mitarbeiter (unofficial collaborator working for Ministry for State Security in the GDR)
MDR   Mitteldeutscher Rundfunk (regional broadcasting company)
N3   (regional television channel)
ND   *Neues Deutschland* (newspaper)
PDS   Partei des Demokratischen Sozialismus (political party)
SED   Sozialistische Einheitspartei Deutschlands (ruling political party in the GDR)
SPD   Sozialdemokratische Partei Deutschlands (political party)
SZ   *Süddeutsche Zeitung* (newspaper)
USV   Upper Saxon Vernacular
ZDF   Zweites Deutsches Fernsehen (national public broadcasting corporation)

1
A Decade of Cultural Disunity: Diverging Discourses and Communicative Dissonance in 1990s Germany

Patrick Stevenson and John Theobald

Introduction

This book addresses cultural complexities and pluralities, unforeseen at the moment of political and economic unification in Germany in 1990, which transformed a euphoric sense of expectation among Germans at the beginning of the decade into a widespread feeling of disenchantment and resentment at the end of it, particularly as far as the development of a new united cultural identity was concerned. Focusing on constructions of Germanness in the 1990s at the complementary levels of discursive and communicative practices, the book seeks both to define more closely and sensitively the processes which have occurred at the cultural/linguistic level, and to suggest that it is at this level that socially valuable diagnosis can take place, and that constructive approaches to Germany's continuing east–west cultural divide can be indicated.

Critical discourse analysis and micro-sociolinguistics are related fields which have advanced in parallel over recent years. Critical discourse analysis has concentrated largely on public discourse, with a particular, but by no means exclusive, emphasis on media discourse. It has seen its role as the illumination of political and ideological agendas, and the relationship between language and power. Micro-sociolinguistics (those areas dealing with individual behaviours and beliefs, especially interactional sociolinguistics and the study of accommodative

1

practices) has explored how particular discourses are articulated and negotiated at the individual and interpersonal levels, and looked at the social outcomes of culturally determined practices and the processes by which these practices are retained, adapted, or rejected.

There is an evident interface between these two lines of investigation at the points where public discourse has its complex effects on everyday language use by individuals (and vice versa), but there have been few attempts to explore the synergy that it could generate. Our main objective in this opening chapter is therefore to chart the twin trajectories of the study of diverging discourses and the study of communicative dissonance in post-unification Germany in such a way as to suggest their common purpose in revealing and analysing the causes, processes, and consequences of social and cultural disharmony. We hope then not merely to juxtapose findings from these two fields of enquiry, but to initiate dialogue between them.

The following chapters collectively offer just such a perspective on the intersection of public and personal discourses. By bringing together diverse approaches to the single question of cultural disunity in contemporary Germany, we hope in turn to stimulate new debates on future ways of counteracting processes of discursive distortion and communicative friction which create misunderstanding and generate conflict.

Diverging discourses

The balloon of a united German national identity, launched with much rhetorical hot air in 1989–90 is, a decade later, struggling to keep aloft, fuelled with diminishing conviction by what increasingly look like empty phrases. We were supposed by now to be soaring over the much-quoted blossoming landscapes with a following narrative wind, telling tales of an eastern German economic and social transformation which made it indistinguishable from the west, where 'east' and 'west' would be mere geographical indicators. Instead, we appear to be riding ever lower over a linguistic wasteland of broken commitments, recriminations, stereotypes and scapegoats.

This may be an over-pessimistic cultural scenario. It is argued by some (for example, Glaeßner 1992) that the process of transformation of the ex-GDR to Western ways was always going to be a lengthy one, and that euphoria was bound to give way to sobriety and moments of gloom once the hard realities of the desired change were imposed. This kind of narrative goes on to demand patience and hard work while the capitalist utopia is postponed into an unspecified future, rather as the communist one was under the previous regime. More recently, Wiesenthal (1998:1) has argued that 'post-unification dissatisfaction' relates predominantly to the older generations, and will thus necessarily slowly diminish.

However, voices are increasingly heard which express serious criticism of the handling of the process of convergence of the two Germanies. In the early post-*Wende* months, these voices were isolated, coming principally from internal critics of the GDR who opposed unification and wished to see a reformed East German state. It was Bärbel Bohley who already in 1990 spoke of the rape of the GDR. These critics were joined by a number of writers and intellectuals from east and west, of whom Günter Grass was the most vociferous. All these were, however, swept aside by the unification campaign and the wave of public unification euphoria which came in its wake (Hofmann 1991) and retained enough momentum to keep Helmut Kohl and his supporters in power in successive elections up to 1998, when disillusionment with the unification process played a key role in his severe defeat.

A second type of criticism is best described as a two-way phenomenon of grass-roots grumbling and has received plentiful media attention since the early 1990s. It sets *Besserwessis* (superior westerners) against *Jammerossis* (moaning easterners), bringing to prominence Peter Schneider's concept of the *Mauer im Kopf* (wall in the head). Here, a western triumphalism and sense of superiority, mixed with resentment at tax increases levied to pay for development in the east, confronted eastern feelings of being taken over, unpreparedness for western ways, and an increasing sense of becoming socially and economically second-class citizens. Media treatment of these issues played a significant role in hardening these perceptions into stereotypes, helping to provoke, then exploit, *Ostalgie*, and unintentionally fuelling the unexpected political revival in eastern areas of the re-formed eastern communist party (PDS). Continuous media concentration on trials of former East German political leaders and on *Stasi* revelations further contributed to the propagation of overwhelmingly negative images of the ex-GDR, which were generally accepted in the west, but which contradicted the subjective individual and collective memories of many easterners, thus promoting divergence rather than convergence between these two sections of the populace.

Thus far, the story is well-known. A third type of criticism, however, is again different in nature, and is located principally in the mid to late nineties. It is the product of the more slowly turning wheels of academia and takes the form of a growing body of critical analysis of the management of the unification process and the first years of unified Germany. There is as yet no critical overview of this increasing body of work; it will thus be useful to set out some examples here.

Jürgen Habermas wrote in 1995 of 'the horrendous asymmetries that became inevitable because of the precipitous unification of East and West' (Habermas 1995:35), and continued:

> The enlarged Federal Republic is the wrong framework for an ethical-political self-understanding that – for compelling internal reasons – ought to be conducted under symmetrical conditions, and from the perspective of a mutual we. But for the time being, there are two unequal parties, one of which is, in many respects, 'evaluating' the other. The apparently magnanimous, but hasty rhetorical leveling of differences between Eastern and Western experiential contexts – differences that will continue to exist for a long time – leads only to false symmetries. To be sure, existing asymmetries also lead to a false affirmation of differences: 'West Germans sometimes approach us', Schorlemmer [a well-known east German protestant churchman and critical commentator (eds)] rightly complains, 'as our treasurers as well as our judges. We East Germans have less and less to say. Hardly anyone is even speaking any more. Once again we are being turned into morons and foreigners in our own country'. West Germans are only too eager to assume supervision of the process by which their brothers and sisters achieve self-understanding.

In comparable vein, the historian Lothar Kettenacker wrote in 1997:

> Post-natal depression is perhaps the best way to describe the mood of Germany six years after the event .... Now that Germany is united, to all intents and purposes, the separate identities of West and East Germany are exposed for the first time ... The melting of the Cold War ice has opened up a mental crevasse between the two Germanies.
>
> Kettenacker 1997:213

He continues, diversifying his metaphors, by saying: 'Unification may be described as an unexpected marriage of two populations, which started with a short honeymoon, only to be followed by a long period of recriminations' (Kettenacker 1997:218). With a stronger implication of 'discursive *Anschluß*' he goes on:

For many East German citizens, the scale of redundancies and the total submission to a new political and economic system are traumatic experiences from which they have not yet recovered. According to a popular phrase, they are now 'foreigners in their own country'. They are made to feel that their life and honest work of forty years have been completely devalued. They know that they need all the help they can get from the West, but that the West does not need them. Their willingness to contribute to a united Germany has been rubbished by the West and dismissed as immaterial: nothing achieved by the old GDR seemed suitable for adaptation by the West. No concessions were made to the feelings of the other half: no new name for the reconstituted whole; no new flag or national anthem; above all, no new constitution. Nor are the East Germans adequately represented on the governing boards of the Federal Republic or in any other prominent positions. Their pride has been deeply wounded.

Kettenacker 1997:220

One of Kettenacker's points reflects the text of the opening section of Margarethe von Trotta's film *Das Versprechen/The Promise* (1995), where it is stated:

Aus einem Volk, das einmal die Wahn erlegen war, die Welt zu beherrschen, wurden allmählich zwei Völker, und bald hielt nur noch die Mauer die Illusion aufrecht, daß nur eine Mauer die Deutschen trennte.

(A people, once mad enough to want to rule the world, slowly became two peoples. And soon only the Wall kept up the illusion that all that divided the German people was a wall.) [Subtitle text]

Outside the crucible of internal German debate, British historians also make critical observations, questioning the wisdom of the unification process. Mary Fulbrook wrote in 1997:

As tensions began to grow between West and East Germans, the euphoria of 1989 gave way to growing irritation and mutual criticism. The civic movements of the revolutionary fall, now castigated as hopelessly idealistic and irrelevant [that is, the real movers and shakers of the East German popular uprising (eds)], faded into insignificance in comparison with the perceived problems of pressure on jobs and housing, the impact of mass population migration, and the mounting cost of reconstruction. Helmut Kohl's promised 'blossoming landscapes' in the East German *Länder* appear increasingly to entail some cost for the prosperous Western brothers and sisters after all, and irritation began to grow with the alleged deficiencies in East German initiative and entrepreneurial abilities.

Fulbrook 1997:184

Fulbrook also emphasizes the crushing of east German sensibilities by the massive west German self-marketing machine under the Kohl government's patronage. She writes:

For triumphalist West Germans after 1989, who had so successfully shaken off the shackles of their own pre-democratic past, the task of energetically 'overcoming' the East German dictatorship was in some sense the measure of their own political maturity as seasoned democrats. In the aftermath of the fall of the Wall, impressions and assumptions along these lines have informed political actions, media discussions, and public debates, and have left their sediments in the emerging academic literature on the GDR. The media have pursued a witch-hunt of former unofficial informers (IMs) for the *Stasi*. Western politicians and bureaucrats have entered the euphemistically termed 'five new *Länder*' and ousted the old officials, administrators, and academics from their former positions, replacing them with Besser-Wessis – the Westerners who always know better ... The general thrust of recent literature on the GDR ... has been to denounce the East German dictatorship, to describe it in black and white terms of oppressor and oppressed.

Fulbrook 1997:179

Konrad Jarausch, the American/German historian, in *After Unity. Re-Configuring German Identities* (1997) collected contributions from largely American or German/American researchers into cultural issues in post-unification Germany. He pulls the debate back from too broad an assertion of west German cultural imperialism by reminding us that the east German electorate voted conclusively for rapid unification in March 1990, and reinforced this in the subsequent united German elections of December 1990 and 1994. He writes:

Due to the disappearance of the GDR as a separate state, the abrupt changes threaten many Easterners with a loss of identity. By rushing to join the successful FRG, instead of creating a hybrid confederation [note that he holds out here the often-denied possibility that things *could* have been done differently (eds)], Easterners forced themselves to adopt the Western model without much chance to preserve their own ways. Initially, the common national identification as Germans, and the familiarity with the virtual reality of Western media helped the transition ... But eventually, the enormity of the transformation, coupled with the devaluation of life experiences, sparked a nostalgic memory of the old GDR that magnified its achievements while forgetting its repressions.

Jarausch 1997b:17

'Vindicated by the accession of the Eastern *Länder*', Jarausch goes on,

the old Federal Republic has continued to set the tone for the united German state ... The West German establishment and population have proven amazingly reluctant to adopt new ways. Much of this response is understandable, since the West holds all the advantages in population size, economic clout, political power, and ideological success. Due to media dominance, the post-unity debates therefore often look like West German affairs that continue pre-1989 conflicts under different auspices.

Jarausch 1997b:17

Later in the volume, Welsh, Pickel and Rosenberg, in a chapter entitled 'East and West German Identities. United or Divided?' record some of the unnecessary human-level changes to everyday life for eastern Germans which also demonstrate the lengths to which the Kohl administration went to rub in the fact that this is no merger, no symmetrical rapprochement, rather an annexation, and to some extent an ironic denial of the democracy and self-determination that had been a key motivation for the Eastern uprising in the first place. The authors state, in terms which are now emerging as a *Leitmotiv* of critical writing:

Thus far, German unification has, however, not led to revaluation of the distortions and elisions of the post-war political polarisation, but to an attempt to simply replace the Eastern version with its Western mirror image.

Welsh, Pickel and Rosenberg 1997:122

Then, following an account of the replacement by a western-German-dominated commission of 'undemocratic' street names in east

Berlin with 'democratic' ones, demonstrating the undemocratic way in which this was done, they add:

> New citizens are unlikely to gain respect for or identify with the 'pluralistic values and West German rules of law and democracy' (the Commission's declared goal) by having their right to vote on neighbourhood issues disregarded.
>
> Welsh, Pickel and Rosenberg 1997:133

The three waves of criticism just described combine to form a growing counter-hegemonic discourse which sees post-unification Germany as a place which is, in Peter Pulzer's phrase 'unified but not united' (Pulzer 1995: chapter heading). These alternative narratives are, as they gain in currency, in the process of puncturing the dominant western story, and by this very act, creating space for the expression of other memories, experiences and historiographies, and the emergence of alternative discourses. Chapters 2 to 9 of this book are part of the analytical creation of such discourses. They broadly apply critical discourse analytical methods to materials which, when analysed, reveal progress, or the need for progress, from thought patterns caught in 'superior/inferior', 'winner/loser' west/east polarities.

As such, they are taking forward a tradition of socially active linguistic analysis and criticism of public discourse which spans the twentieth century. Critical Discourse Analysis (CDA) is the current repackaging and re-definition for the current state of cultural debate and media-dominated social context of an approach to texts which formerly confined itself to products of high culture as the main bearers of significant cultural messages and advances in thought. It thus takes as its theme as much the dissemination of ideas as their origination. It extends the critical agenda not only to textual analysis of products of popular and everyday culture, but also to detailed illumination of the power structures, genre determinants, and contextual factors behind their discourses. There is a concern to show that dominant discourses are not the only discourses, or necessarily more correct or accurate on account of their dominance. While dominant discourses may be challenged, alternative discourses may be taken correspondingly more seriously by CDA practitioners, attempting to shift the balance of power from the hegemonic in the direction of the counter-hegemonic. There may be a range of ideological motivations behind such analysis, but the mainstream would claim to be acting in the interests of democratic pluralism and freedom of information, and against the manipulation of information and ideas in the interests of powerful elites.

The broad critical approach of which CDA is a part goes back to the beginning of the twentieth century and the writings of the Viennese satirist and cultural critic Karl Kraus (Theobald 1996, 1999). Its themes were taken up by Gramsci, followed by the Frankfurt School. The post-war and early Cold War periods consigned issues of propaganda, thought control, and manipulation of language to the totalitarian enemy, and such issues applied to 'free' societies only became (briefly) salient again with the sixties generation and its luminaries such as Herbert Marcuse and Marshall McLuhan in the USA. The seventies and eighties saw the rise to prominence of the Glasgow Media Group, the Birmingham School of Cultural Studies, and critical linguists at the University of East Anglia in the UK, Foucault and Habermas in main-land Europe, and the Chomsky/Herman collaboration in the USA.

The late eighties and nineties then saw a confluence of factors which provoked a rapid expansion of interest in CDA and related areas, mani-festing itself both in terms of public concern and in terms of research, reflection and consciousness-raising amongst the intelligentsia. On the one hand, the end of the Cold War opened doors to renewed radical internal criticism of western ideology and practices. On the other, the increasing marketization and concentration of ownership of media production and distribution on a global scale became an ever-greater matter for concern. Previously, the western media had been able to present themselves as beacons of free thought and pluralism relative to the state-controlled propaganda put out by authoritarian societies. Now they themselves started to be perceived increasingly as a threat to the democracy they purported to defend. The volume of argument and counter-argument grew to industrial levels as Media and Cultural Studies expanded as university subjects and research fields. While Noam Chomsky and Ed Herman stepped out of academia into the arena of public debate in the USA with *Manufacturing Consent* (1988), Pierre Bourdieu did likewise in France with *Sur la Télévision* (1996), as did Robert McChesney, again in the USA, with *Corporate Media and the Threat to Democracy* (1997). In the UK, and mainland Europe, the specific development of CDA had a number of exponents; foremost among these were Teun van Dijk in Amsterdam, Ruth Wodak in Vienna, and in particular Norman Fairclough, with *Language and Power* (1989), *Discourse and Social Change* (1992), *Critical Discourse Analysis* (1995) and *Media Discourse* (1995). Furthermore, the critical work of radical journalists such as John Pilger – *Hidden Agendas* (1998) – and media and communications specialists such as Bob Franklin – *Newszack & Mass Media* (1997) – aroused considerable interest as, in particular, the grip of Rupert Murdoch and his News Corporation on public life appeared to tighten.

Given the synchronicity of the end of the Cold War and its media centrepieces, the Fall of the Berlin Wall and German Unification, with the rise of globalized media power and the radical critical reaction to it, there is a certain inevitability about the application of the critical instruments of CDA to 1990s Germany.

There is rich evidence of this in the current volume. Ulrike Meinhof demonstrates clearly the operation of western hegemonic discourse in unified German television current affairs broadcasting, while Kathrin Hörschelmann analyses a parallel process at work in television drama, relating the west–east patterns of domination to male–female, and colonizer–colonized metaphors. Susanne Schrabback identifies significant differences in press coverage of events showing eastern self-assertion in her comparative analysis of coverage in the *Süddeutsche Zeitung* as opposed to the eastern *Neues Deutschland* of the hunger strike of the eastern Bischofferode miners in 1993, while John Theobald shows that a whole alternative construction of the GDR and view of its future, as manifested in the journal *Grenzfall,* as well as the courageous activities of those who inconveniently promoted reform of the GDR rather than its disappearance, can be silenced or reduced to insignificance.

Helen Kelly-Holmes turns to analysis of the medium of advertising to provide a barometer of eastern integration into, or resistance to, westernized marketing of, in her examples, eastern beers and wines. She shows how manufacturers have varied their marketing approach to eastern consumers in line with perceived attitudinal shifts which reflect attitudes to unification, and presents a picture of increasing, but not wholehearted, integration into western consumer behaviour.

Beth Linklater, while using oral histories as her material for analysis, looks carefully at the individual discourses in relation to media discourses, thus working at the interface between the public and the private. She shows that eastern children of the post-*Wende* generation describe the GDR in similar ways to their parents, who in turn show similarities with media constructions, emphases and omissions, albeit mitigated by needs for self-justification on the one hand, and perceptions of what is acceptable to the interlocutor on the other.

Finally, the role of humour and satire as a way of negotiating one's way out of the eastern frying pan into the unified German fire is the subject of both Joanne McNally's and Gerd Reifarth's contributions:

while the former concentrates on the post-unification programmes of the east Berlin-based Die Distel (The Thistle), the latter contrasts the satirical and linguistic inventiveness of Matthias Biskupek with the stubborn utopian imagery of Volker Braun. Both McNally and Reifarth perceive in their subjects a continuing assertion of eastern identity and a rejection of integration into western patterns. Eastern self-assertion as well as self-mockery through satire may just be an effective cultural/discursive way to lance the twin boils of western arrogance and eastern self-pity.

The collective evidence from these contributions is that hegemonic attempts to smother eastern German identity and promote western constructions of the GDR, the *Wende*, and subsequent phases of the unification process are alive and well, but that since the spectacular successes of 1989–90, partly because of their arrogant, patronizing or humiliating nature, they have met with a certain level of east German resistance. While most east Germans are accommodating with varying degrees of obligation or pragmatism to western discourses, many have also used their GDR experience to construct strategies of discursive autonomy and resistance in an attempt to salvage self-respect, faced as they are by constant messages proclaiming their present second-class status and the worthlessness of their past lives. While this may be seen as a positive manifestation of resilience and pluralism, it is also mis-shapen by the fact that it is reactive to unsubtle manipulations of history, false promises about the benefits of unification, and distorted east–west definitions – all based on western triumphalism, and thus on unhealthy asymmetries of perception.

Communicative dissonance

In the last days of 1989, the leading GDR linguist Wolfdietrich Hartung wrote what he clearly imagined would be the final chapter in the 40-year debate on the 'unity and diversity of the German language', in which he expressed the doubt whether in six months' time many people would be interested in the subject, since it would then be of no more than historical interest (Hartung 1990:447). Ten years later, however, the theme of linguistic difference in east and west is still very much alive and kicking: the comprehensive bibliography on language and communication in Germany since the *Wende* in Hellmann (1999) lists over 700 titles, and while the overwhelming majority of these publications deal with the post-*Wende* period, the GDR past remains an essential component of the research context.[1]

Yet Hartung's prophecy was not as misjudged as it may seem with hindsight. Well before the *Wende*, the debates between linguists (and others) in East and West on the question of whether or not two distinct languages had evolved in the GDR and the FRG had run their course. A consensus had finally been reached that these debates had been more interesting as a barometer of the political climate between the two states than as a measure of the actual divergence between German in the East and German in the West (for critical accounts of these debates as 'histories of the history of the language', see Hellmann 1989 and Stevenson 1993).

However, no sooner had this file on East–West differences closed than another file opened. While linguistic interest in the 1949–89 period had focused on cataloguing semantic change and the growth of vocabulary specific to one speech community or the other, now observers turned their attention either to the gathering of the ephemeral phenomena of 'disposable' lexical innovations, or more importantly to the deletion of 'east German' terms from the new 'united German' lexicon.[2] This work on lexical developments has made an important contribution to the linguistic history of German and more broadly to the study of language change. It has also played a significant part in the conservation of key facts and artifacts of the post-1945 era in German social history, and the importance of this role is sometimes unjustly neglected. However, the collection of this kind of data need not be an end in itself: what is ultimately more important than the linguistic products of social change is the effect of the processes of change on the users of the language. On the one hand, it was widely assumed (at least after the hysterical rhetoric of the 1950s and 1960s) that the accumulation of lexical and semantic differences represented no more than minor changes in the overall substance of the language, and that they were confined overwhelmingly to certain domains and to official discourses and public contexts. By the same token, the rapid disappearance of these differences would scarcely be noticed, since it would be merely a normal adaptive response to changes in what Townson (1992) calls the 'communicative environment'.

On the other hand, the lesson of the first decade of the unified German speech community is that the new communicative environment is new only for east Germans, for many of whom it is a strange and bewildering place. As the east German linguist Ulla Fix points out, not only have the changes affected both language form and language use, but the process of change has been almost unprecedentedly rapid and thorough (Fix 1997a:34). The wind of economic, political and social change transported the population of the former GDR abruptly, without the luxury of a transitional phase of adjustment, into a new *Kommunikationskultur* (Fix 1997a:35).

The nature and extent of the psychological impact of these changes on many east Germans, who experienced them as a mixture of loss and alienation, have manifested themselves in different ways. Helmut Schönfeld (1993), for example, argues that what for the dispassionate linguist may seem like a superficial and readily interchangeable component of an individual's linguistic inventory is actually an integral element of their self-understanding that is truly appreciated only when it is taken away. Outside observers may refer dismissively to the pathos of his examples (such as the displacement of the east German *Kinderkrippe* 'for kindergarten or nursery' by the west German *Kita*, short for *Kindertagesstätte*), but insiders attest to the feeling of being bereft at the 'loss' (or 'confiscation') of words that had been part of their common currency and that had literally represented those things that were the cornerstones of their everyday lives. For the same reason, they felt ill at ease with the strange new vocabulary that represented, in some cases, even stranger new concepts (especially in institutional contexts such as education and social security: for examples, see Schröder 1992).

Particularly long-lasting consequences were in those areas of language use that in GDR times had been more profoundly characterized by what Fix (1992) calls ritual communication, and by what Stevenson (1995) refers to as the discursive penetration of official textual patterns. As these and other studies (for example, Lerchner 1992b) have shown, the widely held belief in the essential superficiality of lexical difference and change and in the restricted validity of vocabulary related to aspects of life in the GDR was seriously misjudged. Take the example of education and the institution of the school, which played such a central role in the construction of the socialist state. As Fix (1994:131) argues, even everyday conversations about education were inevitably saturated with expressions deriving unmistakably from Party doctrine. Texts of every kind, generated as part of the routine of school life, all show the imprint of the official discourse, and not only at the lexical level. For instance, one of the most familiar textual moves in the official discourse was the characterization of performance in any sphere (industrial output, sporting achievement, research developments) as 'good but not yet good enough'. Fix (1992:56) gives an example of this, quoting the former Education Minister Margot Honecker: ' "Die Schlüsselfrage – und das ist die Meinung vieler Lehrer

– besteht *weiter* darin, an der *noch solideren* Ausprägung des grundlegen-
den mathematischen Wissens und Könnens zu arbeiten." ' (The key
issue – and this is what many teachers think – continues to be the need
to work on establishing even more soundly basic mathematical knowledge and ability.) In their analyses of a wide range of everyday texts
from school archives, Fix (1992) and Stevenson (1995) show that this
pattern was absorbed into the sociolinguistic repertoire of teachers and
pupils alike and appeared routinely in everything from teaching plans
to pupils' class reports.

Before the *Wende*, for obvious reasons, research into actual language
use in these and many other contexts and domains in the GDR (that is,
other than the largely taxonomic analysis of public texts such as articles in the national, state-controlled newspaper *Neues Deutschland* or
political speeches) was severely constrained, and such empirical sociolinguistic research as was done at that time was generally driven by the
broader social agenda of the state (see Stevenson 1997b:6–9). The
opening of archives of all kinds (from the modest collections of individual schools to the vast records of the Ministry for State Security, the
Stasi) has made very substantial amounts of material freely available for
the first time, and there remains considerable scope for analysing these
texts (for work on the *Stasi* files, for example, see Henne 1995,
Bergmann 1996, 1999). However, these are all written texts, of course,
and actual oral texts (in the sense of everyday speech) can no longer be
recovered. Yet making sense of the present relations between east and
west Germans depends to a large extent on interpreting and understanding such archaeological evidence of the relationship east
Germans had to (their) language as can be salvaged, in order to identify the sociolinguistic continuities that bridge the discontinuity of the
Umbruch (radical social change). This can be done in two ways: first by
talking to east Germans about their experience of language in the past,
and second by investigating actual interactional behaviours to see what
traces of past practices have survived the superposing of new ones.

By 'experience of language', we mean speakers' evaluations of different speech forms (for instance, regional and standard varieties, or age-
and gender-related varieties), their awareness of the social constraints
on the use of certain forms and the consequences of ignoring them,
the effects on their personal biographies of adopting different linguistic
strategies in their daily lives, the abiding connotations of specific
words or collocations, and the extent to which the particularities of
their linguistic repertoires represented formative influences in their
development of an understanding of self and other. Although a

number of studies (for example, Schlosser 1992, Beneke 1993, Reiher 1996, Schönfeld 1996, Gansel and Gansel 1997) have explored various aspects of these questions, they have by and large not been integrated into attempts to construct a 'bigger picture'. For example, in a simple but revealing experiment conducted in late 1989/early 1990, and which would be interesting to repeat now, Julia Liebe Reséndiz (1992) explored claims that east and west Berliners could recognize speakers from the 'other side' in each case, purely through speech characteristics. Apart from obvious markers such as GDR- or FRG-specific vocabulary, participants in the study (especially east German ones) seemed particularly sensitive towards prosodic features and other aspects of speech performance, such as fluency and 'vitality'.

In a more subtle and methodologically more refined study of east Germans' language awareness, Fix (1997a, 1997b) has used narrative interviews to explore individual 'language biographies'. Rather than attempting a representative analysis in a quantitative sense, she takes these individual accounts as entry points into collective 'communities of memory', and constructs two fundamental prototypes in terms of how interviewees situate themselves in relation to their (GDR) past: 'conformists', who see themselves as having been active participants in the project that was the GDR and who use their narratives to justify their past, and 'non-conformists', who consider themselves to have been more observers than participants and who confine themselves to describing and explaining their understanding of the past. One aspect of this study that is particularly significant in the present context is the picture that emerges of a rather differentiated sociolinguistic profile of the GDR speech community, which is at odds with the simple 'public versus private' model that west German linguists, in particular, have frequently referred to (see, for example, Schlosser 1990:176). One interviewee, for example, categorizes the varieties in the common repertoire in the following terms (Fix 1997a:38):

Ich hab' weniger die Erfahrung gemacht, daß das also die Ideologiesprache war, also das ganz offensichtliche Parteichinesisch, das einen zur Anpassung sozusagen forderte, sondern es war so ein Zwischenglied zwischen dieser in der DDR typischen Sprache der Intimität und dieser hochoffiziösen Ideologiesprache. Es gab so eine Sprache der Gemeinplätze, die zwischen den beiden Sphären vermittelte, die zwischen Ideologie und Intimität kompatibel war.

(In my experience it wasn't the ideological language, you know, the really obvious Party jargon that sort of forced you to conform, it was a kind of intermediate form between that language of intimacy that was so typical of the GDR and the official ideological language. There was a language of platitudes, which mediated between the two spheres, which was compatible with ideology and intimacy.)

At the same time, some interviewees claimed to have shrugged off the straitjacket of this rigidly layered repertoire and to have developed individual patterns of speech behaviour as what Le Page and Tabouret-Keller (1985) refer to as 'acts of identity' (Fix 1997a:39):

> Ich hab' mich immer bemüht, wenn ich Inhalte ... übernehmen mußte oder übernehmen wollte, weil sie mir sinnvoll erschienen, die dann selbst zu formulieren. Und das enthielt natürlich immer ein gewisses Risikopotential, denn man konnte mit der eigenen Formulierung ... zeigte man unter Umständen einen zusätzlichen Gedanken oder die Richtung eines Gedankens, die nicht der offiziellen Festlegung entsprach, und das wurde natürlich registriert.
>
> (I always tried, when I had to or wanted to adopt ideas that seemed sensible to me, to formulate them myself. And of course there was always a potential risk in that, because with your own formulation you could, you maybe showed an additional idea or perspective, which didn't conform to the official position, and that was obviously noted.)

Whether these reflections are an accurate portrayal of the speakers' actual behaviour in the past, or a partly fanciful retrospective construction of defiance, is clearly impossible to determine now. The important point in the present context, however, is that personal narratives such as these do offer compelling evidence to support Wolfgang Thierse's assertion (1993:116) that east Germans had 'nicht eine andere Sprache als die Bundesdeutschen, sondern ein anderes Verhältnis zur Sprache' (not a different language from the West Germans, but rather a different relationship to language).

The legacy of this 'special relationship' with language is revealed in recent empirical research on interactional behaviours of east and west Germans in particular settings. Two major studies, which together with Fix's work on ritual communication and language biographies constitute the wide-ranging project 'Fremdheit in der Muttersprache' (foreignness in the mother tongue; based at the universities of Halle, Hamburg and Leipzig), have investigated in great detail to what extent and in what ways east Germans have been able to cope with unfamiliar speech events (or genres, to use Auer's term: see Chapter 10) such as job interviews and counselling sessions, and the differences between east and west Germans in terms of communicative performance. Both of these communicative genres are extremely important for east Germans, since one of the immediate consequences of economic restructuring in the east has been a high rate of unemployment, and since advice is frequently needed to deal with the plethora of new demands of everyday life (from understanding insurance forms to applying for business subsidies). They are also quite unfamiliar to most east Germans, because formal competitive interviews were not used as a normal means of placing people in jobs in the GDR and there were no sources of advice on personal matters outside the official agencies of the state.

On the basis of transcriptions of both role-played and authentic job interviews on the one hand, and telephone calls to a counselling service provided by a local newspaper on the other, Peter Auer, Gerd Antos and their colleagues have identified striking contrasts in the assumptions that the respective participants appear to bring to these encounters and in the communicative strategies they use to accomplish their roles within the encounters. For instance, as Auer shows in Chapter 10, while west German job applicants know that the interview must be seen as an opportunity to sell themselves and accordingly aim to present their experience and skills in the best possible light, the east Germans observed in the study appear to see the interview as a fact-finding exercise on the part of the employer and are often disarmingly frank in their assessment of their strengths and weaknesses. In the counselling sessions, west German counsellors tended to concentrate on the facts of the situation and on setting out the options, maintaining a detached stance towards their callers in keeping with their 'expert' status, whereas their east German counterparts took a more interventionist approach, explicitly guiding their callers towards particular courses of action (see, for instance, Antos and Schubert 1997).

In Chapters 11 and 12, Grit Liebscher and Stephan Elspaß provide (in quite different ways) further empirical explorations of the interactional performance of identities. By studying specific features of talk in public contexts (the use of local deictics in television talk shows, and markers of uncertainty and vagueness in Bundestag speeches), they offer insights into the conversational construction of context and into patterns of accommodation by east Germans in public settings dominated by west German communicative norms, which have implications over and above the particular focus of their respective research projects. Elspaß shows that there are deeply ingrained conceptions of 'eastern' and 'western' speech styles, and that, while making allowances for individual characteristics, we can see how east Germans' chances of success in the public domain (but very likely also in most semi-public contexts such as the workplace) depend to a large extent on their ability to 'play the game' according to western rules. Similarly, by extrapolating from Liebscher's microscopic analysis of the concepts 'here' and 'there', we can see how complex the dynamics of perspective may be in the negotiation of understanding between east and west Germans.

The critical consensus underlying the studies on communicative interaction and language attitudes in this volume is the recognition that while 'the common language' of the Germans (in the sense of its formal structures – its grammar and vocabulary) is still intact, there are at least perceived to be profound differences in communicative practices and behaviours between east and west Germans, and it is these that constitute a significant continuing barrier to the project of bringing a united (if still highly heterogeneous) Germany into existence. Mutual incomprehension is generally no longer the issue: while Colin Good (1993) was able with some justification, if rather extravagantly, to talk of a *Kultur des Mißverständnisses* (culture of misunderstanding), this no longer seems tenable at the end of the 1990s. It is less a problem of *mis*communication than one of *meta*communication: what messages do particular linguistic practices and behaviours convey, and what does adapting to western patterns represent for east Germans?

As Birgit Barden shows in Chapter 13, linguistic accommodation is not necessarily a simple linear process of adaption. Individuals' linguistic behaviour may respond in subtle and quite complex ways under unstable social conditions, and there is a close relationship between achieving personal benefits from changed circumstances and a willingness to distance oneself from previously secure sources of identification. But while individual language *behaviour* may fluctuate, Jennifer Dailey-O'Cain demonstrates in Chapter 14 how in their *evaluations* of speech varieties east Germans appear to be unconsciously subject to hegemonic pressures to collude in sustaining the standard language ideology of the dominant social force, and so undergo an inexorable shift towards conforming to western norms.

So there continue to be conflicting sociolinguistic responses to both the concrete and the less tangible challenges of life in contemporary Germany. This has resulted in a tension for east Germans between avoiding shibboleths of identifiably eastern manners of speaking (whether accent, vocabulary, or speech style) on the one hand, and rejecting accommodation towards 'western' talk as an unacceptable form of self-denial on the other. There may be isolated flashes of the subversive spirit that fired the linguistic revolt of 1989 (such as the rebranding of *KIM-Eier* [*KIM* eggs], where *KIM* stood for *Kombinat Industrielle Mast* [industrial feed combine], as '*KIM-Eier* – *Köstlich Immer Marktfrisch'* [delicious and always fresh]; Kühn and Almstädt 1997:205), but as yet there is no discernible 'new' east German speech that could either supersede the moribund GDR speech repertoire or compete with the imported western speech styles.

Notes

1   In addition to the individual studies referred to in this chapter, a number of anthologies dealing with various aspects of linguistic issues before, during and after the *Wende* are worth noting: for example, Burkhardt and Fritzsche (1992), Reiher (1995), Lerchner (1992a), and Barz and Fix (1997); and special issues of the journals *Muttersprache* (103/1993), *Germanistische Linguistik* (110–11/1992), *Der Deutschunterricht* (1/1997), and *Deutsche Sprache* (2/1997).
2   Clyne (1995: chapter 3) provides a concise summary of studies on post-1989 lexical change. For definitive commentary on 'GDR vocabulary', see Schröder and Fix (1997). On the so-called '*Wende-Wortschatz'* (vocabulary of the *Wende*) see, for example, the brief survey in Ludwig (1997) and the more substantial studies Herberg *et al.* (1997) and Hellmann (forthcoming) on the massive '*Wende-Korpus'*, which contains vocabulary drawn from newspapers published in 1989–90 and was compiled by the Institut für Deutsche Sprache in Mannheim.

References

Alter, Reinhard and Peter Monteath (1997) *Rewriting the German Past. History and Identity in the New Germany* (New Jersey: Humanities Press).
Antos, Gerd and Thomas Schubert (1997) 'Existenzgründung nach der Wende. Verbalisierungsprobleme von Präsuppositionen bei der sprachlichen Bearbeitung des Wissenstransfers in telefonischen Beratungsgesprächen', in Barz and Fix (1997), 233–62.
Barz, Irmhild and Ulla Fix (eds) (1997) *Deutsch-deutsche Kommunikationserfahrungen im arbeitsweltlichen Alltag* (Heidelberg: Winter).
Beneke, Jürgen (1993) '"Am Anfang wollten wir zueinander ..."' – Was wollen wir heute? Sprachlich-kommunikative Reflexionen Jugendlicher aus dem Ost- und Westteil Berlins zu einem bewegenden Zeitthema', in Reiher and Läzer (1993), 210–38.
Bergmann, Christian (1996) 'Über das "Herausbrechen" und "Zersetzen" von Menschen. Semantische Verschiebungen im Sprachgebrauch des Ministeriums für Staatssicherheit der ehemaligen DDR', in *Muttersprache* 4, 289–301.
Bergmann, Christian (1999) *Die Sprache der Stasi. Ein Beitrag zur Sprachkritik* (Göttingen: Vandenhoeck & Ruprecht).

Berry, David (ed.) (1999) *Ethics and Media Culture* (Oxford: Focal Press).

Born, Joachim and Gerhard Stickel (eds) (1993) *Deutsch als Verkehrssprache in Europa* (Institut für Deutsche Sprache Jahrbuch 1992) (Düsseldorf: Schwann).

Burkhardt, Armin and Klaus Peter Fritzsche (eds) (1992) *Sprache im Umbruch. Politischer Sprachwandel im Zeichen von 'Wende' und 'Vereinigung'* (Berlin, New York: de Gruyter).

Clyne, Michael (1995) *The German Language in a Changing Europe* (Cambridge: Cambridge University Press).

Fix, Ulla (1992) 'Rituelle Kommunikation im öffentlichen Sprachgebrauch der DDR und ihre Begleitumstände', in Lerchner (1992a), 3–85.

Fix, Ulla (1994) 'Sprache vor und nach der "Wende": "Gewendete" Texte – "gewendete" Textsorten', in Heringer *et al.* (1994), 131–46.

Fix, Ulla (1997a) 'Die Sicht der Betroffenen. Beobachtungen zum Kommunikationswandel in den neuen Bundesländern', in *Der Deutschunterricht* 1, 34–41.

Fix, Ulla (1997b) 'Erklären und Rechtfertigen. Die Darstellung der eigenen sprachlich-kommunikativen Vergangenheit in Interviews', in *Deutsche Sprache* 2, 187–94.

Flood, John, Paul Salmon, Olive Sayce and Christopher Wells (eds)(1993) *'Das unsichtbare Band der Sprache'. Studies in German Language and Linguistic History in Memory of Leslie Seiffert* (Stuttgart: Akademischer Verlag).

Fulbrook, Mary (1997) 'Reckoning with the past: heroes,victims and villains in the history of the German Democratic Republic', in Alter and Monteath (1997), 175–96.

Gansel, Christina and Carsten Gansel (1997) 'Zwischen Karrierefrau und Hausmann. Aspekte geschlechterdifferenzierenden Sprachgebrauchs in Ost und West', in *Der Deutschunterricht* 1, 59–69.

Glaeßner, Gert (1992) *Der Schwierige Weg zur Demokratie* (Opladen: Westdeutscher Verlag).

Good, Colin (1993) 'Über die "Kultur des Mißverständnisses" im vereinten Deutschland', in *Muttersprache* 103, 249–59.

Habermas, Jürgen (1995) *Die Normalität einer Berliner Republik* (Frankfurt: Suhrkamp), translated (1998) as *A Berlin Republic. Writings on Germany* (Cambridge: Polity).

Hartung, Wolfdietrich (1990) 'Einheitlichkeit und Differenziertheit der deutschen Sprache', in *Zeitschrift für Germanistik* 90, 447–66.

Hellmann, Manfred (1989) 'Die doppelte Wende: Zur Verbindung von Sprache, Sprachwissenschaft und zeitgebundener politischer Bewertung am Beispiel deutsch-deutscher Sprachdifferenzierung', in Klein (1989), 297–326.

Hellmann, Manfred (1999) *Wende-Bibliografie. Literatur und Nachschlagewerke zu Sprache und Kommunikation im geteilten und vereinigten Deutschland ab Januar 1990* (Mannheim: Institut für Deutsche Sprache).

Hellmann, Manfred (forthcoming) *Wörter in Texten der Wendezeit* (Tübingen: Narr).

Henne, Helmut (1995) 'Hassen. Legendieren. Abschöpfen. Das Wörterbuch der Staatssicherheit', in *Zeitschrift für germanistische Linguistik* 23, 210–14.

Herberg, Dieter, Doris Steffens and Elke Tellenbach (1997) *Schlüsselwörter der Wendezeit. Wörter-Buch zum öffentlichen Sprachgebrauch 1989/90* (Berlin, New York: de Gruyter).

Heringer, Hans Jürgen, Gunhild Samson, Michel Kauffmann and Wolfgang Bader (eds) (1994) *Tendenzen der deutschen Gegenwartssprache* (Tübingen: Niemeyer).

Hofmann, Michael (1991) 'The unity train', in Nowell-Smith and Wollen (1991), 56–68.

Jarausch, Konrad (ed.) (1997a) *After Unity. Re-Configuring German Identities* (Oxford: Berghahn).

Jarausch, Konrad (1997b) 'Reshaping German identities: reflections on the post-unification debate', in Jarausch (1997a), 1–23.

Kettenacker, Lothar (1997) *Germany since 1945* (Oxford: Oxford University Press).

Klein, Josef (ed.) (1989) *Politische Semantik* (Opladen: Westdeutscher Verlag).

Kühn, Ingrid and Klaus Almstädt (1997) 'Rufen Sie uns an: Sprachberatung zwischen Sprachwacht und Kummertelefon', in *Deutsche Sprache* 3, 195–206.

Le Page, Robert and Andrée Tabouret-Keller (1985) *Acts of Identity* (Cambridge: Cambridge University Press).

Lerchner, Gotthard (ed.) (1992a) *Sprachgebrauch im Wandel* (Frankfurt/Main: Lang).

Lerchner, Gotthard (1992b) 'Broiler, Plast(e) und Datsche machen noch nicht den Unterschied. Fremdheit und Toleranz in einer plurizentrischen deutschen Kommunikationskultur', in Lerchner (1992a), 297–332.

Liebe Reséndiz, Julia (1992) 'Woran erkennen sich Ost- und Westdeutsche? Eine Spracheinstellungsstudie am Beispiel von Rundfunksendungen', in *Germanistische Linguistik* 110–11, 127–39.

Ludwig, Klaus-Dieter (1997) 'Wortschatzveränderung nach 1989 und ihre Widerspiegelung in aktuellen Wörterbüchern des Deutschen', in *Der Deutschunterricht* 1, 77–85.

Nowell-Smith, Geoffrey and Tana Wollen (eds) (1991) *After the Wall* (London: BFI).

Pulzer, Peter (1995) *German Politics 1945–1995* (Oxford: Oxford University Press).

Reiher, Ruth (ed.) (1995) *Sprache im Konflikt* (Berlin, New York: de Gruyter).

Reiher, Ruth (1996) 'Ein Ossi – ein Wort; ein Wessi – ein Wörterbuch. Zur Bewertung von Sprache und Sprachverhalten der Deutschen in Ost und West', in Reiher and Läzer (1996), 32–54.

Reiher, Ruth and Rüdiger Läzer (eds) (1993) *Wer spricht das wahre Deutsch?* (Berlin: Aufbau Verlag).

Reiher, Ruth and Rüdiger Läzer (eds) (1996) *Von 'Buschzulage' und 'Ossinachweis'. Ost-West-Deutsch in der Diskussion* (Berlin: Aufbau Verlag).

Schlosser, Horst Dieter (1990) *Die deutsche Sprache in der DDR zwischen Stalinismus und Demokratie. Historische, politische und kommunikative Bedingungen* (Cologne: Verlag Wissenschaft und Politik).

Schlosser, Horst Dieter (1992) 'Mentale und sprachliche Interferenzen beim Übergang der DDR von der Zentralplanwirtschaft zur Marktwirtschaft', in *Germanistische Linguistik* 110/111, 43–58.

Schönfeld, Helmut (1993) 'Auch sprachlich beigetreten? Sprachliche Entwicklungen im zusammenwachsenden Berlin', in Reiher and Läzer (1993), 187–209.

Schönfeld, Helmut (1996) 'Heimatsprache, Proletendeutsch, Ossi-Sprache oder? Bewertung und Akzeptanz des Berlinischen', in Reiher and Läzer (1996), 70–93.

Schröder, Marianne (1992) 'Lexikographische Nach-Wende. Ein Überarbeitungs-
bericht', in Lerchner (1992a), 263–96.
Schröder, Marianne and Ulla Fix (1997) *Allgemeinwortschatz der DDR-Bürger*
(Heidelberg: Winter).
Staab, Andreas (1998) 'Xenophobia, ethnicity and national identity in eastern
Germany', in *German Politics* 7/2, 31–46.
Stevenson, Patrick (1993) 'The German language and the construction of
national identities', in Flood *et al.* (1993), 333–56.
Stevenson, Patrick (1995) '*Gegenwartsbewältigung*: coming to terms with the
present in Germany', in *Multilingua* 14/1, 39–59.
Stevenson, Patrick (ed.) (1997a) *The German Language and the Real World*, revised
edition (Oxford: Clarendon Press).
Stevenson, Patrick (1997b) 'The study of real language: observing the observers',
in Stevenson (1997a), 1–24.
Theobald, John (1996) *The Paper Ghetto. Karl Kraus and Anti-Semitism* (Frankfurt/
Main: Lang).
Theobald, John (1999) 'Radical mass media criticism: elements of a history from
Kraus to Bourdieu', in Berry (1999).
Thierse, Wolfgang (1993) '"Sprich, damit ich dich sehe". Beobachtungen zum
Verhältnis von Sprache und Politik in der DDR-Vergangenheit', in Born and
Stickel (1993), 114–26.
Townson, Michael (1992) *Mother-tongue and Fatherland: Language and Politics in
German* (Manchester: Manchester University Press).
Trotta, Margarethe von (1995) *Das Versprechen* (feature film) (Bioskop-Film/
Odessa Films/Les productions J.M.H./WDR-Fernsehen).
Welsh, Helga, Andreas Pickel and Dorothy Rosenberg (1997) 'East and west
German identities: united or divided?', in Jarausch (1997a), 103–36.
Wiesenthal, Helmut (1998) 'Post-unification dissatisfaction, or why are so many
Germans unhappy with the new political system?' in *German Politics* 7/2,
1–29.

2
The New Germany on the Screen: Conflicting Discourses on German Television

Ulrike Hanna Meinhof

Introduction

The context of this chapter needs to be set with a brief account of some of the events of 3 October 1998 and of the way they were represented to us on some German television channels. On this day, Germany celebrated the eighth anniversary of its (re-)unification. The date 3 October is a public holiday in Germany, carrying the name 'Tag der deutschen Einheit' (Day of German Unity). This nomenclature is not without its problematic resonances. Originally coined in West Germany at the time of the Cold War, 'der Tag der deutschen Einheit' used to be celebrated annually on 17 June, but only in West Germany. It was to remember that day in 1953, when an attempted uprising against the East German regime and its Soviet backers was quashed by military force. With unification becoming official on 3 October 1990 – nearly 11 months after the storming of the Berlin Wall, and the subsequent collapse of the border and of the GDR itself – this 'day of German unity' was transferred from June to October, and its function changed from commemoration of a defeated uprising to celebration of the successful unification of Germany to create a single political system with 16 federal states – a political achievement identified in particular with one man, the conservative Chancellor Helmut Kohl.

On 3 October 1998, the (rotating) public ceremony to mark this event took place in Hanover, because in 1998 the Federal State of Lower Saxony happened to hold the presidency in the German Second Chamber, the *Bundesrat*. Shown live on some of the public service channels, it was riddled with the ironies and pitfalls that are so very typical of post-war German political life. During the celebrations, the cameras zoomed in many times on Chancellor Kohl, the 'forger' of German unification, listening in the front row to the speeches not just by Roman Herzog, the German president whom he himself had helped to appoint, but also by the Minister-President of Lower Saxony, who happened to be Gerhard Schröder. Schröder's party had just won the Federal elections and he was about to displace Kohl and his party coalition of Conservatives and Liberals by a new Red–Green alliance. But this was only one aspect of the irony present in the day's celebrations.

A more poignant irony was the reaction to the day's events by the CSU, Kohl's successful Bavarian coalition partner, which stayed away from the celebrations in protest. The reason for its absence – an objection to a piece of music played between the speeches – provides a wry comment on the unity being celebrated. The musical interlude included a piece which had been specially commissioned from a contemporary composer, who had risen to the occasion by blending fragments of music from various sources. The advance publicity for this piece had sparked off protests from the Bavarian regional government. The composition not only quoted pieces of the German national anthem which had been retained by the West Germans during the time of division, using the inoffensive wording of stanza three 'Einigkeit in Recht und Freiheit' (unity in right and freedom), it also included a brief musical reference to the former East German national anthem, as well as a reference to the Brecht/Weill satirical song 'Surabaya Johnny'. The composer, Michael Bardo Henning, pointed out in a television interview for B3 (the regional Bavarian third channel which also transmits supra-regionally via the Astra satellite) that he had responded to this commission for a piece of symphonic music 'as a composer on a stroll through history', and that he had incorporated positive references to this history whose meaning should also be appreciated in Bavaria. This turned out to be wishful thinking. The Bavarian President and his representatives were not amused, and stayed away from Hanover and its celebration of German unity, preferring instead to commemorate the tenth anniversary of the death of their long-serving president, Franz Josef Strauss, an ardent Cold War warrior as well as an ardent supporter of re-unification during his long political life. The report of this other commemoration from Strauss's native Munich appropriately hogged the Bavarian television channel for several hours.

The symbolic celebration of German unity was thus symbolically undermined by these new echoes of disunity, set in motion by an attempt at integrative and conciliatory musical quotation from GDR history – a few lines of musical notation which one reporter described as 'ein paar drängende Triolen' which sounded 'ziemlich schräg' (a few intrusive triplets which sounded rather out of place). But this was not the only piece of problematic symbolism which we were told about on television that day. Bernd Niebruegge, reporting for B3 when the channel finally did turn its attention to what was happening in Hanover – was speaking in front of a newly built replica of the Wall, which – commissioned graffiti and all – had been erected in the city centre of Hanover as a mnemonic symbol. Noting the absence of fanfares, fireworks, dances and festivity in general, Niebruegge sensed instead a reflective mood about what he referred to as 'German–German misunderstandings':

> deutsch–deutsche Missverständnisse. Der symbolische Wiederaufbau der Mauer hinter mir steht für die in den Köpfen der Deutschen noch immer lebendigen Trennung zwischen Ost und West. Zum einen wegen des wirtschaftlich-sozialen Gefälles, zum anderen wegen der vielen persönlichen Opfer vor und seit dem Fall der Mauer.
>
> (German-German misunderstandings. The symbolic reconstruction of the Wall behind me represents the ongoing division between east and west which is still alive in the minds of the Germans. On the one hand this is due to the economic and social disparity, on the other to the many personal sacrifices before and since the fall of the Wall.)

The metaphoric play with the image of the wall which still exists in people's heads – one of *the* most hackneyed phrases in post-unification German rhetoric – had thus found its material expression.

By contrast, the second German national channel ZDF tried hard to create a more celebratory mood by covering live the contributions of marchers, dancers and flag-wavers (the latter, we were told, were actually in the *Guinness Book of Records* for having achieved 12.5 hours of continuous flag-waving) from all 16 federal states, including the Bavarians, who had gathered in Berlin. Here at last, the image of the Brandenburg Gate without the divisive Wall provided some salient symbolism for the day's celebrations. But here, too, the acknowledgement of tensions between east and west remained a major theme through the day's reporting.

   This account of what is after all a most serious anniversary of a most significant event may sound somewhat personalized and frivolous, but many other individual Germans will doubtless recognize signs of the difficulties which surface whenever historical events need to be officially marked but cannot simply be wrapped inside the warm flags of national sentiments. The unease which many Germans feel about their horrific past in the Third Reich and their discomfort about the historical role of the GDR, and its subsequent demise, are unresolvable legacies, albeit of a different order. By historical juxtaposition, they are inextricably associated with each other, not only in comparative political analysis, but through another commemorative date, 9 November. This day did not only mark in 1989 the opening of the Berlin Wall and thus the beginning of the end of the GDR and the prospect of a united Germany, for 9 November 1938 was also the night of the 'Pogrom' (or 'Kristallnacht', as it used to be known) against the Jews in Nazi Germany.

   How news reports about the significance of this doubly commemorative day can be seen as representative and symptomatic of the unresolved tensions within contemporary Germany is the main subject of this chapter. Examples will be taken from television news items (ZDF) from three different days: (1) an extract from the original reporting on the day of 9 November 1989 (synchronous reporting); (2) the subsequent re-representations and re-framings of the event five years later; and again (3) nine years later. In focusing on these reports and on their interplay between the visual and the verbal, it will be shown that the initial synchronous reporting constructed the event as joyful and euphoric, with the camera seemingly taking on the role of the eye-witness. By contrast, the report of the fifth anniversary in 1994 re-embedded the original footage in a deeply problematical context (broken discourses). A further comparison with the ninth anniversary of the fall of the Wall (9 November 1998), which is also the 60th anniversary of the Pogrom night, will once more reveal a different emphasis and point to a society still deeply torn by its history.

Synchronicity: the camera as eye-witness?

One brief extract from a ZDF news report from the 9 November 1989, the night when East Germans breached the Wall for the first time, shows people climbing and sitting on the Wall, and then focuses on some jubilant men and women. One of them is waving a bottle of sparkling wine, and the group is bursting into a well-known German chant: 'So ein Tag, so wunderschön wie heute, so ein Tag, der dürfte nie vergehn' (Such a day as wonderful as today, such a day should never end). In terms of a television camera playing eye-witness to some momentous historical event, this is about as close as one can get. Theorists from Nietzsche (1967, sections 481, 521, 604) to Barthes (1986:127–54) and Foucault (1970:46–77) have destabilized the notion of an event as separate from a system of interpretation, by pointing out that events do not precede explanation but are indeed constructed by them. Here, on the other hand, we seemed to be in the presence of the opposite, a truly spontaneous event, with the television camera there to record it on behalf of its viewers. Millions watched the images of exuberant people, who for the first time in 28 years were able to cross into West Berlin without hindrance, shared their euphoria, and participated in the sense of liberation from a repressive regime. This television item seemed to give its viewers a very direct and immediate participation in the raw moment of history-in-the-making. There was, to use terms from linguistics, a temporal synchronicity between the event and its representation, and there was less editorial manipulation than is often the case in news reporting, since so much of what was being shown was both spectacular as well as self-explanatory.

Becker (1995:632), referring to the Dayan and Katz (1992) study of ritual, says that ceremonial events collapse 'the individual or private experience into a public and shared identity'. Here something similar seemed to be at play, but in an entirely spontaneous fashion, with the camera providing the access point through which people at home could also participate in this great moment, where the people from East and West Berlin fell into one another's arms. As with reality television, the camera seemed simply to observe what was going on in front of its lenses rather than to construct the event for its viewers. When journalists proudly refer to television as providing an objective window on to the world, it is sequences such as these that they have in mind.

Yet, of course, we are not at all in the presence of any kind of unmediated event. First of all, the media, and especially television, had already been implicated in the fall of the Eastern Bloc states before this climactic moment. When East German viewers in August 1989 saw via West German television how Hungary further liberalized its border regulations to allow East Germans to cross into Austria, this was only one of many similar reports about the reform and eventual disintegration of the Soviet Union and its allies, where television took on the double role of agent and archivist with a specific angle and perspective. Second, the symbolic construction of the moment as one of total joy excluded, of course, other versions and assessments of this event, albeit less photogenic ones. When, for example, individuals' experience of the *Wende* was one of total shock – one of the East German informants in Meinhof and Galasinski (forthcoming) described it as if she were 'standing in front of a long tunnel, a long dark tunnel', and as if she were 'breaking through ice and drowning' – their non-participation in the rush through the wall also meant their absence from the visual representation of the event. Third, the one-sided construction of the historical significance of this event was short-lived, as other accounts and other suppressed social realities found their voice. Five years and again nine years later the complexities and complications of commemorating that day gave rise to very different televisual mediations (for a related discussion of the representation of May 1968, see Barthes 1986a:149–56).

Broken discourses

A sharp contrast to the celebratory mood of 1989 can be observed in the more broken and uneasy representations which we can witness annually in the television reports about 9 November anniversaries. News reports taken from two years, one from 1994, the other from 1998, demonstrate this in two ways. These two years correspond to different ritualistic moments in the time sequences. In the logic of ritualistic commemoration certain reoccurrences are marked as more important than others; the first and the fifth and the tenth anniversaries of an event are given more significance than, say, the third or the sixth or the ninth. Following that same logic, ZDF in 1994 foregrounded the fall of the Wall (fifth anniversary) whereas in 1998 they highlighted the Pogrom (60th anniversary). The commemoration of 9 November thus has to come to terms with its two competing legacies, that of the Pogrom and with it the relationship of contemporary Germany and Germans to their darkest history, and that of the fall of the Wall in Berlin, and with it the assessment of the GDR, its collapse, and the subsequent emergence and development of a united Germany. For each report the coexisting, though less ritualistically foregrounded, other anniversary provides an uneasy foil.

In 1994, the ZDF news programme *heute* decided to wrap both legacies into one news item, which they broadcast as item number two, only preceded by the report of the US mid-term elections. The way it was constructed highlights the ambivalences caused by juxtaposition of these events.

Text: ZDF, *heute*, 9 November 1994

Studio: 28 Jahre war sie das Symbol der deutschen Teilung. Heute vor fünf Jahren stürzte sie ein: die Mauer in Berlin. Für viele wurde ein Traum wahr, an jenem Abend des 9. November 1989. Die ersten Schritte Richtung Freiheit – Jubel, Freude, Verbrüderung.

Gesang: 'So ein Tag, so wunderschön wie heute, so ein Tag, der dürfte nie vergehn.'

Studio: Der neunte November ist aber nicht nur ein Tag der Freude, sondern auch ein Tag der Mahnung, der Erinnerung an die Pogromnacht gegen die Juden vor 56 Jahren.

Voice-over: Dort, wo vor fünf Jahren gegen 20.15 Uhr sich das erste Stück Mauer aufgetan hatte, an der Bornholmer Brücke, da wo sich die Berliner damals in die Arme fielen, mahnt heute abend eine Lichterkette eindringlich zum Brückenschlagen zwischen Ost und West.

Ein Tag in Berlin, der für die politischen Repräsentanten der Stadt mit dem Gedenken an die vielen Opfer der Mauer begann; ein Jahrestag als Mahnung daran, daß Freiheit täglich errungen werden müsse, gerade in Berlin die Opfer von Gewaltherrschaft in diesem Jahrhundert niemals vergessen werden dürfen.

Offizielle Freude aber ebenso lautstarker Protest: seit heute ist die Oberbaumbrücke, eine der wichtigsten Ost-West Verkehrsverbindungen wieder offen. Die Brücke im Kreuzberger Kiez heftig umstritten; die neue Straße bringe nur Lärm, Dreck und Autogestank. Störaktionen der Szene, die Nischenidylle von damals soll erhalten bleiben. Denken aus Mauerzeiten, so der Regierende Bürgermeister Eberhard Diepgen, das überwunden werden muß.

Diepgen: 'Jetzt ist die Mauer weg, Gott sei Dank, in den Köpfen von vielen Menschen besteht aber offensichtlich noch die Mauer. Aber wir alle Berliner werden den Versuch unternehmen, diese Mauer endgültig verschwinden zu lassen.

Voice-over: Der Gang durchs einst zugemauerte Brandenburger Tor, Symbol der deutschen Einheit über Jahrzehnte: Rudolf Scharping und die SPD-Parlamentarier wollten ihn an diesem Tag als zweifachen Appell verstanden wissen. Gerade die Deutschen müßten mit dem historischen Datum 9. November äußerst sorgsam umgehen.

Scharping: Wir haben aber eine Erbschaft, die Erbschaft der Schuld und der Scham und die Erbschaft des Erfolges im Durchsetzen von Freiheit und Demokratie. Für beide Erbschaften müssen wir einstehen.

Voice-over: Der neunte November, für Ignatz Bubis heute aber ein Tag, an die traurige Tatsache zu erinnern, daß viele in Deutschland die Nazigreuel einfach nicht wahrhaben oder relativieren wollen.
Bubis: Wenn auch die Freude über die deutsche Einheit groß ist, so muß man auch wissen, für die jüdische Gemeinschaft ist der 9. November 1938 eben ein besonderer Tag des Trauerns.
Voice-over: Trauerfeier zur Stunde im Haus der jüdischen Gemeinde zu Berlin. Gedenken zum 56. Jahrestag der Pogromnacht der Nazis. Gegen das Vergessen und Verdrängen, der Aufruf zur Wachsamkeit gegen Antisemitismus und Rassismus.

(*Studio:* For 28 years it was the symbol of German division. On this day, five years ago, it collapsed – the Wall in Berlin. For many a dream came true, on this evening of the ninth of November 1989. The first steps in the direction of freedom – jubilation, joy,
5   fraternization.
Song: 'Such a day, as wonderful as today, such a day should never end.'
Studio: But the ninth of November is not only a day of joy, but also a day of admonition, of remembering the night 56 years earlier, the
10   night of the pogrom against the Jews.
Report/Voice-over: At this point, where five years ago at 8.15 pm, the first bit of the wall opened, at the Bornholm bridge, where the people of Berlin fell into each others' arms, at this point a chain of lights reminds us today with fervour that we should build a bridge
15   between East and West.
For the political representatives, this day in Berlin had started with a commemoration of the many victims of the wall; an anniversary to remind everyone that liberty needs to be fought for every day, that especially in Berlin the victims of terror regimes must never be
20   forgotten.
Official joy accompanied by the voices of noisy protest: since today, the Oberbaum Bridge, one of the most important traffic connections between East and West, has reopened. This bridge in Kreuzberg is causing a lot of dispute: [opponents say] the new road will only
25   bring noise, dirt and car fumes. But, according to Eberhard Diepgen, the Mayor of Berlin, these protests are subversive actions of people from the Berlin 'scene', who are attempting to hold on to their idyllic niche, people with a frame of mind belonging to the days when the Wall was still there, a way of thinking that needs to be
30   overcome.

Diepgen: Now the Wall has gone, thank God, but it seems that we still have a Wall in the minds of many people. But all of us Berliners must try once and for all to make this wall disappear.

Voice-over: Walking through the once bricked-up Brandenburg Gate,
35 symbol of German Unity for decades for Rudolf Scharping and the MPs of the Social-Democratic Party this walk has a double meaning. The Germans, more than anyone else, need to be extremely careful with this historical date of the 9th of November.

Scharping: We have an inheritance, an inheritance of guilt and
40 shame, and an inheritance of success in establishing freedom and democracy. We need to bear witness to both of these inheritances.

Voice-over: For Ignatz Bubis, the ninth of November is a day to remember the terrible fact that many people in Germany do not want to recognize the Nazi terrors or want to play down their
45 unique horror.

Bubis: However much joy there is about German unification, one needs to know that the 9th of November 1938 is a special day of grieving.

Voice-over: A Memorial Service is taking place at this moment in the
50 house of the Jewish Community in Berlin. A commemoration of the 56th anniversary of the pogrom night of the Nazis. Against the forgetting and repressing of memories, a call to watchfulness against antisemitism and racism.)

[The numbering of the English texts will be used in the following discussions.]

Connecting themes

German news items on the public service channels normally follow one of three patterns: they use a studio introduction by a newscaster to introduce a subsequent report on scene; they restrict an item to the news studio without a subsequent report; or – and this is where German news conventions differ from, say, British versions – a studio item may be followed by a report about a different news item which has not previously been introduced by a newscaster. The news item under consideration here does not quite follow any of these three established patterns. Here, the studio newsreader appears twice: first to introduce theme number one (lines 1–5), the anniversary of the fall of the Wall, followed by a brief report-on-scene (lines 6–7), and subsequently to introduce theme number two, the anniversary of the Pogrom. However, it is the first theme which is followed up by the report, subsequent to the second studio introduction. Theme two, introduced by the newscaster (lines 8–10), is only fully followed up by a report at the very end of the news item (lines 42–53), although I will show that the voice-over text and what is being said in the commemorative speeches reverberates with mnemonic allusions to the second theme, albeit in a submerged form.

Let us now look at this in some detail. The item opens in the studio with the newsreader introducing theme number one: the fifth anniversary of the fall of the Wall in Berlin. This theme is immediately reinforced by the quotation from the ZDF's own news reports from 1989 which have been discussed earlier in this chapter. Now the sequence showing a group of jubilant people is recontextualized by the voice-over, which places and interprets it as a moment in the past which was then for many 'a dream come true', describing the excursion into West Berlin as stepping into freedom, and the mood at the time as one of 'jubilation, joy and fraternization'. After this upbeat introduction, the item unusually returns to the studio where the newscaster introduces the second theme. She now contrasts the two anniversaries, one as 'Tag der Freude' (day of joy) the other a day of 'Mahnung' (admonition).

Only after this double introduction does the main reporting of the day's events begin. What becomes immediately obvious by contrast with the original report in 1989, and the embedded extract from that earlier report, is the almost complete absence of the vocabulary of joy or any other evidence of positive celebration. The only happy reference is the one already mentioned, a quotation of past rather than present-day exuberance. Instead, the vocabulary of 'admonition' dominates. The idea appears three times altogether. Apart from its initial introduction in relation to the Pogrom night (lines 8–10), it reappears in relation to the need for greater unity between Germans (lines 11–12), and a third time in relation to both legacies of 9 November (lines 14–17). In the second instance, the need for greater unity – metaphorically expressed as a need to build bridges – is linked to and visually represented by the real bridge across the river Spree, the Bornholm bridge. Here, the voice-over tells us, the first bit of the Wall had opened up in 1989, and here today rows of candles are being lit, creating a chain of candle light, which is there to act as admonition: '*mahnt* eine Lichterkette ... zum Brückenschlagen zwischen Ost und West' (translated here idiomatically as 'a chain of lights reminds us ... that we should build a bridge between east and west'). Lines 14–17 continue with the theme of admonition, now set into the full context of what the date means. The anniversary is itself an admonition. Now the admonition is for the first time set in relation to the victims of terror regimes.

Here we have the first joining of the two themes: Nazi terror and its acts of violence are associated with acts of violence committed by the GDR regime. The voice-over loosely suggests this connection by the mnemonic wording 'Opfer von Gewaltherrschaft' (victims of terror regimes). However, the visuals over which this text is spoken tendentiously show the Mayor of Berlin, Diepgen, laying a wreath against a cross where people died in their attempt to escape from East Germany. Visually at least, only one reading of the 'terror regime' – that of the GDR – is represented.

Text	Reference in text	Reference in image	Image
Ein Tag in Berlin, der für die politischen Repräsentanten der Stadt mit dem Gedanken an *die* vielen Opfer der Mauer		GDR	Mayor of Berlin lays wreath on crosses
vielen Opfer der Mauer	GDR		
begann; ein Jahrestag als	GDR and	GDR	zoom in on cross;
Mahnung daran, daß	Nazi		inscription reads:
Freiheit täglich errungen	Germany		Maueropfer 1961
werden müsse, gerade in Berlin *die Opfer von Gewaltherrschaft in diesem Jahrhundert* niemals vergessen werden dürfen.			

The same double reference is present in the voice-over (lines 31–5) and in the speech by the then leader of the SPD Rudolf Scharping (lines 36–8), again in his use of emphasis and mnemonic phrases:

* *especially the Germans* need to be extremely careful with this *historical date*
* *inheritance/legacy of guilt and shame*

The only positive reference appears in the other part of Scharping's speech where the inheritance of guilt and shame is paired with the

* *inheritance/legacy of the success in establishing freedom and democracy*

The item then concludes with an activation of the main theme introduced in lines 8–10: the reference to the Pogrom night in 1938 with
extracts from a memorial service in the Jewish community house, and
a speech by the late Ignatz Bubis, head of the Central Council of Jews
in Germany. Bubis also mentions joy about German unification, but
sets this in contrast to the grieving which the memory of the pogrom
night brings.

• *Bubis: However much joy there is* about German unification, one needs
  to know that 9 November 1938 is *a special day of grieving*.

It should be obvious from the discussion so far that the historical
accident of the double anniversary of 9 November brings with it two
legacies which make any reporting of these events deeply problematical for the news media. Although the word 'joy' appears twice in the
text, there is no witnessing of any such joy in the way the item is constructed; on the contrary, the tone is one of deep solemnity. At the
very beginning of the item, a cheerful sequence taken from 1989 is
ring-fenced by a discourse of admonition which links the memory of
the Nazi past with the memory of the victims of the GDR regime, and
both with the difficulties which, in spite of unification, still divide the
east and the west.

This ongoing division is emphasized by one further sequence right in
the centre of the news report (lines 21–30) focusing on the ceremonial
opening of yet another bridge (the Oberbaumbrücke). The building of
this bridge – which materially as well as metaphorically is a vehicle for
connecting former East and West Berlin – is shown to be deeply divisive. The response to its opening (again symbolically on 9 November)
gives rise to the most confused and confusing part of the news item.

The voice-over contrasts official joy with loud protests against this
bridge, listing arguments for and against the bridge in rapid succession,
without making it at all obvious to whom the various sentiments are to
be attributed. The sequence below (lines 23–30) moves from a general
observation about the dispute caused by the bridge ('This bridge in
Kreuzberg is causing a lot of dispute') to a report of what the protesters
might say – in indirect speech identifiable by the subjunctive mood of
the verb in German ('the new road will only bring noise, dirt and car
fumes') – to a dismissal of the protesters ('subversive actions of people
from the Berlin 'scene' who are attempting to hold on to their idyllic
niche, people with a frame of mind belonging to the days when the
Wall was still there'), which only at the end is identifiable as the opin-

ions expressed by Mayor Diepgen. This is all spoken without any pause, stringing together in one continuous voice-over the conflicting sentiments about the event expressed by different groups of people. Visually the sequence shows us the paraphernalia of civil unrest: protest posters, policemen with dogs, a young man with long hair beaten and dragged away by police, a heavily guarded Mayor speaking from behind a set of bullet-proof shields. In the extract from his address we hear Diepgen not at all as the representative of 'official joy'; instead his words provide a most telling and highly contradictory account. The protesters are identified as the subversives of Berlin (the *Szene*), as people who want to hang on to their old niche-idyll (East Germany was often referred to as a 'niche-society'), as people who still think in the old ways of before unification, and as people who still have the Wall in their heads. Following on from a sequence where the voice-over to Diepgen's laying of the wreath for victims of the Wall linked the GDR with the Nazi past, these further allusions to the GDR again reinforce the sense that the tensions with history continue into the present day, rather than promoting any joyful celebration of unity achieved (see also Meinhof 1998:16–24).

9 November 1998

Four years later, and 9 November 1998 sees the ninth anniversary of the fall of the Wall in Berlin coincide with the 60th Anniversary of the Pogrom. Now the significance of temporal reoccurrence moves the commemoration of the Pogrom more to the foreground, and almost entirely replaces references to the other anniversary. However, as the order of the first seven news items of ZDF of that day shows, other events relating to the GDR have now become the focus of this anniversary.

1 Taxation reform
2 Trade union item: tackling unemployment
3 *Commemoration of the Pogrom night*
4 *Stasi documentation centre opened*
5 *The PDS and its constitutional status (Party of Democratic Socialism)*
6 EU foreign ministers in Brussels
7 Agreement about Kosovo

Other events of the day pushed the commemoration into third place on the agenda. But more importantly, as the texts below show, the Pogrom anniversary is now taking up a report of its own. Instead of the ambivalence between joy and admonition of the report four years earlier, and the genuine unease about how to account for the legacy of the GDR itself, we have two consecutive news items which foreground the deeply problematical nature of the German relationship to the past.

Item 3 highlights the continuing difficulties of how to come to terms with the Third Reich in present day Germany.

Texts: *heute,* 9 November 1998

Item 3: Gedenken an die Pogromnacht
Studio: Heute vor 60 Jahren begann die organisierte Verfolgung der Juden. In der Pogromnacht vom 9. auf den 10. November zündeten Nazis Synagogen an, zerstörten Häuser und Geschäfte jüdischer Familien. Der Begriff Pogrom stammt aus dem Russischen. Er bedeutet Vernichtung oder Verwüstung. Heute war die zentrale Gedenkveranstaltung in der Berliner Synagoge am Prenzlauer Berg.
Voice-over: Um Erinnerung und Wachsamkeit ging es heute Abend: mehrere tausend Berliner auf einem Schweigemarsch zum jüdischen Gemeindehaus. Beklemmender Bezug zur Gegenwart: in der Nacht hatte es wieder antisemitische Übergriffe gegeben. Vor genau 60 Jahren zerstörten Nazi-Schergen Tausende von Synagogen, Gebethäuser und Geschäfte in jüdischem Besitz. 91 Menschen wurden getötet. Dem Menetekel, das zeigte, wozu die Nazis imstande waren, sahen viele tatenlos zu. Bundespräsident Roman Herzog mahnte: Dieser Schlag in das Gesicht der Menschlichkeit dürfe sich nicht wiederholen.
Herzog: Durch Verdrängen, durch Vergessen, durch Auf-sich-beruhen-lassen werden wir mit dieser Katastrophe der Zivilisation nicht fertig werden.
Voice-over: Herzog forderte aber auch die Erinnerung, gerade für jüngere Leute in verständlicher Form wachzuhalten:
Herzog: Wer mich kennt, weiß, daß ich alles eher wünsche als ein Verschweigen, aber auch Abstumpfung ist bei dieser jungen Generation eine Gefahr, die wir nicht gering ansetzen dürfen.
Voice-over: Heftige Kritik am Schriftsteller Martin Walser, der zuletzt eine politische Instrumentalisierung von Auschwitz beklagt hatte, übte ein sichtlich verbitterter Ignatz Bubis. Der intellektuelle Internationalismus sei nicht frei von Antisemitismus, meinte er.
Ignatz Bubis (Zentralrat der Juden in Deutschland): Diese Verbrechen waren nun einmal da und werden durch das Vergessen-Wollen nicht verschwinden, und es ist eine geistige Brandstiftung, wenn

jemand darin eine Instrumentalisierung von Auschwitz für gegenwärtige Zwecke sieht.
Voice-over: In Dresden begann mit dem Spatenstich symbolisch der Neubau einer Synagoge. Sie entsteht unweit vor dem Ort, wo vor 60 Jahren die Semper Synagoge zerstört worden war. Ein Judenstern aus Kerzenlicht am Brandenburger Tor. Der 9. November hat, gerade in Berlin, zwei Gesichter.

(Commemoration of the Pogrom night
Studio: 60 years ago to the day the systematic persecution of the Jews began. In the pogrom night from 9 to 10 November, Nazis set fire to synagogues, destroyed houses and businesses of Jewish families. The term Pogrom comes from the Russian, and means destruc-
5 tion or devastation. Today the main commemoration took place in the Berlin Synagogue located in the Prenzlauer Berg district of Berlin.
Report/voice over: Commemoration and watchfulness were the themes of this evening: several thousand people from Berlin took
10 part in a silent march to the Jewish community centre. A disturbing connection to today: once again during the night there had been antisemitic activities. Exactly 60 years ago, Nazi henchmen had destroyed thousands of synagogues, houses of prayer and shops owned by Jews. Ninety-one people were killed. Many people wit-
15 nessed this 'writing on the wall', which showed what the Nazis were capable of, without doing anything. President Roman Herzog warned: This slap in the face of humanity must never be repeated.
Herzog: We will not cope with this catastrophe of civilization by repression, by forgetting, by letting things rest.
20 *Voice-over:* But Herzog also asked that memory be kept alive in a comprehensible form especially for younger people.
Herzog: Anyone who knows me, knows that I would have anything rather than concealment. But for this young generation there is also a risk which we cannot take lightly, of the impact becoming blunted.
25 *Voice-over:* A clearly bitter Ignatz Bubis vehemently criticized the writer Martin Walser, who had recently deplored a political instrumentalization of Auschwitz. He said that intellectual internationalism was not free of antisemitism.
Ignatz Bubis (Central Council of Jews in Germany): These crimes really
30 happened and they won't disappear by wanting to forget them, and it is arson of the mind when someone sees in this an instrumentalization of Auschwitz for contemporary purposes.

Voice-over: With the cutting of the turf, the rebuilding of the Dresden Synagogue was symbolically launched. It will be erected
35   not far from the spot where 60 years ago the Semper synagogue had been destroyed.
A Star of David in candle-light at the Brandenburg gate. Especially in Berlin, the 9th of November has two faces.)

The report in this item which follows the studio introduction draws on different aspects of that day, both present and past:

- a silent march commemorating the Pogrom (lines 9–10)
- a reference to antisemitic activities in present day Berlin (lines 11–12)
- report/historical footage from the Pogrom night in 1938 (lines 12–16)
- extracts from the commemoration in the synagogue in the presence of the German President and Ignatz Bubis (lines 16–32)
- the symbolic cutting of the turf for the building of a new Synagogue in Dresden to replace the one burnt down by the Nazis 60 years earlier (lines 33–6)
- a concluding brief reference to the double anniversary of the 9th of November (lines 37–8)

This is a very different report from the one in 1994. The issue which implicitly and explicitly dominates it is the row sparked off by the German writer Martin Walser in his acceptance speech of the peace prize of the German publishers, where he had referred to the 'instrumentalization of Auschwitz'. The problem is symptomatic of the unresolved difficulties of accounting for the German past. Like in the famous 'Historikerstreit' (historians' dispute) in the 1980s, any discussion of the horrendous crimes of the Holocaust which seems to excuse or relativize them, or which suggests that Germans have done enough to atone for past crimes and that they should now look forward rather than backwards, is bound to bring to the foreground unhealed wounds and divisions. For Walser publicly to enter the debate with such a polemical expression as the 'Instrumentalisierung von Auschwitz' has to be seen – at best – as misguided, even if in the context of his speech he may have intended something less crude than the subsequent interpretation. That Bubis picked up on this in his speech by declaring it as 'arson of the mind', a phrase he later withdrew, places Walser implicitly in line with antisemitic and racist agitation. The term *Brandstifter* (arsonist) intertextually recalls a famous play by the Swiss writer Max Frisch, *Biedermann und die Brandstifter*, about the gradual spread of violence in a liberal society which cannot be bothered to check it; the play is usually understood as an allegory about the rise of fascism. President Herzog's speech tries to defuse the conflicts by juxtaposing the two poles. On the one hand, he points to the danger arising from trying to deny the memories of the Holocaust through repression, forgetting, letting things rest (line 18–19), concealment (line 23); on the other, he also warns of the risk that young people may lose interest by overexposure to the Holocaust crimes, so that the impact becomes blunted (lines 23–4). These are carefully chosen formulations which signal to the listeners a possible compromise in the row since the first is clearly identifiable with the Bubis, the second with the Walser position. Such general phraseology belongs to the acceptable rhetoric of German political discourse about these highly sensitive issues, part of the same set as *Mahnung* (admonition), *Wachsamkeit* (alertness), *Schuld* (guilt) and so forth, a rhetoric which is dulled by its very familiarity.

If we compare this reporting of the anniversary of 9 November to the one that preceded it by four years, the total absence of reference to the fall of the Wall becomes notable. Only at the very end, in the cryptic reference of lines 37–8, is there an allusion to the double legacy of the day: 'A Star of David in candle-light at the Brandenburg gate. Especially in Berlin, *the 9th of November has two faces.*'

However, the next item of that day's news, item four, explicitly mentions the anniversary of the fall of the Wall, but not in the context of celebration or even commemoration, but by explicitly problematizing GDR history. Instead of the (symbolic) opening of a bridge between East and West as in 1994, we have the (equally symbolic) opening of a documentation centre about the GDR's secret service, the *Stasi*.

Item 4: Stasi-Dokumentationszentrum (Opening lines only)

> Das Ministerium für Staatssicherheit. Es galt als Schild und Schwert der DDR. Die Stasi als Machtinstrument der SED-Diktatur, darüber informiert jetzt ein Dokumentationszentrum in Berlin. Heute, am 9. Jahrestag des Mauerfalls war die Eröffnung.
>
> (The Ministry for State Security. It was seen as sword and shield of the GDR. A documentation centre in Berlin informs us now about the Stasi as an instrument of power of the SED dictatorship. Today, on the ninth anniversary of the fall of the Wall, it opened to the public.)

The next item, number five, implicitly continues the theme of the GDR by focusing on the PDS which had emerged after the *Wende* as successor of the defunct Socialist Unity Party (SED), and which is achieving respectable success with the electorate in some of the new federal states (that is, in former GDR territory) though none at all in the old ones (that is, in west Germany). Here the question is raised whether or not the Federal Constitutional Court needs to continue to observe the party to test its democratic credentials. Again it foregrounds the problematic legacy of the GDR.

Item 5

PDS Beobachtung: Müssen die Verfassungsschützer die PDS weiter im Auge behalten? Innenminister Schily will prüfen, ob die Nachfolgepartei der SED weiter beobachtet werden soll. Es ist eine vertrackte Situation, wenn die PDS, wie in Mecklenburg-Vorpommern an der Regierung beteiligt sei und gleichzeitig observiert werde. Bisher stuft das Bundesamt für Verfassungsschutz die PDS als linksextremistisch ein.

(PDS observation. Must the protectors of the constitution still keep an eye on the PDS? Minister of the Interior, Schily, wants to check whether the party which grew out of the SED needs to remain under observation. According to him, it is a tricky situation, when the PDS forms part of a government as it does in Mecklenburg-Vorpommern, and yet it is still under observation. Up till now the Constitutional Bureau has assessed the PDS as a left-extremist party.)

The theme of the Stasi documentation centre was revisited later that evening in the ZDF news magazine *heute*-Journal, again by deliberately drawing on the double significance of the date of 9 November. Intriguingly, the contrasting pair used in the 1994 report (joy versus shame) reappears in the journalist's introduction, but it is now not clear whether 'shame' refers to the Nazi past or to the shamefulness of the GDR's secret service.

heute-Journal

Es ist ein seltsamer Zufall der deutschen Geschichte, daß ein Datum des Sich-Schämens mit einem Tag der Freude zusammenfällt, denn heute vor neun Jahren fiel die Mauer in Berlin. Die Fundamente der DDR waren gebrochen, und Licht drang in so manches finstere Gemäuer. So mancher Bürger erfuhr, daß es über ihn geheime Akten gab, aber nicht alle Geheimnisse eines zugemauerten Staates sind heute zugänglich und offen.

(It is a strange accident of German history that a date of shame coincides with a day of joy, because it was today, nine years ago, that the wall in Berlin fell. The foundations of the GDR were broken and light shone behind more than one set of dark walls. Quite a number of citizens found out that there were secret documents about them, but not all secrets of a walled-in state are today openly accessible.)

Conclusion

What the extracts from the news reporting of *heute* on 9 November 1998 demonstrate is that the rhetoric of unity, which still provided one discursive thread during the news reporting of 1994, has given way in 1998 to an open problematizing of the GDR and its past. The absence of joy in the reporting was already noticeable on the fifth anniversary, which was dominated by the discourse of admonition about the different legacies of the German past. By 1998, and undoubtedly influenced by the fact that the year coincided with the 60th anniversary of the Pogrom, there is even less optimism to be registered. Any joyful commemoration of the bringing down of the Wall and any celebration of unity between east and west has been superseded by grim and divisive memories of the GDR, a struggle to find new (political) roles in a united Germany, and a continuing deep unease about the legacy of the Third Reich. The double commemorations of 9 November and their reporting in the news media will undoubtedly continue to offer insights for discourse analysts into the nature of the divisions in contemporary Germany. Where commemorative discourses about the fall of the Wall and what this signifies provide us with an interpretation of east-west disunities, the commemorations of the Pogrom night will add to this the pains of an unresolved past for all Germans.

References

Barthes, Roland (1986a) 'From history to reality', in Barthes (1986b), 127–54.
Barthes, Roland (1986b) *The Rustle of Language* (ed. R. Howard) (Oxford: Blackwell).
Becker, Karin (1995) 'Media and the ritual process', in *Media, Culture and Society* 17, 629–46.
Dayan, Daniel and Elihu Katz (1992) *Media Events: The Live Broadcasting of History* (Cambridge, MA: Harvard University Press).
Foucault, Michel (1970) *The Order of Things. An Archaeology of the Human Sciences* (London: Tavistock).

Frisch, Max (1962) *Biedermann und die Brandstifter* (Frankfurt/Main: Suhrkamp).

Meinhof, Ulrike Hanna (1998) *Language Learning in the Age of Satellite Television* (Oxford: Oxford University Press).

Meinhof, Ulrike Hanna and Dariusz Galasinski (forthcoming) 'Photography, memory, and the construction of identities on the former East–West German border'.

Nietzsche, Friedrich (1967) *The Will to Power*. Translated by W. Kaufmann, and R. J. Hollingdale (New York: Vintage Books).

3
'Go East, Young Man ...' – Gendered Representations of Identity in Television Dramas about 'East Germany'

Kathrin Hörschelmann

Introduction

> Amerigo Vespucci the voyager arrives from the sea. A crusader standing erect, his body in armor, he bears the European weapons of meaning. Behind him are the vessels that will bring back to the European West the spoils of a paradise. Before him is the Indian 'America', a nude woman reclining in her hammock, an unnamed presence of difference, a body which awakens within a space of exotic fauna and flora.
>
> de Certeau 1988:xxv

In his preface to *The Writing of History*, Michel de Certeau describes the first encounter of West European 'discoverer' Vespucci with the 'New World', America, based on an etching by Jan van der Straet. The continent is depicted here as a nude woman,

> a *nuova terra* not yet existing on maps – an unknown body destined to bear the name, Amerigo, of its inventor. This is *writing that conquers*. It will use the New World as if it were a blank, 'savage' page on which Western desire will be written. It will transform the space of the other into a field of expansion for a system of production.
>
> de Certeau 1988:xxv–xxvi

Why start with such an example? Is it not too far removed from the time and place of German (re)unification? I believe not. Present day discourses on German identity not only manufacture a difference between the 'old' and the 'new' Länder that comes close to mirroring the encounter between *terra nuova* and *terra antigua* described above; they also proceed with a strictly comparable gendering method that projects traditional western views of femininity onto the east German 'other', which is seen as nude, a blank page 'waiting' to be inscribed. Similar to de Certeau's analysis of ethnography's construction of the 'other', this feminization revolves around two, apparently divergent images: a diabolical, feminine body on the one hand and a 'paradise lost' on the other (1988:233–4). Both these images arise from and inform an eroticization of the other's body, a nude female figure that fascinates and threatens at once (227–32).

In contemporary discourses about German identity such constructions of western masculinity versus eastern femininity work on both a direct personified, and an indirect metaphorical, level. The reader, listener or viewer is confronted either with a female *figure* symbolizing 'the' east or with *metaphors* that mirror gendered attributes in such a way that they 'naturalize' an argument. In the first case, the female 'other' becomes a 'metaphor for her land' (Shohat in young 1996:20–1), while in the second an implicitly gendered opposition makes the discourse more 'intelligible'.

In this chapter a number of films broadcast around the seventh anniversary of German (re)unification in 1997 will be analysed. They illustrate how visions of east and west German unity draw on gendered constructions while still excluding east German *women as active personalities*. The films operate with relations of gender in *partially* subversive ways. None the less, they utilize traditional binaries and marginalize those groups that apparently do not 'fit'.

Although the 'new world' might have seemed like a 'blank page' to its so-called European 'discoverers', of course it had its own varied histories and did not easily consent to the process of colonization that was to ensue. In eastern Germany the same must be seen as true. It would result in an over-estimation of the perceived power of present dominant discourses if only those of the media were to be considered. This chapter will therefore conclude with a consideration of audience members' own reactions to such representations and of how they describe *their* experiences with unification from a socially embedded, yet personal perspective.

Visions of unity

Representations of post-unification Germany often start out from an explicit understanding that the 'east' and 'west' remain specific in socio-cultural/economic characteristics and are still largely split. In the following section four films broadcast around 3 October 1997 that appear to envisage *unity* in a somewhat different way will be analysed. These television dramas were situated during and after autumn 1989, and addressed the issue of unification directly. They shared a range of narrative characteristics such as their illustration of conflicts of economic ownership, 'development', and romantic/sexual encounters between east and west Germans. Gender relations played an important part in all of them. (The first film, *Stilles Land*, will be treated individually, while the other three will be analysed comparatively. Brief synopses are provided.)

Stilles Land (Silent Land)

Set in the period of autumn 1989, this film tells the story of a theatre-group from Anklam (near Berlin) caught in the middle of political change. While their country is getting ready for revolution they prepare a performance of Waiting for Godot *but do not take part in any of the demonstrations or activities. None of the actors is particularly motivated or gifted as a performer. A few weeks before the premiere, however, the Berlin Wall collapses. Claudia, assistant and girlfriend of director Kai, decides to go to Berlin and returns, four days later, with Thomas, a young and fashionable man from the west. He is excited about the theatre right from the start and manages to motivate everyone in the group (apart from Kai). As a consequence the performance improves radically, but the audience is still small on the opening night. Despite seeming undecided at first, Claudia splits from Kai in order to move with Thomas to Hamburg. The film ends with a positive outlook on the future of the theatre none the less. In the final sequences Kai is shown as he looks optimistically into the auditorium.*

Stilles Land presents an empathetic view of people in East Germany during the 'revolution'. However, it works with relations of gender and 'othering' similar to those discussed in the introduction and the plot establishes a basic structure, which reappears in the films to come. The story sets up a clear distinction between the politically inactive, unmotivated and incapable theatre group with their unattractive, impulsive and somewhat fanatical director, and the fashionable, bright young man from the West, whose introduction marks a radical shift of events. In a crucial scene, he is thus shown surrounded by the whole group who keep their eyes glued on him as he describes the 'wonderful' opportunities lying ahead of them. Thomas, portrayed as the generous helper from West Germany, represents a complete antithesis to Kai. He is smartly dressed with a bright red pullover and a black leather jacket, talks calmly, smiles a lot and has his blond hair neatly cut. Kai, on the contrary, never wears anything but a dark-grey hand-knitted jumper and worn-out jeans. His thin long hair is untrimmed, he often talks with an aggressive, frustrated voice and makes inconsiderate, depressing comments to the group. Only in the final scenes, *after* Thomas's assistance has led to a better performance, does Kai's face light up a little and his speech adopts an excited tone. He has to admit defeat, nevertheless, as Thomas 'wins' Claudia's love and friendship from him. Claudia leaves Kai as well as the group *behind* to start a new life with Thomas in the West.

The film deals with more than just a general story of change and romantic conflict. It constructs an image of East Germany as impotent, needing 'development' aid from the masculine West, not just in financial but also 'mental' terms, and having to trade in female protagonists in return. By not interrogating this construction critically, the film repeats the theme of sexual/reproductive robbery masked by solidarity impulses that were displayed in many colonialist tales of the nineteenth century. It points towards unity as having only *one* option for successful completion: eastern Germany's subservient accession to the system of patriarchal, western 'potency' and an unquestioning acceptance of its traits.

Interestingly, the films to follow play with gender divisions in quite the opposite way, while still employing metaphors of femininity and masculinity in their depictions of east and west Germany. A strictly sexual-romantic plot facilitates all of their narratives, but the direction has now changed.

Amerika

Lilly, a young waitress from Hamburg, inherits a restaurant in 'Amerika'. Her initial excitement is followed by shock when she discovers that this is a small village in Saxony and that the 'Alter Krug' is a completely run-down hot-dog canteen. Nevertheless, she decides to 'develop' it into a posh restaurant with the help of her uncle Otto, Karla and Thien, who were formerly running it. In addition to financial problems, Lilly soon meets competition from a west German property management firm. Her relationship to Otto, Karla, Thien and Rudi, a young local man who initially wanted to buy 'Alter Krug', also proves difficult. In the course of the film, however, Lilly and Rudi develop a romantic relationship, culminating in a 'happy ending'. The restaurant slowly turns into a success, yet at its height it is blown up by the competitor firm. Lilly's dreams are shattered. She goes back to Hamburg, but six months later the 'Amerikans' visit her and ask her to come back to 'Alter Krug', which they have managed to rebuild. The film ends with a picture of them walking together into the sunset.

Reise nach Weimar (Journey to Weimar)

Young and beautiful Mafalda from Munich travels to Weimar with her mother (ex-East German) and her grandfather (Italian) in order to inspect a house that they intend to buy and turn into a money-making pizzeria. On her first day in Weimar Mafalda meets Hauke, an unemployed, ex-communist teacher who has a reputation for 'flirtatiousness', impulsive behaviour and alcohol-addiction. The two fall in love but their romance is destroyed when Hauke learns about Mafalda's commercial ambition. He reacts with fury, injures the property manager and is finally arrested by the police. Mafalda returns to Munich with her mother, disappointed but still in love. She splits from her previous partner and moves to Italy to live with her grandfather. The latter, however, has already initiated a plot to bring the couple together again and to end the restaurant plans. When Mafalda applies for an executive secretarial job with a mysterious Russian businessman (a friend of her grandfather), she meets 'personnel manager' Hauke for an interview. Their passionate reunion concludes the film.

Ein Schloß für Rita (A castle for Rita)

The plot evolves around conflicts of economic and personal/romantic competition. Central protagonist Rita, who works as a successful book-keeper for a high-profile property-developer in Frankfurt/Main, is sent to Erfurt by her ex-lover/boss Eberhard in order to choose and purchase a suitable property for building a themed holiday-park. She soon finds out that this is just a ploy to get rid of her but falls in love with an old castle near Erfurt, which she decides to develop into an up-market hotel on her own. Needing the support of a 'native' to get planning permission, Rita turns to the local stonemason Hubert, whom she convinces to take on a DM16 million investment plan. Hubert approaches Rita romantically but separates from her after discovering that she works for his west German rival (Eberhard) and has only used him to achieve her own egoistic goals. Rita, however, does not give up so easily. Utilizing her inside knowledge of the Frankfurt firm, she reveals Eberhard's hidden bankruptcy to his creditors, who immediately withdraw all their loans. Eberhard has to give up the project and flees to Switzerland, while Rita and Hubert are happily reunited, forming a partnership on both business and personal levels from now on.

One of the main points in common between these films is their cen-
tredness on romantic/sexual encounters between young, west German
women and east German men. The women are portrayed as dissatisfied
with their life in the west, looking for a fresh challenge and potentially
a new romantic relationship. They all come to the east with a specific
project in mind. 'Developing' restaurants or hotels 'over there'
promises to be an adventurous way to achieve personal growth, liberation and economic upgrading. None of the women have any doubt
about the justification of their plans. They only see the great opportunities presented to *them*:

Lilly: Ich will aus diesem Laden hier was machen, mit Euch zusammen. Den Leuten sollen die Augen übergehen, wenn's hier fünf-
gängige Menüs gibt, frische Forellen, Fasanen, Mousse au Chocolat.
(*Lilly*: I want to make something of this place with you. People will
be amazed when there are five-course dinners on the menu here,
fresh trout, pheasants, mousse au chocolat!)

Mafalda: Mama, dieses neue Lokal möcht ICH führen.
Mutter: Was?
Mafalda: Ja!
Mutter: Aber wofür hast de 'n dann so lange studiert, Kind?
Mafalda: Ich weiss es nicht. Jedenfalls möcht ich hier dieses Lokal
aufbaun. Darf ich?
Mutter: Aber ja, Mafalda!
(Mafalda: Mum, *I* would like to manage this new restaurant!
Mother: What?
Mafalda: Yes!
Mother: But why have you studied for so long then, girl?
Mafalda: I don't know. In any case, I would like to build up this
restaurant. May I?
Mother: Of course, Mafalda!)

Rita: Das wird MEIN Schloss! ... Ich hab mich auf den ersten Blick in
dieses Schloss verliebt.
(*Rita*: This will be MY castle! ... I fell in love with this castle at first
sight.)

All of the women approach the east like heroes approached the
colonies in late-colonialist films:

The Empire provided a narrative space for the realization of manhood, both as action and maturation. The colonial landscape is expansive, enabling the hero to roam and giving us the entertainment of action; it is unexplored, giving him the task of discovery and us the pleasures of mystery; it is uncivilized, needing taming, providing the spectacle of power; it is difficult and dangerous, testing his machismo, providing us with suspense. In other words, the colonial landscape provides the occasion for the realization of white male virtues, which are not qualities of being but doing – acting, discovering, taming, conquering.

Dyer 1988:52

In the films being considered here, however, 'machismo' is not at stake. Rather, they focus on the experiences of *heroines* who have learnt the trades of their male west German partners well and now see their first chance for 'testing' them. The women, while adopting 'masculine' tricks and developing such interests, are also still cast as very 'feminine'. This gives them access to a double role as competitors *as well as* romantic love-objects.

Initially, Lilly, Mafalda and Rita are drawn in terms of binary opposition to the men they encounter in east Germany. These men carry the stigma of having lived in rigid, failed socialism and of having had to struggle more or less successfully to cope with the changes. In *Amerika* the main male protagonist is depressed, aimless, secretive and corrupt, while Hauke in *Reise nach Weimar* spends most of his time drinking, doing odd jobs and reminiscing about the GDR, where people were treated 'equally' and working-class kids could receive a good education in secondary schools like his own. Hubert, by contrast, has been more successful in developing his own business after the *Wende*. His attitudes, however, remain stuck in the casual, informal, non-entrepreneurial styles associated with GDR times. As a consequence, Hubert's meetings with Rita are characterized by his humorous attempts to win her respect and by her efforts to *train* him in the behaviour of west German business men. In all the three films, the east German men appear as less polished, rougher, not quite so civilized and needing to be 'tamed'. Rita does this in the cruellest way. She actually runs 'classes' to train Hubert. Yet Rudi and Hauke also receive significant 'help' to reconfigure their lives and to discover their self-esteem via Lilly's and Mafalda's love. The women's relationships with them take on aspects of the same responsibility that Dyer has described in his analysis of *Simba*:

Colonialism, as a social, political and economic system, even in fictions, also carries with it challenges of responsibility, of the establishment and maintenance of order, of the application of reason and authority to situations.

Dyer 1988:52–3

Dyer's description also parallels the binary construction of *mise-en-scène* in the films above. In each of them, landscapes of the east are set off strictly against those in the west in characteristic spatio-temporal imagery. The symbols employed manufacture a contrast between modernity/civilization/progress versus backwardness/nature/failed development. This is notable with respect to the lighting strategies, which make places in the west appear clearly visible, clear, flashy and light, while Amerika, Weimar and most of Erfurt come across as dark, shadowy and overcast. It often rains in these places (*never* in the west), and even the film quality seems to decline with pictures becoming blotchy and more diffused. Elements of a journey *from* west *to* east, and often back, are significant in each film, again mirroring Dyer's analysis:

The credit sequence ... uses aerial shots moving through space, rather than pans with their fixed vantage point; it emphasises the view from above, not that from the ground, and the modernity of air travel after the primitivism of the machete. It also brings the hero to Africa ..., brings the solution to the problems of deceptive, unfixed appearances set up by the pre-credit sequence.

Dyer 1988:52

The most explicit 'time-travel' metaphors are employed in *Amerika*. Lilly's first trip to Saxony is cast as a successive downward journey by train. Starting off from a very modern station and in an extremely fast, comfortable Intercity-Express, she changes into ever slower and less serviced trains, finally sitting in one that can be overtaken by a cyclist and has no comfort at all. Its lack of service is epitomized in the waiter, a sweaty, unclean, poorly dressed man who has nothing on the menu but hot-dogs. Lilly herself has dressed the part of an early-century female traveller, carrying old-fashioned suitcases and wearing a retro-style dress and hat. It is as though she expected to arrive in a country lagging behind by centuries. The viewer's expectation is framed in a similar way by the television announcer's introduction and the sequence of Lilly's first appearance. An ironic contrast is created both times between US-'America' and 'Amerika' in Saxony. This allows the viewers and Lilly only one reaction: disappointed hope.

Moderatorin: Eine schöne junge Frau, liebe Zuschauer, macht eine Erbschaft, ein Restaurant in Amerika. Eigentlich alles paletti, oder? Eben nicht! Die Sache hat nämlich gleich zwei Haken: Mit Amerika sind nicht die USA gemeint, sondern ein 80-Seelen-Dorf im Osten Deutschlands. Das Restaurant entpuppt sich als heruntergekommener Gasthof. Und zu allem Überfluß sind auch noch Immobilienhaie scharf darauf. Kann Liliane den Alten Krug trotzdem wieder auf die Beine bringen? Sophie von Kessel in einer ganz und gar ungewöhnlichen Liebesgeschichte. Amerika.

(*Announcer, addressing viewers*: A beautiful young woman ... inherits a restaurant in *Amerika*. Sounds great, doesn't it? Well actually no! For there are two catches to this: *Amerika* does not mean the USA but a village of 80 inhabitants in the east of Germany. The restaurant turns out to be a rundown pub. And on top of all that rich estate agents are keen on it. Can Liliane restore the 'Alter Krug' nevertheless? Sophie von Kessel in a totally unusual love-story. *Amerika*.)

Lilly: Ein Restaurant in Amerika. Phh, ich weiss, das klingt albern, aber ...
Notar: Was ich Ihnen dazu noch sagen muss, ist, ...
Lilly: Wissen Sie, wie gross Amerika ist?!
Notar: Es hat etwa 80 Einwohner und liegt in der Nähe von Chemnitz. Ruhig, schön gelegen, saubere Luft. Mein Kollege schreibt, man kann es von Glauchau aus mit dem Zug erreichen.
Lilly: Von Glauchau, mit dem Zug ...?
Notar: Ja, keine 40 Minuten.
Lilly: Und ich bin die einzige Erbin.
Lilly, at the solicitor's; astounded, keeping her hands in front of her mouth, eyes wide open: A restaurant in America. Phh, I know it sounds silly but ...
Solicitor: What I have to add is ...
Lilly: Do you know how big America is?!
Solicitor: It has about 80 inhabitants and is situated near Chemnitz. Beautifully positioned, clean air. My colleague says that one can reach it by train from Glauchau.
Lilly, slow, after moment of silence: By train, from Glauchau ...?
Solicitor: Yes, in less than 40 minutes.
Lilly: And I am the only heir.)

Having heard the solicitor's description Lilly's face drops, her mouth opens in horror and she sits down. There is a succession of further moments of shock, when she arrives at the old station of 'Amerika', walks through the village for the first time, spots the inherited 'restaurant', and finally enters it.

The walk through the village draws on constructions of the hero in Westerns (for example, *Dead Man*), slowly marching through a silent, hostile and morbid place, achieving a maximum of suspense and, in Lilly's case, of irony. The village seems poor, its inhabitants unfriendly, threatening. Children with ragged clothes and sad, dirty faces stand lonely by a gate and gaze at her. Several rough-looking men pose along the side of the sandy, unlevelled street. A cowherd passes in front of Lilly as she looks around in astonishment. The place's ancient and uncivilized impression is further emphasized by the background song (*Night falls*) which adds to both the horror and the irony of this sequence.

Finally, Lilly arrives at 'Alter Krug'. Her suitcase drops as she stares at the derelict, unpainted building that stands alone in a 'desert'. When she eventually enters it, one can almost smell the fatty hot-dogs and potato-salad that make up the menu. The first shot of this sequence is a close-up of a sausage dug into mustard. The camera moves up from here to bring into picture an unfriendly, hostile looking man and finally the rest of the shadowy room.

The impressions of backwardness and morbidity created here are reinforced by the restaurant manager's and assistant's age. Only Thien and Rudi are young and available for possible romance. Lilly's love-interest develops accordingly, yet it is only Rudi who appears as a potential partner. Thien does not even come into the equation and remains a withdrawn, silent figure. Only towards the end is he allowed to prove his capacity, when Lilly discovers that his cooking expertise could actually save her restaurant. Rudi, who is *always* dressed in grey, ex-GDR army clothes, seems equally incapable at first. He does, however, introduce an element of local opposition to Lilly's entrepreneurial plans and romantic advances that has to be overruled by taming in a loving relationship.

Reise nach Weimar and *Ein Schloß für Rita* proceed in exactly the same way. In both films, the east German partners are resistant to western intrusion or 'occupation' and to feeling 'used'. While Hubert moans about Rita's '*Wessi*-methods', reminds her of the existence of not just one (west German) Frankfurt and separates from her because of refusing to be her 'silly *Ossi*', Hauke voices criticism about the two-faced character of western 'assistance'. His love for Mafalda is thrown into disarray because of her 'capitalist' interests. Yet Hauke expresses his resistance to her in a totally uncivilized, impulsive and aggressive manner. It is only with the help of Mafalda's grandfather that he 'comes to reason' and can give their love a second chance. 'Taming' is needed in both cases to enable the men to achieve their aims.

As for the women, their success depends on the employment of 'masculine' tricks while maintaining strong traits of femininity. Although they are given considerable scope for achievement, it is the existence of west German male competitors that frames their actions and forces upon them a 'superior' measurement. They are cast as economically and emotionally dependent on their father, ex-lover or boss, and have to liberate themselves from these men's influence.

Although playing a significant role in all the films, the west German rivals appear as a strange *absence*. They are usually only glanced, shown in quick sequences and presented as not really personally involved with their daughter's or partner's projects in east Germany. A sense of detachment prevails in each case. They achieve a position of superiority that is also enhanced by the women's emotional attachment and remorsefulness for having to oppose or leave them in the course of events. Rita, Mafalda and Lilly all suffer from moments of breakdown and instability. Conversely, this brings them closer to their east German companions. Showing feelings, admitting weaknesses and revealing a 'human face' appear to be as much preconditions for a loving east/west relationship as does the east German men's assertion of power and confidence in the end. In the interest of constructing an image of successful unity, the narratives thus draw on both partners' social inferiority that can be partially overcome by 'solidarity'. The films provide some scope for opposition and alternative action, yet also still rely on given power-relations, because the west German men's overwhelming control is weakened for a *fraction* only. It retains its force by remaining the ultimate measure of the protagonists' practices.

The films also gloss over and cast in silence another important social group: east German women figure in none of them as potential competitors. They are either old, insignificant, or simply non-existent. Thus, Hauke, Rudi and Hubert do not have any close relationships with, or deep emotional interests in, an east German woman. They are freely available, it seems. A peculiar lack of resistance from their east German 'sisters' thus enables Mafalda, Rita and Lilly to achieve their economic and personal aims.

This is a significant observation, as it suggests an answer to the question of *who* can hope to profit from German (re)unification. It also leaves one to ask what an east German woman's appearance as leading protagonist would have meant for the narrative development of these films. Their structure would have been irretrievably upset because of the disruptive force that the symbolic presence of such a character would have posed to the romantic one-to-one set-up of marriage-unification tales. Competition to the economic and love interests of the west German female characters would have prevented a successful union, while at the same time making these protagonists' achievements seem less outstanding and unique. Heroines are born, it seems, out of *homogeneous* struggles that position them at the *core* of narrative events. This centrality is destroyed in accounts of multiple conflict because of the diffusion of attention and the construction of 'heroic' achievements as *comparative*. It therefore appears that the substitution of east German women by a black hole highlights the constructedness of these films around traditional narrative parameters that *make sense* of social events by narrowing them down to certain normative structures and by eliminating any forces that could be disruptive to the centrality of a selected tale. This is similar to the way in which stereotypes are created:

> The stereotype is not a simplification because it is a false representation of a given reality. It is a simplification because it is an arrested, fixated form of representation that, in denying the play of difference (that the negation through the Other permits), constitutes a problem for the *representation* of the subject in significations of psychic and social relations.
>
> bhabha 1983:27

The films work within an established grid of narrativity that has achieved 'normality' status and thus enables viewing pleasures as well as glossing over the more complicated aspects of socio-cultural practices. They not only silence the voices of east German women (and of people with 'other' ethnicities), but at the same time neglect completely the possibility of homosexual encounters which would upset the traditional logic of a 'marriage'. Friendships/romances between east and west German women (perhaps on the basis of similar patriarchal obstacles) and *non-competitive* relationships between men are simply not on the agenda.

In the non-filmic realms of social life these are, however, the relations that are assembled alongside and often in contrast to more established practices. 'Viewers' as social subjects *perform* their subjectivity across multiple and ever shifting layers of relativity. Their personal and communal histories position them as part of a complex 'audience' that is never secluded or totally 'suspended in disbelief'. The term can, as Ang (1991, 1996) has shown clearly, be used as nothing more than 'a provisional shorthand for the infinite, contradictory, dispersed and dynamic practices and experiences of television audiencehood enacted by people in their everyday lives ...' (1991:14).

From this perspective, 'viewers' do not simply coincide with the spectators envisaged by discourse analysts and media producers. Research into television interpretations and the formation of subjectivity in Germany (Hörschelmann, 1999), has shown that viewers take pleasure not only from films that totally exclude them or cast them as marginal and inferior; they also shift between different subject positions when watching television representations such as those analysed in this chapter. Women in east Germany thus manage to suspend attention to their feminine construction in order to enjoy the degree of 'non-compliance' offered up by depictions of east German men as successful. In other situations they align themselves with west German female protagonists in their struggle against male domination. Nevertheless they usually point out what appears to them as an exclusionary structure in these and other films or media reports:

H: Ne, also die Frau muß arbeitslos sein, geschieden, eh,vergewaltigt, mißbraucht, eh, 'n Kind, daß ein, ein katastrophaler U-, Unfall passiert und, eh, jemand Anverwandtes hat 'ne schwere Krankheit und dann ist er auch noch aus 'm Osten, ne, so. Das kommt da noch mit dazu. Und, eh, daß, daß also, wenn, wenn 'ne Frau dargestellt wird, dann ist es 'n Einzelschicksal. Sie wird immer als defizitäres, benachteiligtes Etwas dargestellt und als Krönung ist sie aus 'm Osten. Um noch mal, daß sie also nicht ganz ist. Also wird der, der Mangel wird auch produziert, ja. Und nicht als Zugewinn oder als Bereicherung ... Aber oftmals ist 'n, also Problemlagen, also Probleme, die Frauen haben, ... Dann fänd ich's ganz spannend, eh, 'ne Fernsehreportage zu machen über Frauenbiographien mit diesen sogenannten Sozialisationsbrüchen durch die Wende, das mal zu thematisieren und nicht unter, auf dieser Jammertour, sondern also diese Vielfalt zu zeigen, was da auch noch gewachsen ist an neuen Sachen. Und auch 'ne Dokumentation über Frauengruppen, Frauen,

Wende, Bewährung, 'ne, aus deren Sicht, und sie nicht 'n, ausschließlich immer zu darzustellen, als, das sind die 'Verliererinnen der Einheit'. Was sie mit Sicherheit sind, aber nicht immer wieder dieses, weg von diesem defizitären Blickwinkel.

(Hörschelmann 1999)

(*H*: No, well the woman has to be unemployed, divorced, um, raped, abused, um, a child that a, a catastrophic accident has happened and, um, some relative has a serious illness and then on top of that she's from the east. There's that as well. And, um, that, well, that, if a woman is represented, than it's as an individual case. She is always represented as a deficient, disadvantaged something and on top of that she's from the east. To repeat again, then, that she is not whole. Thus the, the lack is also produced, yeah. And then it's not as a benefit or an enrichment, ... But usually it's, well, problem situations, problems that women have ... Then I would find it quite interesting to make a television report about women's biographies with these so-called socialization ruptures because of the *Wende*, to thematize this and not only through, in this whingeing way, but to show this plurality, what has also grown there in the way of new things. And also a documentation about women's groups, women, *Wende*, proof of success, well, from their perspective, and not to, to exclusively represent them as, being the 'losers of unification'. Which they surely are, but not always to repeat this, away from this deficit angle.)

This quotation clearly expresses the tension between the need for different representations, which take account of the diversity of east German women's experiences, and the need to recognize forms of social marginalization such as the loss of the extensive child care system, high rates of unemployment and ensuing financial dependence on men. In contrast to the images described above, however, many women *actively* try to manage the changes that have occurred in the course of (re)unification. They participate in social or political groups and, even if unemployed, have found ways of re-establishing or maintaining contacts in the community that lend them confidence. The account of a former public relations manageress from Erfurt summarizes these contradictory sentiments clearly. It also indicates the sheer complexity of situations in which women in east Germany are often caught:

E.H.: Und da ist die Entwicklung dann so gewesen, ja, daß ich '93 arbeitslos geworden bin, hab eben gleich gedacht, das kann's nicht, also 's kann's nicht gewesen sein. Ja, also in meinem Kopf hat sich so manifestiert, und das ist auch heute noch da, ich sag, also ich bin nicht Verlierer der Nation. Und das ist, hat sich so fest eingekramt, daß mich das immer wieder neu aufgebaut hat.

(Hörschelmann 1999)

(*E.H.*: The situation developed in such a way then that I, yes, that I became unemployed in '93, I thought to myself straight away, this cannot, well, this cannot have been it. Yes, in my head it became clear, and this is still there today, I say, well, I'm not the *loser of the nation*. And all this, it has dug itself in so deeply that it has always put me back on top again.)

The job centre promised to put her on a retraining course within the following three months. However, the course was postponed several times and in the end did not take place at all. While waiting for the course to begin, Mrs E.H. applied for a place on a job-creation scheme (*Arbeitsbeschaffungsmaßnahme*) with the local women's centre. She was accepted together with three other women, who made a good team and hoped to stay on for a longer period. However, the scheme was terminated after one year:

E.H.: Also wir hatten alle noch keinen Draht irgendwie nach 'ner neuen Arbeit oder, keine Chance. Hch, und wir haben dann die Möglichkeit ins Auge gefaßt, aus uns selber einen Verein zu gründen. 's waren damals so Vereinsgründer. Haben dann an einem Seminar teilgenommen ... So, nach den zwei Tagen hatten wir den Hefter mit Vordrucken, wie das Gehalt zu rechnen ist, wie, eh, welche Wege gegangen werden müssen also bis das Ganze auf 'm Papier stand, erstmal den Verein gründen mit Satzung und Eintragung und Finanzamt, Registeramt, also, stand eben 'n unheimlicher, eh, Weg vor uns. So, und dann ist das Ganze mehr oder weniger, ... und am 19. 8. war Verein Cecilia gegründet.

(Hörschelmann 1999)

(*E.H.*: Well, we all had no access to a new job yet or, no chance. Um, and then we started to consider founding a social club ourselves. It was a time for founding such clubs back then. [We] took part in a seminar then ... So, after two days we had the folder with sheets on how to calculate the salary, and, er, how to proceed until the whole thing was down on paper, founding the club first with a contract and registration at the tax office, registration office, well, we really had a long way ahead of us. Well, and then the whole thing [went ahead] more or less ... and on the 19 August the *Cecilia Club* was founded.)

Finance for the club was unclear until six months later. But the women's consistent enquiries finally led to the granting of funds from the Thuringian ministry for social affairs. The interviewee and her colleagues now run the only rural social club around Erfurt with events for senior citizens, women and children.

Conclusion

The four films discussed in the first part of this chapter work with metaphors of 'marriage' or romance to construct images of successful unity. They utilize relations of gender to make their narratives more intelligible, pleasurable and seemingly 'natural'. The social inferiority of central protagonists enables an emancipatory solution, while also leaving traditional 'technologies of gender' (de Lauretis 1987) *intact.* The films fabricate an image of the western male as *controlling absence* on the one hand, and of east German women as *non-fitting, aged, ignorable* or *tradable* items on the other. They remain caught within the frame of western dominance *versus* eastern inferiority because of their spatio-temporal starting point, their allocation of normativity to the west and their portrayal of the east as a resource for adventure, personal growth and economic bargaining. As such the films produce a logic of 'commodifying the other' that echoes clearly bell hooks' remarks on 'eating the Other'.

Hooks notes that commodification eradicates whatever difference the 'other' inhabits *via* exchange. It is a form of cannibalism that 'not only replaces the Other but denies the significance of that Other's history through a process of decontextualisation' (1992:31). Desires to inhabit the world of the 'other', if only temporarily, have led the (white) post-modern West to sustain romantic fantasies of the 'primitive' and to search for a real primitive paradise, whether in a country or a body (1992:27–8). Contrary to how it represents itself, such fetishism in the interest of consumption is *not* an appropriate means to build 'democratic' and 'empathetic' relationships. Instead, the 'other's' sexuality and ethnic difference become commodified in such processes as a 'resource for pleasure'. Hooks clearly demonstrates the problems raised by western attempts to talk *about* the 'other' or to hear the 'other' speak:

Often this speech about the 'other' annihilates, erases. *'No need to hear your voice when I can talk about you better than you can speak yourself. No need to hear your voice. Only tell me about your pain. I want to know your story. And then I will tell it back to you in a new way. Tell it back to you in such a way that it has become mine, my own. Re-writing you I write myself anew. I am still author, authority. I am still colonizer, the speaking subject and you are now at the centre of my talk'.*

(hooks 1990:343)

Audience responses, however, show that different stories *can* be told, even if alternative visions of life histories and futures may be difficult to maintain in the midst of a social discourse that works to marginalize east Germans' very talk and that denies the radical potential of their *differences* while at the same time trying to capitalize on them.

References

Ang, Ien (1991) *Desperately Seeking the Audience* (London: Routledge).
Ang, Ien (1996) *Living Room Wars. Rethinking Media Audiences for a Postmodern World* (London: Routledge).
bhabha, homi (1983) 'The other question', in *Screen* 24, 18–36.
Certeau, Michel de (1988) *The Writing of History* (New York: Columbia University Press).
Dyer, Richard (1988) 'White', in *Screen* 29, 44–65.
Lauretis, Teresa de (1987) *Technologies of Gender. Essays on Theory, Film and Fiction* (London: Macmillan Press).
Hörschelmann, Kathrin (1999) *Placing 'the East' in the German Nation: Representations of Otherness in German National and Regional TV, PhD, University of Bristol.*
hooks, bell (1990) *Yearning. Race, Gender and Cultural Politics* (Boston, MA: South End Press).
hooks, bell (1992) *Black Looks. Race and Representation Politics* (Boston, MA: South End Press).
Sharp, Ingrid (1994) 'Male privilege and female virtue: gendered representations of the two Germanies', in *New German Studies* 18, 1/2, 87–106.
Shohat, (1991) 'Gender and the Culture of Empire: Toward a Feminist Ethnography of the Cinema', in: *Quarterly Review of Film and Video* 3, 45–84
young, lola (1996) *Fear of the Dark. Race, Gender and Sexuality in the Cinema* (London: Routledge).

Films

Amerika (3:sat, 3 October 1997)
Reise nach Weimar (3:sat, 30 September 1997)
Ein Schloß für Rita (ARD, 1 October 1997)
Stilles Land (3:sat, 7 October 1997)

4

Diverging Discourses of East German *Kabarett*: Cultural and Linguistic 'Misbehaviour'

Joanne McNally

Introduction

Although cabaret as a cultural phenomenon originated in France at the end of the nineteenth century, it is within Germany that it has developed into a distinct medium for political and cultural satire referred to as *Kabarett* (Vogel:1993). *Kabarett* can be perceived as reflecting and responding to the *Zeitgeist* in a mischievous way, through a discourse style which is generally characterized by distortions, exaggerations, incongruities and ambiguities. The style can, at times, be more agitative than playful. Indeed, opposition and provocation are traditionally the key defining features of *Kabarett*. (See Greul 1971 for a detailed historical account of the development of *Kabarett*.)

The aim of this chapter is to illustrate the way one particular group, Die Distel (The Thistle), has adapted its operation and style in order to re-locate itself in a changing cultural, social and political environment, and to contribute critically to the emerging issues and problems since unification. The discussion will show that some of its strategies can be perceived as cultural and linguistic 'misbehaviour'.

Kabarett: Some defining features

Traditional ensemble *Kabarett* consists of a programme of texts and draws on theatrical, literary, musical and media-related forms as vehicles for the satire. These texts are often self-contained, to a large extent re-arrangeable, and linked by music or a unifying theme. Although

Kabarett draws on issues from its immediate socio-political context, it is not about the events and issues themselves but rather the public's attitude towards them. Thus, in terms of operational levels it depends heavily on the knowledge and attitudes of its audience and this sets it apart from other art forms. This, in turn, means that *Kabarett* is potentially an indicator of the 'mentality of a nation' (Hofmann 1976:250), a notion which will be of particular relevance when investigating attitudes towards unification.

This dependency on audience interaction has been developed into a theory of *Kabarett* as 'Spiel mit dem erworbenen Wissenszusammenhang des Publikums' (Play with the acquired knowledge of the audience) (Henningsen 1967:31), which at times can be 'destructive' (Fleischer 1989:49). Henningsen's definition is based on the view that people's 'storage' of knowledge and experience is not, in actual fact, as integrated as it appears to be, but has 'Bruchstellen' (cognitive dissonance). In the case of problematical areas such as certain periods and events of German history, he argues: 'Das Bewußtsein salviert sich, indem es nicht integriert, sondern trennt' (the consciousness heals itself by separating, not integrating), and that consciousness can therefore easily be played with: 'Er (der Kabarettist) spielt damit auf einem sensiblen und leicht verstimmbaren Instrument' (He [the cabaret artist], thus plays on a sensitive instrument which can easily get out of tune) (Henningsen 1967:34). *Kabarett*, however, is not just a 'pedagogical institution' (Henningsen 1967: 9), it also attempts to be an instrument of social change, providing new insights and perspectives on problems. In particular, the fact that *Kabarett* authors and performers address highly sensitive issues, and, for provocative effect, re-deploy stereotypes, prejudices, and clichés, and also appropriate and/or modify slogans, quotations and sayings for satirical effect, can be regarded as cultural and linguistic 'misbehaviour'.

German unification and its effect on East Germany (GDR) and on the way east Germans perceive themselves within the 'new' system has been a recurring topic of concern with Die Distel since 1990. Before embarking on a discussion of Die Distel it will be helpful to contextualize the group against the background of *Kabarett* in the GDR, especially with regard to function, style and themes.

Kabarett in the GDR

In the GDR professional *Kabarett* was officially founded to promote positive satire in the aftermath of the uprising of 17 June 1953. Die

Distel in Berlin was the first state-funded group, soon to be followed by the Pfeffermühle (Pepper Mill) in Leipzig. By the time the Wall fell in 1989 there were twelve professional *Kabarett* groups and over 600 amateur groups. A further indication of the significance of *Kabarett* is the fact that performances from the seventies onwards were usually sold out with a waiting period of a few years to acquire tickets. *Kabarett* often had a larger audience than the theatre and fulfilled a social need: that of providing a *Lachventil* (safety valve) for coping with the daily frustrations under communism (Jacobs 1996:56). Indeed, it was one of only a few institutions in the GDR in which a negotiable range of taboo themes could be critically addressed.

East German *Kabarett* retained the more traditional style of ensemble *Kabarett*, whilst the solo style became more popular in West Germany from the sixties onwards. Additionally, the music and artistic dimensions of satire within East German *Kabarett* continued to play an important role and drew on the traditions of some Weimar *Kabarett*. Such elements often had a critical function, and according to Otto Stark (director of Die Distel between 1968 and 1990): 'Was man nicht mehr sagen kann – wird gesungen. Was gesungen immer noch zu hart klingt – wird getanzt' (What can no longer be said – is sung. If what is sung is still too critical – then it is danced) (Jaeger 1984:89).

A typical style of *Kabarett* in the GDR was the *Nummernkabarett* (a mixture of songs, scenes, and monologues on an assortment of themes) with an opening and closing number – 'Entree' and 'Finale' – which dealt with the main theme of the programme and usually involved all the performers on the stage. The programmes also had to include *Westnummern*, targeted against the capitalism and politics of the West. Parallels can be drawn here with the specific role of the West Berlin radio *Kabarett* group Die Insulaner (The Islanders) of the American-backed German-language station RIAS. The group was founded by Günter Neumann to agitate against the East and lift the spirits of the West Berliners at the time of the Berlin Blockade and during the Cold War (van Sweringen 1995).

While on the surface the groups appeared to support the 'Party line', criticism of the GDR's economic and ideological structures was possible, so long as politicians were not mentioned. Targets of the satire included daily problems in the GDR, officialdom and 'polit-speak': themes which were not allowed to be criticized in the media and in politics. The texts and performances were subject to strict censorship controls, whereby all scripts had to be shown to the authorities in advance. In the case of Die Distel, situated on the Friedrichstraße in

Berlin, this meant censorship from both the 'Bezirksleitung' and 'Zentralkommittee' (the Local and Central Party Committee). It is for this reason that it was perceived by the West, especially in the eighties, as the 'Hauskabarett der Staats- und Parteiführung' (House *Kabarett* for the State and Party leadership) (Jacobs 1996:60).

Despite the censorship, criticism of the regime was still possible, even in Die Distel, due to the fact that the audience often perceived what they wanted to hear. Seemingly harmless texts gained allegorical and critical potential by being carefully chosen for and presented in the *Kabarett* context (Erika Mann's exile group Die Pfeffermühle (1933–7) operated with similar techniques to criticize Hitler and the Third Reich). Subtle allusions within a text would be picked up by an active audience eager to search for critical comment against a common target (Ensikat 1998:128). For instance, an element of opposition towards the authorities could be signalled by the use of alienation techniques (for instance, if a scene was set in the Stone Age, the audience transported it automatically into the present), or by the use of Saxon dialect, due to the fact that most of the SED ministers came from Saxony. Other strategies included using subtle 'insider' language, for example expressions such as 'die Firma' (The Firm), 'männliches Pärchen' (male couple) or 'lange Ohren' (long ears) to signal the *Stasi* (*Staatssicherheitsdienst* – the GDR State Security Service). The audience's eagerness to read between the lines and re-interpret resulted in a certain conspiracy between them and the cabaret artist. Other devices for signalling things which could not be said directly but which the audience wanted to hear included pauses, slips of the tongue, the strategic use of homonyms and the positioning of the *Pointe* (punchline/twist) in the middle of the text, rather than at the end[1]. Indeed, the East Germans were used to reading between the lines of official statements and recognizing implicit threats, and were also used to speaking a different language within the family from the one used in public.

Due to the censorship process texts were not necessarily up-to-date. They also possessed a timeless quality because of the stagnation of the political conditions, which meant that many key texts could be performed within the different *Kabarett* groups throughout the GDR and over a period of years. This stands in stark contrast to the more 'journalistic' *Kabarett* in the FRG represented by such groups as Die Münchener Lach- und Schießgesellschaft (The Munich Society for Laughing and Shooting).

A turning point for East German *Kabarett* was 1988, a period of political awakening amongst citizens in the GDR, when many texts and programmes were banned due to the increase in direct criticism of the Party. Die Distel also injected their 1988 programme 'Keine Mündigkeit vorschützen' (Don't pretend to be adult; a play on the saying 'keine Müdigkeit vorschützen' – Oh, don't tell me you're tired!) with a sharp critical content against the socialism of the GDR, which resulted in a banning of the programme after the dress rehearsal. In November 1989 Die Distel tried to revive this programme. By this time, however, historical events were overtaking ideological debate, and public attention was directed elsewhere.

Kabarett in the nineties

The nineties have seen an increase in the popularity of stand-up comedy and comedy in general. German unification has provided fertile ground for satire, especially in the east, and for the re-establishment of a more traditional and 'classical' ensemble *Kabarett* with music, songs, scenes and monologues as its core elements.

The re-emergence of the more 'classical' style of *Kabarett* can be attributed mostly to the survival of the East German *Kabarett* groups. Although they have been subjected to economic cuts they have largely managed to maintain artistic quality. Despite an initial period of disorientation for these groups, due to the loss of targets for the satire and a loss of audience, most have now become privatized with prominent groups such as Die Distel and Pfeffermühle successfully performing within a unified Germany, and to mostly full houses in the east and west. By contrast, west German groups like Lach- und Schießgesellschaft and Stachelschweine (porcupines) have lost their orientation and satirical bite, and, to some extent, their discerning audience; it has indeed been announced that the former is to close. Many of the established authors and performers from the GDR period are still engaged at the former *Kabarett* theatres (for example, both Inge Ristock and Peter Ensikat have returned to Die Distel), and indeed, a certain traditionalism seems to have paid off for the *Kabarett* groups. In a climate in which a re-assertion of east German identity is gaining popularity, familiar names from the past help to attract the return of the audience from before unification and also attract a new younger audience dissatisfied with the present system.

In contrast to west German groups, east German groups also have a constant target for satire: the 'westernization' of the east, and the continuing discrepancy between ex-Chancellor Kohl's promise of 'blühende Landschaften' (blossoming landscapes) for the east and the stark reality of massive unemployment, economic stagnation and social disadvantage. This provides particularly sharp and biting satire.

Die Distel since 1990: the effect of the wider socio-political changes on the styles and content of its programmes

The year 1990 marked a watershed for Die Distel. It was no longer subject to political censorship, but it also no longer had the security of state funding. In order to survive, it was forced to reduce staffing numbers from approximately 65 to 20. Moreover, it had to reckon with a new kind of constraint: the market economy, in which the audience determined the style and content of the programmes to a far greater extent (Ensikat 1998:129). Whereas in the GDR there was a common target for the satire, 'die da oben' (them upstairs/those at the top) (Ensikat 1998:21), the new situation meant that Die Distel had to find fresh targets for the new heterogeneous audience of the early nineties, whilst also addressing the major issues confronting a unified Germany. As regards the style and content of the programmes, this resulted in an initial period of disorientation and uncertainty, followed by new confidence and new stylistic directions since the mid-nineties.

The programmes of the early nineties were characterized by the familiar structure of *Kabarett* in the GDR, the *Nummernkabarett*. However, there were some major changes as regards the content and presentation. For the first time Die Distel explored the media to react critically to the rapidly changing events and appeared every two months with *Scharfer Kanal* (Sharp Channel – an allusion to the GDR television current affairs programme *Der Schwarze Kanal* (Black Channel) which habitually contained venomous comments against the West) on Ostdeutscher Rundfunk Brandenburg (ORB) until 1991, sharing similarities with Dieter Hildebrandt's *Scheibenwischer* (Windscreen Wiper). Some of the texts from *Scharfer Kanal* were also integrated into its standard programmes. A news-type approach was adopted to deal with the rapidly changing events, and the themes were characterized by their immediacy and topicality. Fairy tales and 'news broadcasts' were text-types frequently adopted during this time. The 'news broadcast' provided an authentic frame for the satirical comment, whereas fairy tales could be updated by using different names and playing on audience familiarity with the plot. Recurring themes included aspects of the former GDR, loss of security and identity, the effect of unification on east German women, the emerging east/west hostility and the rise in racist sentiments. Honecker and other East German politicians (especially Modrow, Krenz and Krause) were frequently ridiculed, alongside Chancellor Kohl. Socialist songs and the GDR national anthem were used as vehicles for the satire, in a way which had not been permitted under communism. In terms of linguistic play, the Saxon dialect was no longer confined to parodying the SED regime, but was employed to symbolize the GDR and an east German identity; stereotypical phrases and clichés from both west and east Germany were ridiculed. A closer look at two programmes from this period will help to illustrate some of these strategies.

The programme *Uns gab's nur einmal* (We were unique) (1990) represents a critical appraisal of both the GDR and unification as well as the new freedom associated with capital and the D-Mark. It was televised several times in the early nineties on 3 October, the Day of German Unity. The old regime is symbolically buried, whilst the new marriage between the GDR and FRG is perceived as starting off in an inauspicious way. This is due first to the poverty of the bride (an allusion to the run-down state of the GDR economy), and her need to hire a wedding gown for her second marriage: 'Wenn Helmut wüßte, daß das Brautkleid aus dem Leihhaus ist ... Der Alte hat doch alles "runtergewirtschaftet"' (If Helmut knew that the bridal gown comes from the pawnshop ... the old boss ruined everything). Second, it is due to the fact that the marriage has been joined by Kohl (the groom) rather than a third party, and alludes to the fact that the marriage was not necessarily by mutual consent, echoing the notion of the GDR being annexed: 'Erst neulich verführt, heut schon treulich geführt, rollt der Jubel unerbittlich weiter. Denn der Mensch soll nicht scheiden, was Kohl zusammengefügt!' (Only just seduced and already married today, the cheering continues relentlessly. What Kohl has joined together, let no man put asunder), a distortion of the saying in the marriage ceremony (extracts are taken from the sketch 'Das Traumpaar'/The Perfect Couple).

The sense of east Germans being second class citizens is captured sarcastically in the final verse of a fairy tale: 'Wir weißen Neger – wir Eingebornen dieser Kolonie!' (We are the white negroes – we are the natives of this colony) (from the sketch 'Ein letztes Märchen'/A Final Fairy Tale). The disillusionment with western identity and thence the lack of a new identity is reflected in the sketch 'Das Loch' (The Hole), and summarized with the line 'Ick fühl' mir selber schon wie'n großes, schwarzes Loch, in das nischt is' (I feel like a big black hole, in which there is nothing). The continual updating and exchange of texts within this programme reflects the state of turmoil in which east German citizens suddenly found themselves and stands in clear contrast to *Kabarett* under the old GDR regime.

Although the Gulf War was the impetus for the programme *Wir sind das Letzte* (We Are The Pits) (1991), with the human race in general heavily criticized, many texts still deal with the problems in the east. The programme begins in the Garden of Eden and ends in Noah's Ark with biblical quotations and ecclesiastical music recurring throughout. The programme is especially critical of the eastern 'bunker mentality' and is intended to provoke the east Germans into coming to terms with the present and the past, in order to play a decisive role in shaping the future. 'Wir Zauberlehrlinge' (We, the sorcerer's apprentices), a politicizing of Goethe's 'Der Zauberlehrling', depicts the east Germans as apprentices within the new system which they initially wanted but which is now sweeping them aside. Towards the end the optimism of the government (represented by four of its leading figures) is sarcastically undermined, while there is also a warning about a nostalgic attitude towards the type of socialism prescribed by the SED, with *Sozialismus* pronounced with a Saxon accent:

> Kohl und Waigel, Lambsdorff, Rühe –
> alle rufen: Optimismus!
> Gebt euch doch ein bißchen Mühe!
> Oder wollt ihr Sozialismus?
> (Kohl and Waigel, Lambsdorff, Rühe –
> all calling for optimism!
> Come on, muster up some effort!
> or would you rather Socialism?)

The new east/west German animosity at this time is ridiculed in a series of songs, often using stereotypical phrases. In a medley of popular songs with a new satirical content 'Die deutsche Wiedervereinigung' (German re-unification) is represented as 'die deutsche Wiederverfeindung' (German 're-enemyfication'), the title of the medley. The first six verses are sung alternately by east and west with each respective group redeploying prejudices and clichés such as: 'Alle Ossis sind so doof' (All easterners are stupid) and the next verse 'Alle Wessis sind nur da, um uns zu beklauen' (All westerners are only here to rob us) and both referring to each other as 'Schweinehund' (swines/'bastards'). The medley ends with the biting comment: 'Also – schlagt euch, wo ihr euch trefft' (hit each other, wherever you meet each other), an echo of the leftist slogan from the thirties 'Schlagt die

Faschisten, wo ihr sie trefft' (Smash the Fascists, wherever you meet them), and also an allusion to Kurt Tucholsky's 1932 satirical song 'Küßt die Faschisten, wo ihr sie trefft' (Kiss the Fascists, wherever you meet them).

Despite the elements of caricature, this programme introduces a shift in methods which reflects the situation in the new Germany with many serious tones often presented as monologues and soliloquies, particularly when referring to the effect of unification on individuals within east Germany at this time. Uncomfortable questions are often placed in the final lines of the texts. For instance, the monologue 'Die Schichtarbeiterin' (the [female] shift-worker) ends with the poignant phrase: 'komisch, wir hatten keinen Krieg, und trotzdem haben wir eine Nachkriegszeit' (Funny, we never had a war and yet we have a post-war period). In the poem 'Die Trümmerfrau – kein Berliner Original' (The Rubble-clearing lady – not a Berlin original) searching questions reflect the mentality of many older east Germans at this time:

> Ob sie nun glaubten, sich selbst nur belogen –
> man hat sie um ihr zweites Leben betrogen.
> Und sie fühlen bei allem noch eigene Schuld –
> war es Feigheit, war's nur Geduld?
> Wir Jüngeren schaffen vielleicht noch die Wende.
> Doch wer überlebt schon zweimal sein Ende?
> (Whether they now believed, they'd only deceived themselves –
> they'd been cheated out of their second life.
> And they nevertheless still feel their own guilt –
> was it cowardice or was it just meekness?
> We younger ones may make it through the *Wende*
> And yet who can survive a second defeat?)

Metaphor and personification are used for the serious existential problems experienced by most citizens in the monologues 'Angst' (Fear), 'Frust' (Frustration), 'Wut' (Fury) and 'Schuld' (Guilt). In the monologue 'Schuld', about a border guard, the term *Klassenfeind* (a cliché word much used in the GDR newspapers to describe a 'class enemy') is employed in its original way with serious intent: 'Ich hab's fertig gebracht, mir einzureden, daß Kai Uwe nicht so'n armes DDR-Schwein abgeknallt hat ..., sondern daß er ... "einen Klassenfeind unschädlich gemacht hat"' (I managed to convince myself that Kai Uwe didn't gun down a poor GDR swine ... but that ... he neutralized a class-enemy instead). In the *Kabarett* programmes of the GDR such 'polit-speak' had often been a vehicle for satire.

In general, the programmes of the early nineties can be regarded as primarily of interest to an east German audience, and often lack a broader vision in the face of changing events, resulting in a more serious and direct kind of satire. In contrast to the programmes written under censorship, targets are often clearly identifiable and named, with little attempt at disguise. This can be attributed to the fact that knowledge about the new system was being simultaneously and constantly acquired both by the cabaret artists and the audience, making subtle allusions to the present situation virtually impossible. This also meant that the audience did not have to listen so acutely, as had been the case with *Kabarett* under communism.

From the mid-nineties onwards, Die Distel programmes have experimented with different structures and forms, against the backdrop of what appear to be deteriorating east/west German relations. The focus has shifted to the internal structures of Germany; new perspectives for social and political change and new strategies towards the east-west division are explored. There is a break with the traditional *Nummernkabarett* structure, and themes of concern for both east and west, such as capitalism (*Im Westen geht die Sonne auf* /The Sun rises in the West, 1995), the justice system (*Lebenslänglich auf Bewährung* /Life-long Probation, 1996), entertainment (*Wir lachen uns tot – ein bunter Abend* /We're laughing ourselves to death – a varied programme, 1996), unemployment (*Das haben wir nicht verdient* /We didn't deserve this, 1997) and personal relationships (*Alle Brüder werden Menschen*/All brothers will become people, 1998), provide the leitmotif and the target for the satire in the programmes. Social and economic problems are no longer culturally polarized into east and west, but rather are reviewed in terms of policies, laws and practice and often from a more critical distance using alienation techniques for the whole programme. Problems of particular concern to the east are alluded to *en passant* within texts, rather than being the focus of whole texts. Political symbols such as 'Standort Deutschland' (Business Location – Germany), and 'der große Lauschangriff' (the great bugging offensive) become the recurring targets of the satire, alongside Christian Democratic Union (CDU) politicians, especially Kohl and Waigel, and media personalities. Lines from songs, slogans and quotations associated with GDR socialism are subtly employed for satirical effect, reflecting a certain distance from the past and also maintaining the feelings of the audience as being part of an 'in-group'. For instance, in an allusion to Chancellor Kohl, the quotation by Rosa Luxemburg 'Freiheit ist die Freiheit des

Andersdenkenden' (Freedom is the freedom to dissent) is modified to imply dishonesty: 'Das ist nämlich die Freiheit des Andersdenkenden, daß er anders spricht, als er denkt' (That is namely the freedom of the dissenter – that his speech dissents from his thoughts). A closer look at two programmes from this period will help to illustrate some of these strategies.

In the programme *Im Westen geht die Sonne auf* (1995) Die Distel criticizes western democracy as defined by capitalism by adopting a loose plot. This represents a stylistic break with previous programmes. The main techniques are alienation and reversal. Events since 1989 are strategically placed in America, with the newly elected president Johnny Walker calling for *perestroika* and *glasnost* in all areas of American society. The Germans react to this new world order with passive resistance, while Germany's government sets up a 'Krisenstab zur Währung der Kontinuität' (Crisis Committee for the Maintenance of Continuity), and demonstrates confidence in its current policies, with the slogan: 'Das Kapital in seinem Lauf halten weder Ochs' noch Esel auf!' (Neither ox nor ass can halt the march of capital) placed here in the mouth of ex-Finance Minister Theo Waigel, and providing an ironic twist of Honecker's words (quoting August Bebel) just before the Wall fell, 'den Sozialismus in seinem Lauf halten weder Ochs' noch Esel auf!' (Neither ox nor ass can halt the march of socialism).

The alienation effect allows the past and present to be reviewed in a new light in order to move forward provoking ideological debate. Regardless of whether the system is characterized by 'Demokratur' ('democtatorship') or 'Diktatie' ('dictocracy'), or by 'Stasi' or 'Verfassungsschutz' (GDR and FRG names for the security police) the recurring theme is that there are no real changes for the citizens. Both west and east Germans are united by their uncertainty and fear of change: 'ein ganzes Volk abwickeln – das kann man doch nicht machen' (you can't wind up a whole nation; a new usage of a verb which is usually used to signify the closing down of institutions, factories and so forth). This is the first attempt to unify the diverging profiles of eastern and western cultures into one programme, also demonstrated by the employment of both Bavarian and Saxon accents for humorous effects. In terms of reversal, the final twist comes towards the end with the concession: 'Es war doch nicht alles schlecht in der BRD' (not everything was bad in the FRG), re-orienting the popular cliché associated with the GDR.

Particularly sensitive themes such as the *Stasi* are playfully alluded to, while parallels to the present system with regard to observation techniques are mischievously set up. For instance, before the interval –

'Lauschpause' (bugging/eavesdropping interval; an allusion to both Western and Eastern illicit surveillance practices) – the cabaret artists request the audience to act as their 'UM – also unsere unbekannten Mitarbeiter' (UM – our unknown collaborators; a play on IM – Inoffizielle Mitarbeiter/unofficial collaborators, as employed by the *Stasi*) and to use their performance tickets as *Verpflichtungserklärungen* (signed declaration to work for the *Stasi*) with the rejoinder: 'Keine Angst, im Ernstfall wird alles vernichtet./Der Verfassungsschutz hat aus den Fehlern der Staatssicherheit gelernt./Wir legen keine Akten an. Uns reichen Ihre Daten' (Don't worry, should the situation become serious then everything will be destroyed./The Constitution Defence Authority [West] has learnt from the mistakes of the State Security [East]./We will not start any files. Your data is enough for us.). The implication is that there is no guarantee of data protection, indeed 'Das Volk denkt, der Mann am Datenspeicher lenkt' (The people are thinking, but the man in charge of data storage is in control; a play on the proverb 'Der Mensch denkt, Gott lenkt'/Man proposes, God disposes). However, such connections between dictatorship and democracy may be too discomforting.

The recognition that unification has failed to create one Germany results in attempts at unification of a different kind by Die Distel. They perceive the way forward for both the east and west Germans as laughing together. This is the aim of the programme *Wir lachen uns tot – ein bunter Abend* (1996), with entertainment the common denominator and target of the satire, and popular songs the vehicle for much of the satire. Indeed, the 'we' in the title of the programme reflects an 'integrated' east/west identity. The clichés of the east and west are provocatively undermined in 'Verrückte Welt' (Crazy World): 'Weißt du warum die Wessis noch gefährlicher sind als die anderen Ausländer? Man erkennt sie nicht' (Do you know why the west Germans are even more dangerous than the other foreigners? You can't recognize them), thus implying that there is, in fact, no difference between east and west Germans. This is also reflected in the final text 'Letzte Antworten auf allerletzte Fragen' (Last answers to the very last questions) in which Germans in general are criticized:

– Aber wir waren doch mal das Volk!
– Ja, das Volk waren wir mal, jetzt sind wir nur noch ein Volk und zwar ein ziemlich bescheuertes.
(– But we were once the people!
– Yes, we were once the people, but now we're only one people, and a fairly stupid one at that.)

Socialist language such as 'Klassenfeind' is redeployed in a playful way: 'Was in der DDR der Klassenfeind war, ist in der BRD ... die Langeweile' (What the class-enemy was in the GDR ... is in the FRG ... boredom) with a strategic pause after 'BRD' to allow the audience to jump to their own conclusions first. The ideological past of Die Distel and of many east Germans is not completely abandoned. There is a sense that SED warnings about capitalism have come true with the prophecy at the end: 'komisch, der Sozialismus ist daran gescheitert, daß er keiner war. Der Kapitalismus könnte daran scheitern, daß er wirklich einer ist' (funny how socialism failed because it wasn't what it claimed it was. Capitalism could fail because it really is). In a recent programme *Alle Brüder werden Menschen* (1998), there is a return to the image of personal relationships and marriage to symbolize the state of affairs between east and west Germany in the sketch 'Sofa II':

> – Mit Ost und West ist es wie mit dir und mir – wir müssen uns nun endlich mal abfinden, daß wir geheiratet haben, bevor wir uns erkannt hatten.
> – Es war eben eine Liebe vor dem ersten Blick.
> – Und jetzt heißt es wie in jeder normalen Ehe – Augen zu und durch!
> – Das siebte Jahr haben wir hinter uns, und es war nicht viel schlimmer als das sechste.
> (– With East and West, it's like with you and me – we must finally come to terms with the fact that we married, before we slept together.
> – It was love before first sight.
> – And now it's just like any normal marriage – close your eyes and see it through!
> – We've survived the seventh year and it wasn't much worse than the sixth.)

This implies sardonically that such relationship difficulties are normal and that it is down to individuals to make Germany as one nation work.

Conclusion

Many of the sensitive issues and attitudes associated with a unified Germany can be traced in the cultural and linguistic misbehaviour of east German *Kabarett*, particularly as exemplified by the programmes of

Die Distel. The misbehaviour is not merely for entertainment's sake, but rather to make the audience more receptive to critical comment, and to question the status quo. Alongside the setting up of provocative parallels between past and present systems, clichés and stereotyped thinking relating to the immediate socio-political context are redeployed within the *Kabarett* context, often relying on the audience to reinterpret and make evaluations.

Thus, *Kabarett* is ultimately dependent on the audience for its effectiveness, with the prevalent political climate playing a major role in determining the directness of the criticism and the type of 'reconstruction' required of the audience. Audiences of East German *Kabarett* during the GDR period wanted to listen, wanted to pick up fine nuances and reconstruct the critical comment with a distinct target in mind. Indeed, in order to circumvent censorship, the misbehaviour of East German *Kabarett* under the SED often relied on strategic ambiguity with multi-valenced intentions, one directed to one addressee and one to another. In this way, the audience supplied the critical content triggered by a keyword or a certain pronunciation.

Despite a stylistic break with the GDR and new themes of interest to both east and west, socialist ideals have not been abandoned. In east German Kabarett since unification there is, to a certain extent, a continuity of strategies with the past; former socialist slogans and songs are also redeployed for satirical effect. This, in turn, reinforces an east German identity and, with respect to cultural misbehaviour, can be perceived as promoting an 'in-group' with which the west will not always be able to identify. Although *Kabarett* as a form of misbehaviour is largely contextually sanctioned and, at times, even regulated, nevertheless its effectiveness can extend beyond the intimacy of the performance. This is achieved by the bringing together of thoughts and opinions which may be particularly disquieting, and by criticizing political systems, not just their manifestations. In the current German context, the functioning of *Kabarett* generally as an art form which both reflects and questions attitudes towards the status quo makes it a significant factor in challenging hegemonic discourses in a unified Germany.

Note

1. It has recently emerged that Die Distel's artistic co-director and cast member Gisela Oechelhaeuser was an IM. This adds a further layer of interpretation to the lines she uttered on stage.

References

Ensikat, Peter (1998) *Hat es die DDR überhaupt gegeben?* (Berlin: Eulenspiegel).

Fleischer, Michael (1989) *Eine Theorie des Kabaretts: Versuch einer Gattungsbeschreibung* (Bochum: Universitätsverlag Dr Norbert Brockmeyer).

Greul, Heinz (1971) *Bretter, die die Zeit bedeuten: die Kulturgeschichte des Kabaretts* (Munich: dtv).

Henningsen, Jürgen (1967) *Theorie des Kabaretts* (Ratingen: A. Henn Verlag).

Hofmann, Gerhard (1976) *Das politische Kabarett als geschichtiche Quelle* (Frankfurt: Haag & Herchen Verlag).

Jacobs, Dietmar (1996) *Untersuchungen zum DDR-Berufskabarett der Ära Honecker* (Frankfurt/Main: Lang).

Jaeger, Joachim (1984) *Humor und Satire in der DDR* (Frankfurt/Main: R. G. Fischer Verlag).

van Sweringen, Bryan (1995) *Kabarettist an der Front des Kalten Krieges* (Passau: Wissenschaftsverlag Rothe).

Vogel, Benedikt (1993) *Fiktionskulisse* (Paderborn: Ferdinand Schöningh).

Primary sources

Von der Wende bis zum Ende (1990) (Berlin: Edition Hentrich).

Das Letzte Ende (1991) (Berlin: Edition Hentrich).

Uns gab's nur einmal (1990) unpublished.

Im Westen geht die Sonne auf (1995) CD (Berlin: Berolina Tape).

Wir sind das Letzte (1991) audio recording (Berlin: Deutsche Schallplatten GmbH).

Wir lachen uns tot (1996) CD (Berlin: Berolina Tape).

Lebenslänglich auf Bewährung (1996) CD (Berlin: Berolina Tape).

Das haben wir nicht verdient (1997) CD (Berlin: Berolina Tape).

Alle Brüder werden Menschen (1998) CD (Berlin: Berolina Tape).

5
Can Oil Unite with Water? Braun and Biskupek on German Disunity

Gert Thomas Reifarth

There's a wall between you and what you want and you got to leap it.
Tonight you got the power to take it, tomorrow you won't have the
power to keep it.

(Dylan 1994:651)

Introduction

German unification was shortsightedly designed by West German
politicians and desired by the East German masses. Politicians got
caught in the so hastily woven web of their promises, and the masses
quickly became disillusioned. The most serious effect of this is the
increasing difficulty (see *Der Spiegel* 27/95:41) of removing what has
been labelled the *Wall in the Head*. 'Inner' German unity was, and still
is, blocked. The old GDR largely became 'atlanticized' (that is,
glorified in retrospect) (see *Der Spiegel* 27/95:43) or was even viewed as
returning or only now coming into being (Groschopp 1996:23;
Rutschky 1996:1), and new developments have often been condemned
and rejected. The blame for difficulties was always put on the respective 'other' Germans. East Germans find it hard to get accustomed to
the *Gemütsarktis* (Arctic of the soul) (Demski 1992:105) which they
encounter in the west, while they are increasingly 'seeing their old
experience become a closed chapter' (Reed 1993:234). As the GDR
moves further and further away into history, it does not, paradoxically, get smaller proportionally as it should (see Stölzl 1997:9) and
has therefore not, as a critic in *The Irish Times* suggests, 'been ...
swiftly forgotten' (Staunton 1997).

Literature which engages in contemporary issues should not only express the author's views, but also offer readers paths of thought and even advice, solutions, guidelines, consolation, justifications or explanations. East German readers in particular learned to expect as much from their writers. The question to be addressed here is how the Saxons Volker Braun and Matthias Biskupek are contributing in these respects. Why this choice of authors? The intention is to introduce two views which are both significant and representative, and yet opposed to each other. Furthermore the works chosen should explore practical consequences for the everyday relationship of east and west Germans. Finally, frequently forgotten whenever east German literature is discussed after unification, the writing should be aesthetically and artistically of high value. Braun and Biskupek meet these criteria.

Volker Braun

Braun after 1989

In GDR times, Braun, born in Dresden in 1939, developed a critical and questioning attitude towards the state in which he lived as 'an intellectual prisoner' (Subiotto 1991:196) and which he measured against the communist utopia in which he believed. Since the *Wende*, the situation has not become easier for Braun. While fellow poets explicitly or implicitly refer to him in their poetry – Barbara Köhler (1991:229) seeing him as a Rumpelstiltskin in a satirical poem (*Rumpelstilz*), Yaak Karsunke (*den hochverdienten dichtern*, to the poets of great merit, 1992:98) accusing him and others of having led a morally doubtful existence in the GDR – critics, often misleadingly, portray him as facing grave artistic and ideological problems since the end of the GDR. Reed says that Braun's 'commitment has lost all meaning now that the [GDR] society has vanished' (Reed 1993:236). Emmerich diagnoses Braun as suffering from '*Furor melancholicus*' (Emmerich 1996:16, 460). Wehdeking (1996:24) calls Braun's post-*Wende* texts 'Seismogramme vorübergehender Orientierungslosigkeit' (seismograms of a temporary loss of orientation). Costabile-Heming thinks that Braun 'began to use his writing as his means to attain inner peace' (Costabile-Heming 1997:3) after unification, and detects 'a plaintive undertone' in his texts which 'read like laments' and 'depict a man who is severely troubled, deeply disillusioned, and very bitter' (Costabile-Heming 1997:205). Reading all this, one could revive a remark which Fritz-Hendrik Melle made in 1985: 'Volker Braun? – Da kann ich nur sagen, der Junge quält sich' (Volker Braun? – All I can say is that this lad is torturing himself) (cited in Pergande 1991:234). As we will see, Braun, 'a staunch idealist, who remained so even after unification was imminent' (Costabile-Heming 1997:2), does not have to change in order to re-establish his position as a writer. He stays, in fact, exactly where he was.

After the *Wende* Braun transferred his attitude – which critically measured reality against the communist utopia – to the new Germany. This utopia is his ultimate template for *any* society. Here Braun stays true to his own principles, particularly to one from *Büchners Briefe* (1977), namely that *every* class society requires a counterbalance (cf. Braun 1993a:296f). This adhesion to his ideals is the first important aspect of Braun's views on united Germany. The second – resulting from the first – is his vehement rejection of the new society. It will be fruitful to examine these two aspects by analysing a series of prose pieces by Braun written mainly in 1990 and 1991. It is remarkable that these pieces have been ignored by many critics, who have reduced their interpretation of Braun's views on the *Wende* to analysis of his poem *Das Eigentum* (Property).

Utopia, land of mammoths

In the ten short paragraphs of *Arbeitsnotizen 16.10.91* (Work Notes) (Braun 1993c:104–6), Braun states his theory of utopia. Utopias are, according to him, like mammoths which may be called extinct but exist in our minds as a reconstruction in many shapes, forever dying in the ice, being dug up and rising to their feet again. They also have a material existence; as skeletons, for example in museums in St Petersburg and East Berlin (1993c:105). As mammoths, utopias tramp paths which might either be the Rue St-Jacques leading to the Seine or the street leading to the Buchenwald concentration camp (1993c:105). Real existing socialism had the communist utopia in its stranglehold and made a complete mess of it (1993c:104f). Reversing the step taken earlier in the century, socialism has now developed back from reality into a utopia (1993c:104). This utopia, however, lies beaten on the ground, which is the position best suited for it (1993c:105). Braun calls the communist utopia an arduous vision, compared to 'die bürgerliche utopie der machbarkeit, der immerwährenden prosperität, der zuwachsraten von adam und eva bis bayer leverkusen' (the bourgeois utopia of the feasible, of long lasting prosperity, of growth rates from Adam and Eve to Bayer Leverkusen): in short, the democracy of greed (1993c:106). It is, however, the overbearing power of this Western style which 'provoziert den aufstand der unterdrückten hoffnung gegen die herrschende idee, auf dem ungewissen, weltweiten, aschgrauen grundstück der zukunft' (provokes a rebellion of oppressed hope against the ruling ideology on the uncertain worldwide ash-grey terrain of the future) (1993a:106).

At the end of his *Leipziger Vorlesung* (Leipzig Lecture) (Braun 1993c:173–92) Braun justifies his continuing belief in utopia:

> die früheren Sozialismen sind vielleicht gescheitert, die Aufbrüche versandet, die Utopien aufgebraucht für ein paar milde Jahrhunderte. ABER, IHR TRÄUMER, GLAUBT IHR WIRKLICH, DER ZERFALL DES HISTORISCHEN KOMMUNISMUS HABE DEM BEDÜRFNIS NACH GERECHTIGKEIT EIN ENDE GESETZT?
> 1993c:192, Braun's emphasis
> (Maybe the former socialisms have failed, the new departures have run into the sand, and the utopias have been used up for a few mild centuries. BUT DO YOU REALLY BELIEVE, YOU DREAMERS, THAT THE DISINTEGRATION OF HISTORICAL COMMUNISM HAS PUT AN END TO THE DESIRE FOR JUSTICE?)

Braun's sketch *Die Kammer* (The Chamber) (Braun 1993c:45–6) provides his utopian beliefs with a material manifestation: a chamber into which he admits nobody else and which he enters every now and again to keep himself alive, finding himself lost in rapt absorption there and often leaving it bruised and dishevelled. Utopia fills the place, a dangerous intoxicating substance (1993c:46).

By no means is Braun, as Costabile-Heming (1997:205f) believes, announcing the death of utopia. On the contrary, he is convinced of its existence in human thinking, independent of time and place, as it is the appropriate manifestation of the human desire for justice. The end of real existing socialism does *not* mean the end or the failure of the socialist utopia. According to Grant, Braun's utopian vision had 'encountered its ultimate rupture' in the GDR (Grant 1995:165). Now, after the GDR, the time seems right for Braun to revive and redirect his utopian vision.

Braun's view on utopia faces strong opposition. Günter Kunert, a GDR writer who left the country in the seventies, regards the communist utopia as mummified, as a joke out of place, a deceptive hope, which ignores the present situation in Germany and the human condition as such (cited in Maier 1991:56). To Wehdeking, Braun's critical discourse in the GDR was 'klüger' (more intelligent) than his present insistence on the possibility of making the utopia real (Wehdeking 1996:24). Furthermore, the GDR population did not want any further socialist experimentation. Emmerich (1996:461) says that 'die Bevölkerungsmehrheit der DDR weder von der genuinen noch von der pervertierten Version der sozialistischen Utopie etwas wissen [wollte]' (the majority of the GDR population wanted nothing to do with either the genuine or the perverted version of the socialist utopia). Costabile-Heming states: 'Yet, an increased desire for freedom superseded these utopian philosophical ideals among the real people of the GDR' (1997:204).

According to Levitas, utopias are two-fold. 'The articulation of dissatisfaction and of a preferred alternative way of being' (Levitas 1997:122) is what may be called the *passive* role of utopia. Also, it has an *active* role, namely *'to inform political action and social transformation'* (1997:122, her emphasis). This would allow utopias 'die *tatsächlich* in die Wirklichkeit eingreifen, *nicht* sich aus ihr abkoppeln' (which really intervene in reality rather than severing themselves from it) (Jucker 1997b:58, his emphasis). Braun's views, however, are not so much of this kind as closer to Jucker's answer to the question why beautiful, simple and harmonious utopias are so much more appealing than the complexities of reality: 'sie kommen dem menschlichen Verlangen nach Bequemlichkeit und Einfachheit entgegen, auch wenn sie mit Wirklichkeit wenig bis nichts zu tun haben mögen' (they comply with the human desire for convenience and simplicity, even if they may have only little or nothing at all to do with reality) (1997b:57f). But it is not so much Braun's utopian belief that points to inadequacies in his position, it is rather what *follows* from this belief.

Living for Atlantis

In *Arbeitsnotizen 27.11.90* (Braun 1993c:104), Braun states that the socialist utopia has (been) turned into a *Fata Morgana*, and if we, being left in a desert, cry for water, we find everything poisoned. There might have been hope had we not given away the soil we had. And yet, bits of this soil stick miserably to our hands.

Braun compares the GDR to the island Atlantis (in the sketch *Atlantis*, 1993c:202–3), originally a happy island in a sea of mocking and hatred (1993c: 202). Later, however, the island became reduced to an ordinary run-down harbour which was given up because of bad business, unbearable bureaucracy and the migration of its labour force (1993c:203). Its disappearance was welcomed by its inhabitants as proof that the island was too weak to withstand the Flood and could now be forgotten about. But Braun claims that the so-called Flood which led to the island's end was merely made up 'aus kleinen Regengüssen, Verhängnissen, Resignation, Gleichgültigkeit und Dulden' (of little showers, misfortunes, resignation, indifference, and letting things happen) (1993c:203). While Braun watches how the last remaining groynes and posts are torn out to erase any trace of Atlantis, he preaches 'Nur ein Erdbeben, meine Kinder, nur ein Erdbeben kann das versunkene Land wieder heben' (Only an earthquake, my children, only an earthquake can raise the sunken land again) (1993c:203). In fact he preaches the possible return of Atlantis, the possible return of the (purified) GDR.

Braun's Atlantis is an unrealistic symbol of a happy life on a fantasy island, the GDR, in which the positive is posthumously emphasized, something which is not untypical of some of the ex-islanders, the former GDR citizens, after the drowning of their state. It is unusual insofar as its inhabitants *survive*. They watch the flooding of their island – but *from where*? From the desert which Braun describes in *Arbeitsnotizen*? In both texts the GDR disappears for lack of idealism, once in water, once in sand. In both texts an idealized GDR, however, survives the catastrophe in one form or another. Bits of soil remain in *Arbeitsnotizen* – do they contain the seeds of a new GDR? Air ('mein Luftkoffer', my suitcase containing air/made of air) is left in *Atlantis* – is it destined to become a wind which will bring with it a new GDR in the future?

Braun's one-page sketch *Die Donauversickerung* (The Danube's disappearance) (Braun 1998:120), written in 1995, puts his Atlantis argument into a different context. Braun describes how the Danube disappears in the state of Baden-Württemberg. The water, he states (with some poetic licence, since the geography is dubious) travels underground and re-emerges from the source of the river Aach. The GDR also has disappeared, but now 'wohin geht die Kunst und das Können, vertut es sich, *strömt* das je wieder *zuhauf*' (where does art go, where the abilities, will they disappear, will they ever re-emerge/come again in large numbers) (1998:120, his emphasis). Here he can be compared with fellow east German writer Joachim Walther, who creates the image of survivors of the wrecked GDR on a raft, about to be saved by the Titanic (Walther 1991).

Braun's rejection of united Germany

In his text *3. Oktober 1990* (Braun 1993c:199–200), originally a speech given on the eve of German reunification, Braun compresses his views on the new Germany into 44 lines. The piece offers far more than Costabile-Heming's reading suggests. Braun is said to have 'criticized the consumerism that East Germans demonstrated after the July currency reform and advised care after unification' (Costabile-Heming 1997:205). Neither argument is to be found in Braun's text! Also, Meinel's claim (1997a:105) that Braun 'verteidigt und erhofft die Uneinheitlichkeit der geeinten Deutschen' (defends and hopes for the non-uniformity of the united Germans) is not an adequate analysis of the piece.

The text is extremely condensed, and the argumentation appears disjointed. Braun, struggling to translate his multi-layered, clustered emotions into the linearity of language, attempts to avoid this transfer altogether by presenting his emotions in their natural disorder. Also, there is the contradiction that the text is very gruff and aggressive in tone, while the mood is rather a mixture of sadness, pessimism and loss. The rendering of mood into tone is strangely paradoxical.

German unification is, to Braun, *not* the start of a new era (Braun 1993c:199) but a swift and rough forcing and nailing together of what is torn apart and forever disagreeing and different. As if unification had been achieved by war, Braun (as does Hochhuth in his play *Wessis in Weimar*: Hochhuth 1994) uses militaristic terms to describe it; it was achieved by the Western democracy *occupying East German territory*, whereas the East German dictatorship simply *surrendered* (Braun 1993c:199, my emphases). The image of war and the following post-war trauma is reinforced in an interview which Braun gave in February 1991 (Braun 1993c:203–8); people *collaborate with the friend* on a massive scale as capitalism *marches into* abandoned East Germany, emptying old shops and immediately installing bourgeois business practices with their full range of unemployment, part-time work, parliamentary demagogy and, as if going with it naturally, *war* (1993c:205, my emphases). More than in the closed GDR, one sees now in the open landscape of the new Germany the monstrous connection between *work and war*, profit and consciousness, power and hunger (1993c:207f, my emphasis). Braun, contradicting the dominant historiographical discourse of the GDR's 'peaceful revolution', sees the German government as *being at war*, and calls upon it to resign (1993c:208, my emphasis). Also, as is clear from Braun's argumentation in the interview, obvious reasons for him to reject the new society are the negative features of capitalism which he takes from Marx's analysis.

To return to the text of *3. Oktober 1990*, Braun stated that in the new capitalist society-in-the-wild where freedom is exercised on the punching ball, east Germans are to guard the treasure of their differences against the drunken (west German) power which levels out any contradiction (Braun 1993c:199f). However, east Germans will have to work like the Turks in the new state – which Braun calls boring, unloved and merely practical (1993c:199f) – while their unemployed souls (deprived of what?) will remember the future and an old common cause which does not have a name anymore (1993c:200). Braun's own political luggage – 'mein Luftkoffer, mein politisches Gepäck' (my case of air, my political baggage) – contains remembrances and expectations which are uncontrolled and subversive and yet drive his steps (1993c:200).

While one can agree with Meinel who comments on this last part that Braun encourages his readers to engage in further political commitment (Meinel 1997a:105), one has to doubt Costabile-Heming's interpretation. She calls Braun's message 'very astute', claiming that 'it grants us insight into the difficult psychological decisions that all must make' (Costabile-Heming 1997:205). Braun is said to note 'that the changes on paper could not alter the forms and visions ingrained in peoples' minds' (1997:205) when he speaks about his political baggage. It has to be asked of this interpretation whether Braun was speaking for *other* people here, or whether he was, in fact, *only speaking for himself*. Costabile-Heming also says of Braun that he 'recognized that time was necessary to heal the wounds of the past' (1997:205). This is, however, expressed nowhere in the text, and there is no evidence that Braun wants the wounds of the past to heal at all.

Braun, in the aforementioned interview, argues that instead of making the differences of the two systems, East and West, productive – which would have meant bringing to light the ideological and materialistic daylight robbery of both systems – one now sees one structure simply laying itself on top of the other like lava (Braun 1993c:206). As he puts it in the poem *O Chicago! O Widerspruch!* (Oh Chicago! Oh Contradiction!) (Braun 1993c:51): 'Der Sozialismus geht, und Johnny Walker kommt' (Socialism goes, and Johnny Walker comes).

In *Der Wendehals* (The Turncoat) (1995) Braun mourns how the most compliant people changed quickly after the *Wende* and even the haggard and godforsaken party comrades were given the chance to become businessmen (Braun 1995:113). Related to this is the theme of the story *Worauf es hinausläuft* (Where it's all going) (Braun 1993c:30–41) where Braun examines post-unification reality by taking a close look at a man who was a high school official in the GDR and is now unemployed. As the story unfolds its Kafkaesque intensity, it appears that the man is obviously two people at the same time; depicted as unemployed and destroyed by the changes on the one hand, and on the other as still in office and able to stay in power as he changed his views willingly and quickly enough (Braun 1993c:39f).

An assessment of Braun's views

According to Costabile-Heming, 'Braun never desired an end to socialism in Germany, but sought instead a progression away from socialism toward the communist utopia' (Costabile-Heming 1997:5) which he kept believing was 'attainable' (1997:204). Volker Braun's views are understandable enough. He is sticking to his Marxist values, although it is remarkable that he should do so when the society which claimed to be working towards their realization, the GDR, has collapsed in failure. The practical implications of this principled position, however, are of questionable usefulness in Germany's current situation. Braun offers his readers a retreat from the new state into the realm of utopia and, along with this, idealistic reasons to reject the new society outright. If put into practice, if readers hear and follow Braun, the consequences are by no means constructive. On the contrary, they are *destructive* as they do not allow for a tolerant or pragmatic living together of Germans in the east and the west.

Apart from being one-sided (only the GDR/utopia perspective is taken, the West has no voice), Braun's ideas represent a refusal to engage with the changed reality. The *terra incognita* of the utopia becomes a substitute for the real world. Braun's defiant reconstruction of communist utopia is asserted as the antithesis of the 'new' society, but his rejection of the new is categorical and not concrete. He says that unity is a flawed project, which is doomed; and then he does *not* propose a practical alternative. United Germany is not given any chance at all. For Braun, the question 'Can oil unite with water?' is beside the point. Preoccupied with ideals and ideology, he puts off dealing with tangible substances such as oil and water, let alone their combination.

Matthias Biskupek

Although Biskupek, born in Chemnitz in 1950, published three volumes of prose in the GDR from 1981 on, he is little known. Books and articles on GDR literature usually ignore him. After the *Wende*, he published *Wir Beuteldeutschen* (We carrier-bag Germans) (1990) and *Biertafel mit Colaklops* (Beer table with cola meatball) (1995), both collections of short satirical sketches, and *Der Quotensachse*. *Vom unaufhaltsamen Aufstieg eines Staatsbürgers sächsischer Nationalität* (The token Saxon. On the unstoppable rise of a citizen of Saxon nationality) (1996), a novel depicting the absurdity of both the GDR system and the system of united Germany (cf. Meinel 1997b:241).

Wehdeking (1996:10) finds in post-unification literature 'hier und da bereits einen spürbar entspannteren, originell humorvollen Umgang mit den deutschen Dingen' (here and there an already noticeably less tense, wittily humorous treatment of the German situation); this is clearly applicable to Biskupek although he is not mentioned. Some of Biskupek's texts concerned with Germany after 1989 will be examined in this section.

Problems of language and identity

Reed remarks that Germans 'are currently hung up on awkward formulations' when trying to name the former GDR and its people (Reed 1993:234). This is comically reflected in Biskupek's texts. He comes up with various names for the people of the former GDR: 'eine ehemals im ehemaligen Bundesaussengebiet lebende Arbeitnehmereinheit' (an employee unit having formerly lived in the area formerly outside the Federal Republic) (Biskupek 1990:127), 'der reversibel einsetzbare mobile Neuganzdeutschländer' (the reversibly usable movable Newwholegerman) (Biskupek 1990:127), 'der Großbundesfesteinge-deutschte' (the firmly naturalised Greatfederalgerman) (Biskupek 1990:128), 'lernwilliger Jungbundesländler' (willing-to-learn Federal-younggerman) (1995:35), 'ein lernfähiger Angehöriger der deutschen Grossraumlande' (an able-to-learn member of the great German lands) (1996:14). The country they live in is called 'früher vormals ehemalige Ex-DDR' (the in former times previous former ex-GDR) (1996:157); re-unification is termed 'Wiedereinheit' (again-unity) (1990:124) or 'grosser Einigkeitsliebestaumel' (big agreementlovingecstasy) (1995:60).

Biskupek goes further. In *Wie ein DDRler jetzt sprechen lernen sollen müsste* (How a GDR person ought now to possibly have to learn to speak) (1990:123–8), he takes a broader satirical look at language and claims ironically that east Germans should move with new words to a new identity (1990:124) and radically erase any old term that makes them recognizable as people from the east (1990:125). Language is to be rigorously purified and completely renewed (1990:124). Furthermore, to sound 'gesamtdeutsch' (standard, unified German), to be linguistically effective and to become fully integrated into the united Germany, east Germans should look knowingly when speaking, nod intelligently, say 'ähm' every now and again and neutralize their accents.

The richness of East German language, 'althochdeedeeerr-deutsch' (old high gee-dee-arr German) (1990:126), is to be sacrificed for the neutral 'Gesamt-Deutsch' (standard, unified German). A few of Biskupek's examples for vocabulary cleansing are: 'Heddleins' instead of 'Schlagworte', 'Team' instead of 'Kollektiv', 'Management' instead of 'sozialistische Menschenführung', 'Positionspapier' instead of 'Programm', 'eliminieren' instead of 'liquidieren' (1990:124–8), in each case substituting a west German borrowing from English for GDR German usage.

In part three of *Sprachlehrgang in drei Aufbau-Stufen* (Language course in three continuous stages) (1990:33–9), called *Wörteraustausch mit dem Ping* (Word replacement with the gong), Biskupek in similar vein proposes a method to enforce and exercise the use of new words. The method involves hitting a gong every time one uses an obsolete word, which then has to be replaced by the new word, whereupon the gong is to be hit again (1990:38f). Biskupek asks east Germans to impose upon themselves west German linguistic patterns. Their own vocabulary, accents, modes of speech all have to go in order to loosen the linguistic bonds that tie people to East Germany. With these satirical proposals Biskupek not only attempts to create awareness of and resistance to artificial cultural-linguistic changes, but furthermore seems to suggest that such changes do not even touch, let alone erase, east German identity.

Biskupek deals with two typical elements of GDR grammar in the first two parts of *Sprachlehrgang* called *Wie wir früher und heute die Zukunft vollendeten* (How we formerly and today completed the future) and *Der Deutsche Demokratische Passiv* (The German Democratic Passive). The future perfect tense is marked as typical of the GDR, expressing the perfect communist future, as well as the present perfect tense, expression of the perfect socialist present. The FRG, on the other hand, used the coming-to-terms-with-the-past tense. Now, in united Germany, this latter form is to be used, as in 'Wir hatten nie mitgemacht' (we were never part of it) (1990:35). The German Democratic Passive ('wir sind belogen und betrogen worden, uns ist tiefes Unrecht geschehen, man hat uns zu Hampelmännern gemacht' – we were lied to and cheated, great injustice was done to us, we were treated like puppets) (1990:36) is now to be replaced by the Militaristic Active Voice ('Augen auf!' – open your eyes!) (1990:37). Biskupek's term *Der Deutsche Demokratische Passiv*, however, refers to people even more than to grammar (note the masculine gender of the term instead of the neuter). He mocks East Germans both for having borne everything passively in the old system – 'Nixsehenhörensagen' (speakseehearnothing) (1995:20) – as well as for now exaggerating the injustice of the old system in wailing laments (1990:36ff). Biskupek indirectly criticizes the need to adapt, both as self-inflicted by east Germans and as inflicted on them by the west. In a satirical way, such manipulated changes are unveiled as superficial, as failing to reach deeper and decisive levels of identity.

Abuse and falsification of the past

In *Wie ich widerstandskämpfte* (How I resistanced) (1990:12–17) Biskupek satirically re-interprets the life of a conformist GDR citizen, turning it into a life of protest and resistance. The knot in his Young Pioneer's scarf, for example, was only perfectly uncreased on the *outside* (1990:13). When the protagonist rose to the rank of staff sergeant in the National People's Army, he did so only to prevent other, maybe less 'resisting', people from occupying the post (1990:13). As a party official, he instigated the expulsion of many a comrade, enabling them to escape the party yoke (1990:14). By contributing to the lies in official party newspapers, he claims to have made the people angry, thus mobilizing them for the revolt (1990:15f).

This is developed further in *Resolution. Für eine VVDDR* (Biskupek 1990:85–7). After having resisted in the GDR, for example by not holding banners straight during May Day demonstrations (1990:86), Biskupek's protagonists, an unspecified 'we', want to found an organization for the victims of the demagogic dogmatic regime ('Vereinigung der Verfolgten des demagogischen Dogmatiker-Regimes' = VVDDR, Organisation for the Victims of the Demagogic Dogmatic Regime) (1990:87) in order to compensate everybody who was wronged in the GDR by having to lead an ordinary life there; in fact the whole GDR population who all suffered for the future (1990:87).

Biskupek's recipe for social advancement in the new Germany has three main ingredients (cf. 1996:139 and passim): use old *Seilschaften* (old boys' networks), falsify and use tradition, exaggerate, falsify and use the *Stasi* past. He thus mocks the abuse of the past, east German laments about the past, and the rejection of responsibility for the past. In its satirical form, this criticism appears all the more serious.

Other themes

In the guise of an ethnological study, the sketch *Die Beuteldeutschen* (Biskupek 1990:88–91) describes the East German invasion of Western shops after the opening of the border. Biskupek hits out at the purely materialistic orientation of East Germans after the *Wende*.

Die Patriarchen der Kleinstadt (The small town patriarchs) (1995:90–4) is a rather serious account of how the unjust practice of dealing with the *Stasi* past after unification can be even more revolting than this past itself. The focus of criticism is on the powerful structures of cowardice, denunciation of others and self-righteousness which the FRG system invites with regard to coming to terms with the *Stasi* past.

Sparschwein&Heiligenschein (Piggy bank and halo) (1995:71–3) describes how the ruling party of united Germany is asking east Germans to buy letters of indulgence to be forgiven the sin of having lived in the GDR as *all* of them are said to have been involved with the *Stasi*. Biskupek here criticizes the western practice of making east Germans feel ashamed of their past.

Erinnerung an unseren ersten gemeinsamen Sommer unter blauweissem Himmel (Memory of our first summer together under a blue and white [Bavarian] sky) (Biskupek 1995:60–3), finally, records a dialogue in which a Saxon reads a notice on a Bavarian campsite, informing guests that unmarried couples are not allowed to sleep in the same tent and that the management would see to it that this law is obeyed. A Bavarian camper is informed that he has stupidly accepted this grave violation of human rights for 40 years, which nobody would have done in the GDR. The West is seen as a society without freedom for over 40 years, and a subservient spirit is ascribed to all west Germans. Of course, facts are completely reversed. Biskupek mocks the west German attitude which is expressed in statements like 'How could you in the GDR ever put up with this? *We* would *never* have!'

An assessment of Biskupek's views

Biskupek shows the faults on *both* sides, east and west. In his texts he stands on *terra firma*, looks at the here and now, faces the new reality and examines what keeps people from accepting it. His satirical treatment of matters has practical implications; it invites us to question, to rethink, to change for the better. Also, it advocates a co-construction of getting accustomed to the new life, coming to terms with the past in an honest fashion and keeping a 'modernized' form of the old identity which does not endanger the process of inner unification. Biskupek's ideas are *constructive* and do not obstruct the view to the future.

As to the question 'Can oil unite with water?', one should expect an optimistic answer from Matthias Biskupek. However, a quote from *Der Quotensachse* gets in the way here: immediately after the *Wende*, east

Germans are reported to have struggled 'Ost und West irgendwie zu vermengen. *Inzwischen wissen wir, dass sich Feuer und Wasser nur dann verbinden lassen, wenn man einen Kochtopf dazwischenstellt'* (to somehow mix east and west. In the meantime we know that one can only unite fire and water if one places a saucepan between the two) (1996:129, my emphasis). Maybe, though, matters are different for *oil* and water? Or, if that is not the case, cannot oil and water *un-united* be ingredients of, say, a very nice salad? This is the implication and tone of Biskupek's work.

Conclusion

The perspectives of Braun and Biskupek are shown here to be competing and conflicting. In the works of both writers we certainly find many reasons why the achievement of 'inner' German unity is difficult, and indeed close to impossible. The crucial difference between Braun and Biskupek is, however, that the former *holds beliefs himself* which block this 'inner' unity, while the latter *addresses* such beliefs.

To be influenced by Braun means to gain insight into and sympathy for the difficult inner processes which were, after the demise of the GDR, going on within those who had invested hope in this state. It is, however, more realistic to leave the impractical utopia behind and cease mourning what might have been.

To be influenced by Biskupek, on the other hand, means for east Germans to look for an appropriate self-definition (other than becoming west Germans) and to take an even-handed view of the past. In Biskupek's opinion, it is time for all Germans to stop blaming the other side for their own problems.

We may conclude from the work of both Volker Braun and Matthias Biskupek that east German oil can never unite with west German water. However, these writers may also make us wonder whether the dissolving of differences is even a desirable end, and suggest to us that a balanced cultivation of the differences is much healthier.

References
Biskupek, Matthias (1990) *Wir Beuteldeutschen. Satiren, Glossen & Feuilletons* (Berlin: Eulenspiegel).
Biskupek, Matthias (1995) *Biertafel mit Colaklops. Satirische Zutaten von Claudia bis Kanada* (Berlin: Eulenspiegel).
Biskupek, Matthias (1996) *Der Quotensachse. Vom unaufhaltsamen Aufstieg eines Staatsbürgers sächsischer Nationalität. Roman* (Leipzig: Kiepenheuer).

Braun, Volker (1993a) *Texte in zeitlicher Folge Band 5* (Halle: Mitteldeutscher Verlag).

Braun, Volker (1993b) *Texte in zeitlicher Folge Band 8* (Halle: Mitteldeutscher Verlag).

Braun, Volker (1993c) *Texte in zeitlicher Folge Band 10* (Halle: Mitteldeutscher Verlag).

Braun, Volker (1995) *Der Wendehals. Eine Unterhaltung* (Frankfurt/Main: Suhrkamp).

Braun, Volker (1998) *Wir befinden uns soweit wohl. Wir sind erst einmal am Ende. Äusserungen* (Frankfurt/Main: Suhrkamp).

Costabile-Heming, Carol Anne (1997) *Intertextual exile. Volker Braun's dramatic re-vision of GDR society* (Hildesheim: Olms).

Demski, Eva (1992) 'Der Hund ist klüger als du', in *Kursbuch, Heft 109: Deutschland, Deutschland* (Berlin: Rowohlt), 101–9.

Dieckmann, Christoph (1998) *Das wahre Leben im falschen. Geschichten von ostdeutscher Identität* (Berlin: Ch. Links).

Dylan, Bob (1994) *Lyrics 1962–1985* (London: HarperCollins).

Emmerich, Wolfgang (1996) *Kleine Literaturgeschichte der DDR. Erweiterte Neuausgabe* (Leipzig: Kiepenheuer).

Fröhling, Jörg, Reinhild Meinel and Karl Riha (eds) (1997) *Wende-Literatur. Bibliographie und Materialien zur Literatur der deutschen Einheit* (Frankfurt/Main: Lang).

Grant, Colin B. (1995) *Literary communication from consensus to rupture. Practice and theory in Honecker's GDR* (Amsterdam, Atlanta: Rodopi).

Groschopp, Horst (1996) 'Im Gespräch mit Jörg Lau', in Keller, Rutschky and Schmidt (1996), 23–39.

Hochhuth, Rolf (1994) *Wessis in Weimar* (Munich: dtv).

Jucker, Rolf (ed.) (1997a) *Zeitgenössische Utopieentwürfe in Literatur und Gesellschaft. Zur Kontroverse seit den achtziger Jahren* (Amsterdam, Atlanta: Rodopi).

Jucker, Rolf (1997b) 'Zur Kritik der real existierenden Utopie des Status quo', in Jucker (1997a), 13–78.

Kaiser, Paul and Claudia Petzold (eds) (1997) *Boheme und Diktatur in der DDR. Gruppen, Konflikte, Quartiere. Katalog zur Ausstellung des Deutschen Historischen Museums vom 4. September bis 16. Dezember 1997* (Berlin: Fannie & Walz).

Kane, Martin (ed.) (1991) *Socialism and the Literary Imagination: Essays on East German Writers* (Providence, Oxford: Berg).

Karsunke, Yaak (1992) 'Fünf sarkastische Sonette', in *Kursbuch, Heft 109: Deutschland, Deutschland* (Berlin: Rowohlt), 97–99.

Keller, Walter, Michael Rutschky and Maruta Schmidt (eds) (1996) *Wie erst jetzt die DDR entsteht* (= *Der Alltag. Die Sensationen des Gewöhnlichen*, Nummer 71) (Berlin: Elefanten-Press).

Köhler, Barbara (1991) 'Rumpelstilz', in Pergande (1991).

Levitas, Ruth (1997) 'Utopia as literature, utopia as politics', in Jucker (1997a), 121–37.

Maier, Gerhart (1991) *Die Wende in der DDR* (Bonn: Bundeszentrale für politische Bildung).

Meinel, Reinhild: (1997a) '"Mein Luftkoffer, mein politisches Gepäck ..."', in Fröhling, Meinel and Riha (1997), 105 [Review of Braun, Volker: *Die Zickzackbrücke*. Halle 1992].

Meinel, Reinhild (1997b) '"Bloss gudd, daß es de Saggsen gäb'm dud"', in Fröhling, Meinel and Riha (1997), 240–2 [Review of Biskupek, Matthias: *Der Quotensachse*. Leipzig 1996].

Pape, Walter (ed.) (1993) *1870/71 – 1989/90. German Unifications and the Change of Literary Discourse* (Berlin: de Gruyter).

Pergande, Ingrid (1991) '"Volker Braun? – Da kann ich nur sagen, der Junge quält sich ..."': New Voices in the GDR lyric of the 1980s', in Kane (1991), 229–46.

Reed, Terence James (1993) 'Another piece of the past', in Pape (1993), 233–50.

Riha, Karl (1997) 'Ein skeptisches Resumee des Mauerfalls', in Fröhling, Meinel and Riha (1997), 231–2 [Review of Braun, Volker: *Der Wendehals*. Frankfurt/Main 1995].

Rutschky, Michael (1996) 'Die Fusion von Berlin und Brandenburg', in Keller, Rutschky and Schmidt (1996), 1–2.

Staunton, Denis (1997) 'Elegy for an unloved state', in *The Irish Times*, 5 May [Review of Fennell, Desmond: *Dreams of Oranges: An Eyewitness Account of the Fall of Communist Germany*. Sanas Publishing 1996].

'Stolz aufs eigene Leben', in *Der Spiegel* 27/1995:40–52.

Stölzl, Christoph (1997) 'Vorwort', in Kaiser and Petzold (1997), 9.

Subiotto, Arrigo (1991) 'Volker Braun: Literary metaphors and the travails of socialism', in Kane (1991), 195–212.

Walther, Joachim (1991) 'Das Floss der Utopia', in *ndl* 1, 42.

Wehdeking, Volker (1996) *Die deutsche Einheit und die Schriftsteller. Literarische Verarbeitung der Wende seit 1989* (Stuttgart: W. Kohlhammer).

6
United Consumers? Advertising Discourse and Constructions of German Identity

Helen Kelly-Holmes

Introduction

> Schokoladcndüftc bis auf die Straße, deshalb keine Reklame.
> (Our chocolate aromas fill the street – that's why we don't need to advertise)

Despite its anti-advertising tactic, this old maxim of the *Café Français*, Leipzig's most famous coffee house which was destroyed in the Second World War, seems like a highly appropriate place to start investigating advertising discourse and the construction of consumer identity since German unification. Paradoxically, the sentiments expressed in the slogan could be applied equally to two contradictory – even dichotomous – strands in the discourse of and about advertising in the period immediately following the *Wende* and unification, both of which, in turn, reflect contrasting worldviews and constructions of identity. On the one hand, we hear echoes of the texts and contexts of the west German advertisers who felt that advertising was barely necessary, the demand for western brands being so great. On the other, there are the east German voices of bewilderment and at times resistance, which met the influx of western advertising texts, questioning the nature, goals and very existence of the discourse. In this chapter, I shall begin by giving a brief overview of the development of advertising as a discourse, first in the GDR, then in the new *Länder*, before going on to look at a number of contemporary campaigns to see if (and how) such texts express or prescribe any distinct east German identity.[1]

Advertising in the former GDR

Of all discourse[2] types, perhaps advertising best symbolized the communicative cleavage between east and west, and their competing constructions of identity. With the introduction of the most capitalist of discourses to what has been described as the most socialist of countries,[3] the clash of ideologies was audible. Of course, 'introduction' is not the most accurate description, since that would imply that there was no advertising in the east, which was simply not the case. In fact, advertising texts played a complex and manifold role in the society of the GDR. To start with, there was the homegrown version, managed by *DeWag* and *InterWerbung*, who produced simple, straightforward and informative texts to – in the words of the Large Soviet Encyclopaedia – 'spread data on commodities, create and foster new wants and tastes in the population, make propaganda for and introduce new commodities' (in Harris and Seldon 1962:190). This was a very alien genre to west German advertising, and it could be claimed that the ubiquity of advertising in the west made the east seem even more distant and foreign, leading not only to communicative but also visual alienation; in the words of Schlosser (1990:76) 'die DDR [war] sehr weit von der bunten Vielfalt westlicher Werbung', (the GDR was very far away from the colourful variety of western advertising). This lack of commercial advertising was both an inevitable consequence of the economic system and the result of a deliberate policy and world view; as Schlosser (1990:76) terms it, '[eine] systembedingte Unterentwicklung kommerzieller Werbung' (an underdevelopment of commercial advertising that was determined by the system). The context for the production and consumption of advertising texts was simply not present (cf. also McNair 1991:87ff). In fact, one of the challenges facing advertisers following the *Wende* was 'to wean readers off their non-advertising mix and their conviction that space is for articles and information, not for advertising' (Hannan 1990:134). More than this, however, the official disavowal of advertising as a capitalist discourse made advertising texts part of the forbidden fruits of the west. The following extract from an academic analysis of West German classified advertisements sums up, better than any official statement, the given ideology regarding Western advertising:

> In vielen Anzeigen dieser Art ist deutlich die Sprachverwendung der kapitalistischen Werbung zu spüren. Nach dem Motto 'je übertriebener, desto wirkungsvoller' werden aufwertende Attribute,

häufig mit intensivierenden oder graduierenden Adverbien, verwendet, um das Selbstbild besonders vorteilhaft zu lassen.

Fritsch 1982:38

(In many such classified advertisements, the language of capitalist advertising is plain to see. Following the motto 'the more exaggerated, the more effective', superlatives, often with intensifying and graduating adverbs, are used, in order to present the individual in as positive a light as possible.)

Added to this was the preponderance of political advertising, making the East Germans world-weary recipients of political slogans and state propaganda. Another factor that came into play was the leakage of West German television advertising as a result of what Lemke (1991) terms the 'doppelte Medienlandscaft' or 'double media landscape' and the effect its creation of a consumption utopia had on the government portrayal of a capitalist dystopia.

Despite all these complexities and, in the words of Bartram and Waine (1983), 'the manifestation, particularly under Honecker, of many of the attributes of a typical "consumer" society', we can still conclude that an advertising culture in the sense that advertising is understood in western societies did not exist in the former GDR and that most of its citizens were inexperienced users of postmodern discourse types such as abstract consumer advertising. Living in a society predicated on the market and its texts, where the assumptions, associations and expected reactions form part of a shared body of subconscious knowledge, which, in turn, forms part of a shared identity, is a very different situation from viewing stolen snatches not just out of context, but in an ideologically opposed context.

Advertising and unification

In the early days of the *Wende*, there was an inevitable rejection of the products and texts of the GDR and a rush to purchase and experience the too-long denied products from the West (cf., for example, *Der Spiegel* 1990a, Atkinson 1993). In the words of one consumer researcher, the finer points of advertising and marketing research could wait until the East Germans had first satiated themselves (*Der Spiegel* 1990a:106). Marketers rushed to fill the vacuum left behind by the texts of actually existing socialism, and, as Cook (1992:16) predicted, advertising and its accompanying capitalist discourses spread across not only east Germany, but eastern Europe as a whole. The lack of an advertising and marketing culture meant that there were no 'home-grown' role models to provide guidance in consumption practices and it was therefore inevitable that many, initially, simply emulated west German behaviour (cf., for instance, Leiss, Kline and Jhally 1990:66).

Due to the level of demand for western products, it took some time for advertisers and marketers to realize that it was in fact a vacuum in which they were operating. A nice illustration of this was the reaction in the east to an advertising campaign for west German chocolate. The campaign's message was that the mother in the advertisement gave the chocolate to her children, just as *her* mother had given it to *her*. Not surprisingly, this left slightly bemused east German advertisees wondering where the mother had got the chocolate (*Berliner Morgenpost* 1997). To the west German advertiser, confronted for the first time with an east-west 'communication gulf', the east German proved a major challenge, unlike his/her 'identikit' counterpart in the west.[4] A key group of texts which supports and gives meaning to advertising texts, namely marketing research reports and data, were absent. This provides a very simple illustration of the fact that the life-world (Habermas 1993), the context – both producer and product of these advertising messages in the west – did not correspond with the life-world and context of the east. The successful strategies of many years were found wanting; worse still, they were seen as seductive, affected, laughable and over-the-top (*Der Spiegel* 1990b). Reimut Vogel, Director of the well-known advertising agency, *Logo FCA*, admitted that it had never even occurred to him and his advertising team that east Germans would think or speak differently and he was genuinely shocked at their inability or unwillingness to deal with the discourse (*Der Spiegel* 1990b). This phenomenon can also be attributed to the disappointment felt by many in their first direct and open encounter with west German media, the credibility of which had understandably been rated highly by many in the east (Lemke 1991:191). Meuschel (1992) too speaks of a 'double disappointment' felt by many in the east: on the one hand, that socialism and its system had failed (and failed them too), and, on the other, that the reality of the alternative, the consumer society, as presented by west German television, was rather different from its idealized, mediatized image.

Once this realization had dawned, advertisers set about the task of constructing a context within which their advertising and marketing texts would have meaning for individuals and groups who had only just begun to think of themselves as consumers. This involved educating and consumerizing citizens through advertising and promotional texts, constructing an intertextual sphere within which texts would have meaning, linking these texts to the new institutions of economic reform, and attempting, once the context of the new *Bundesländer* was complete, to create an all-German context to which east Germans too could relate.

Given the amount of time and effort which advertisers and marketers in consumer societies invest in the process of socializing individuals into the texts of consumption, it is interesting to note the pace at which people in the east developed a complex, sophisticated and discerning approach to consumption and its texts, working out quite definitely what they did and did not like in contemporary advertising: the former being 'exact, informative and "absolutely credible" advertisements', the latter being patronizing (Atkinson 1993; interestingly, this is also supported by research carried out by Saatchi & Saatchi in the former Soviet Union, reported in Davidson 1992).

Research carried out in Leipzig in 1994 also pointed to the development of a new type of consumerism (for full details, see Kelly 1995b). For example, only a minority of individuals rated the two needs which make up the cornerstone of advertising's existence, the need for a choice of products and services and the need to be informed about such products, as very important. Of course, it is possible that these needs had at that stage become somewhat obsolete, given the plethora of goods swamping the shops in the new federal states, and that, faced with this bewildering assortment, many individuals, now distanced from the previous situation, would opt for a slightly less extensive range. Another explanation however could be that, as in so many areas of east German public life, the west German solution did not quite fit. It was perhaps an excessive response to the wishes of east Germans for certainly more choice and availability, but within limits and specific areas.

Over half (57 per cent) of those interviewed in connection with the research expressed a very negative attitude to advertising, while a further 14 per cent held mildly negative views. Almost everyone commented on the increase in the amount of advertising since the *Wende* and the irritating effects and intrusive nature of this. Also evident was the lack of trust in advertising and advertisers, as were the difficulties in dealing with this new discourse. Many doubted the power of advertising, claiming, in keeping with the old *Café Français* slogan, that good products are sufficient advertising in and of themselves. What also impressed was the helpless way people commented on the fact that advertising, although regrettable, was now essential, an inevitable text of the *Wende* and a key text of unification. What the results of the survey pointed to, above all, was the desire for informative, straightforward and literal advertising, which sought to explain rather than to overwhelm, as it was put so eloquently elsewhere, '*Schicki-Micki-Werbung kommt bei uns nicht an*' (cool advertising does nothing for us) (*Der Spiegel* 1990b).

It may be argued that such attitudes could also be applied to certain sections of the west German population (and many people in other consumer societies). While this is true, what is unique about the *Wende* and such reactions is that the introduction of this discourse offered the opportunity to articulate attitudes to consumption (since these were in their early stages of formation), an opportunity which is not always available in an existing consumer society, where people do not necessarily have the same distance.

Another interesting trend that could be observed was the development of 'life-situation'[5] groupings with particular attitudes to advertising and ways of interacting with its texts. These included the 'unification generation', which did not want to be patronized and wished to converge with west German consumer identities; the 'conscientious objectors', who, although relatively well-off, had ideological problems with the texts of consumption and were consciously resisting them; the 'victims', who were bewildered and apathetic in the face of such advertising appeals; and finally the 'survivors', an older group who could see the benefits and were able to use the texts to their own advantage.

Many initial campaigns, in the early days of the *Wende* and unification, tried to overcome these problems by emphasizing or constructing some sort of link with the east and, by extension, a shared past and identity: for example, Dresdner Bank, which pronounced itself proud to be 'back in Dresden'. Others stressed their commitment to the restructuring of the east German economy, for instance, Bayrische Landesbank's slogan 'Wir haben vor ihnen investiert' (We invested before them [other banks and financial institutions]). An important point to make here is that changes also took place in the west German advertising landscape. The *Wende* itself became thematized in advertising and its terminology subverted for advertising purposes. So, in an advertisement for *Der Spiegel*, west Germans were urged to give their friends, relations and newly-acquired brothers in the east 'das grenzenlose Geschenk' (the borderless present). In fact, because the *Wende* and unification, were, for many, among the first shared

German-German experiences – albeit lived through from radically different viewpoints – this period became one of the first linguistic spheres or contexts within which common references and associations became possible, making, for instance, the advertisers' dream of a pan-German pun a reality. A good example was a series run by the non-German Fiat, in which unification was used as a new theme, a joke to which both east and west Germans could relate, reproducing the familiar phrases of unification, such as, 'Auf dem langen Weg zur Einheit' (On the long path to unity) and 'Der 4-Stufen-Plan zur Vereinigung' (the four step plan to unification) in an unfamiliar context. (For a more detailed discussion of advertising strategies during the *Wende*, see Kelly 1995a.)

Many companies attempted to overcome the problems of creating an all-German advertisement, by designing separate campaigns for west and east (cf. Cote 1990, Atkinson 1993), telling eastern advertisees in basic terms what the product costs, what it does and where it can be bought (*Der Spiegel* 1990b). However, in a number of instances this backfired, with the result that the targeted group felt insulted at being offered a 'dumbed-down' version of a west German advertisement (Atkinson 1993). A further consideration was the need for advertisers to, literally, teach east German consumers about products, to give them the vocabulary required, and, where necessary, to create new, positive meanings for this vocabulary of the market, traditionally seen as negative under the previous system (cf. also Stevenson 1993:350 on this aspect). This was particularly evident in advertising for banks and other financial services, in much of which, according to the marketing personnel concerned, the promotional aspect was almost non-existent, so great was the need to 'inform' and 'educate'.

Once east German products began to find a voice again, as disillusionment with things western led in part to mourning for an idealized shared past, appeals to nostalgia and local loyalties, the so-called 'Buy eastern' tactics came into their own. Given that in a 1995 survey (*Der Spiegel* 1995), 45 per cent of east German respondents stated 'I buy eastern products, if at all possible' – the percentage of east Germans deliberately choosing (or admitting to choosing) west German products being just 2 per cent – such appeals were certainly not misplaced. This rejection also marked a new period of greater self-confidence among east Germans as they developed their own brand of consumerism. Examples included RTF, an east Berlin television manufacturer's slogan, 'ostdeutsch, daher gut' (it's east German, so it's good) and Reemtsma's counterpart to 'Test the West', 'Kost die Ost' (savour the East). Berliner Kosmetik, interestingly, appealed to a pan-post-communist identity by using the slogan 'What was good yesterday doesn't have to be bad today' in the Czech Republic, Slovakia, Poland and other countries, as well as east Germany.

Advertising discourse and identity ten years on

How have these aspects developed in the years since unification and how does advertising discourse reflect and construct identity almost a decade since the *Wende*? An examination of the advertising and promotional literature of a selection of east German drinks manufacturers gives interesting answers to these questions. Of the five brands discussed below, the first three, Hasseröder, Glückauf and Ur-Krostitzer, have strong regional/local identities, whereas the other two, Radeberger and Rotkäppchen, have a greater presence throughout the new *Länder* and increasingly in the old *Länder* too.

The first significant feature of this east German promotional discourse is the treatment of the period of the *Wende* and unification, which have almost become mythologized. There is, in all of the advertising materials, a need to acknowledge this time, even to come clean about it. Two approaches dominate: the *Wende* and unification are either heralded as the start of a great new epoch, or glossed over as an unfortunate blip in an otherwise fairly happy continuum. Hasseröder, for instance, adopts the former approach in its advertising literature: 'Der Auerhahn startet zum Höhenflug im Jahr 1990, nachdem bereits eine Brautradition seit 1872 mit wechselvoller Geschichte belegt ist' (The capercaillie soared into flight once more in 1990, after a brewing tradition since 1872 has had to endure a varied history).

Geography and origins are seen as key in determining the identity of all the brands examined. Although the majority of these brands are now either owned by, or in partnership with, a west German brewery, the east German identity is strong and the product is seen as an *Ostprodukt*, an eastern product. The products are mainly sold in the east, and even within this identity, there are strong east German localized identities. In the case of Hasseröder, the fact that the products were originally East German makes it logical that they are *Ost-Marken* or eastern brands in the opinion of the marketing department.

In the straightforward approach of Hasseröder's advertising, we also see the expression of the desire on the part of consumers for straightforward advertising. The anti-advertising, anti-west-German, anti-*Schicki-micki* approach referred to above has also become part of this consumer identity, as expressed in the discourse. Everywhere in Hasseröder's promotional literature, we see the vocabulary of western marketing and advertising, the *Fremdwörter* or English words and mishmashes that have come to characterize marketing-speak in west Germany: *Zielgruppe* (target market), *Marketing-Strategie* (marketing strategy), *Premium-Marken* (premium brands). However, the words seem strangely juxtaposed and do not always sit comfortably with the context of the message, the graphics or the sentiments being expressed. For example, in its PR material, Hasseröder states:

> Hasseröder Premium Pils ist weder Szene-Bier, noch liebäugelt es mit einem hochgestochenen Schickeria-Image. Es positioniert sich nicht in unglaubhaften Scheinwelten mit für Bier unakzeptierten Lifestyle-Kampagnen, sondern bleibt bodenständig.
> (Hasseröder Premium Pils is neither a 'scene beer' nor does it flirt with a pompous, 'in-crowd' image. It does not position itself in unbelievable 'pretend worlds' with lifestyle campaigns that are not acceptable for beer, but instead it remains solidly down to earth.)

What is even more interesting about this approach is that Hasseröder's advertising is designed by the west German parent.

A more direct appeal to constructions of an east German identity is found in the advertising of Glückauf Bier, located in Gersdorf in the Erzgebirge region. The firm is 100 per cent east German and works together with an advertising agency to produce its own texts. The target group consists exclusively of east Germans and all of the turnover is achieved in the new *Länder*. According to the management of the brewery, Glückauf is without question an *Ost-Marke*, because in their own words 'Beer needs *Heimat*'. This *Heimatverbundenheit*, this tie with the *Heimat* or home and roots – in relation to Saxony and in particularly the Erzgebirge – forms the main theme of the advertising and the foundation upon which the beer's identity is built. Through the use of location, slogans and also dialect, the brewery attempts to present the beer as east German. For instance, the slogans 'Wo mit Glückauf gegrüßt wird, wird auch *Glückauf* getrunken' (Where people greet each other with 'Glückauf', they also drink Glückauf) and 'Bei uns wird nicht nur mit Glückauf gegrüßt, bei uns wird auch *Glückauf* getrunken' (Here we not only greet people with 'Glückauf', we also drink Glückauf) rely on localized knowledge of the miners' greeting, 'Glückauf'. Another slogan which leaves no doubt about the regionality and identity of the product is 'Aus dem Herzen unserer Sächsischen Heimat' (From the heart of our Saxon *heimat*/home). The use of *unser* (our) here and *bei uns* (here, among us, in our home) in the previous example relates not just to the brewery of course, but also to the target readers, at one and the same time acknowledging that this is also their identity and inviting them to (re)construct themselves in this way. What is also interesting about Glückauf's campaigns is the less obvious acknowledgement of a break with the past, of the mythology of *Wende* and unification. The only hint is an allusion to the 'wechselvolle Geschichte' or 'varied history'. There is a greater air of confidence in this advertising, a sense that this brand need not feel inferior, but simply different, or even superior.

The third of the local/regional brands is Ur-Krostitzer. Again, 100 per cent of turnover is achieved in the new *Bundesländer*, and the target group consists of east German consumers. As with Glückauf, those responsible for marketing Ur-Krostitzer believe 'Beer needs *Heimat*' and that regional references and ties are important for brands. Although regional in its origins, the beer became a 'national' GDR brand and for this and other reasons the brewery would definitely describe Ur-Krostitzer as an *Ost-Marke*. Here it is the new epoch metaphor of *Wende* and unification that is utilized, albeit as part of the telling of the brewery's history since 1534: 'Die deutsche Einheit ermöglicht den Neubeginn. Seit 1990 erstrahlt Ur-Krostitzer in neuem Glanz' (German unity has made the new beginning possible. Since 1990 Ur-Krostitzer has glittered with a new sparkle).

Although claiming not to use its east German identity as an advertising tactic, the use of geography, history and narrative all produce an effect that unmistakably appeals to an east German regional sense of pride. First, the beer is situated in its (east German) *grüne Heimat* (green homeland), then it is identified with Leipzig. What is interesting about this appeal, however, is that it harks back to a mythical shared past predating the GDR. For example, in slogans such as the following:

Die zurückhaltende Noblesse der sächsischen Traditionsmarke.
(The reserved noblesse of the traditional brand from Saxony.)

Ur-Krostitzer feinherbes Pilsner wird streng nach dem deutschen Reinheitsgebot von 1516 gebraut.
(Ur-Krostitzer Pilsner is brewed strictly in accordance with the German Purity Law of 1516.)

Exzellentes Bier zu brauen ist in Krostitz seit Jahrhunderten
Tradition wie Selbstverständnis.
(For centuries, brewing excellent beer has been part of what we are
in Krostitz.)

Nur etwa fünfzehn Kilometer von Leipzig entfernt, liegt das kleine
Örtchen Krostitz. ... Die Geschichte des Dorfes und seiner Brauerei
sind untrennbar miteinander verbunden – bis auf den heutigen Tag.
Die Silhouette wird geprägt durch Doppelturm und Brauerei.
Eigenwillig und stolz tut sie kund: Das Dorf und sein Bier sind eins.
(Only 15 kilometres from Leipzig lies the tiny village of Krostitz. The
history of the village and its brewery are one and the same – and
this still holds true today. The silhouette is dominated by the
double spire and the brewery. Independent-minded and proud: the
village and its beer are one.)

The whole approach, the language and style all serve to create a much
more formal appeal, which complements the studied and stilted gravitas of the promotional texts themselves and the determined sense of
history. The distancing mechanism of the formal address form *Sie* and
the overly formal register of the following quotation create a slightly
old-fashioned feel, not often seen in today's advertising landscape,
except perhaps within the sphere of parody:

Ur-Krostitzer steht bei vielen Anlässen im Mittelpunkt. Seine Präsenz
schafft Lebensgefühl und prägt den Augenblick. Daß Sie sich wohl
bei uns fühlen, liegt uns am Herzen! Mit freundlicher Empfehlung,
Ihre Krostitzer Brauerei.
(Ur-Krostitzer is at the centre of many occasions. Its presence creates
a feeling of being alive and marks the moment. We want you to
enjoy yourself with us. With best regards, Yours, Krostitzer Brewery.)

Here we see the manufacture of an aristocratic, gentlemanly past, the
brand apparently having been left untainted by the GDR or unification. In this slightly pompous, slightly naive approach, there is,
perhaps, further evidence of an anti-*Schicki-micki*, anti-vulgar and, by
implication, anti-west German appeal.
   The final two brands are better known throughout the rest of
Germany, something which is evidenced by the scale of their advertising presence in a range of media both inside and outside of the new
Länder and the fact that both target consumers in the west as well as in

the east. Furthermore, in an all-German context, they would be recognized as east German brands, with a strong east German identity; however, both declined to define themselves in this way. In the case of Radeberger, the beer and the city of Dresden have become inextricably associated through the advertising texts. This, in and of itself, is noteworthy, indicating that a change has taken place in the advertising and media texts with which all Germans become socialized consumers. The presence of Dresden in the television texts of Radeberger gives young people growing up all over Germany, a fundamentally different view of Dresden from that of their parents; for them the city will simply form part of the taken-for-granted landscape of consumption texts.

The advertising and promotional literature talks of 'Ein Bier, das Geschichte schrieb. Eine Geschichte, die untrennbar verbunden ist mit seiner sächsischen Heimat' (A beer that wrote history. A history that is inextricably bound up with its Saxon home). Here, again, as with all the other examples, we see the importance of the east German *Heimat*. The approach, although more polished, is very similar to that of Ur-Krostitzer. The emphasis is on a very particular aspect of Radeberger's tradition, namely its role as *Hoflieferant*, a purveyor to the court – again, in all aspects of the public relations material, this regal, pompous gravitas is the main motif: 'Die Faszination, erster deutscher Pilsbrauer zu sein und mit dieser Kompetenz bis heute nur nach Pilsner Brauart zu brauen, gibt uns ein erhabenes Gefühl – und die Tradition lebt' (The fascination of being the first German Pils brewer and, in this position of authority, of brewing Pils to this very day only in accordance with the Pils method makes us feel exalted – and the tradition lives on). There is no acknowledgement of the GDR, of any break in continuity since the glorious past; in the world of Radeberger, the GDR did not really exist. The Dresden presented in the advertising and public relations material is not the Dresden of actually existing socialism, but the Dresden of this golden age: regal, sophisticated, cultured. Rather than modern-day sponsors and celebrity testimonials, we are given the recommendations of Friedrich August III von Sachsen and Otto von Bismarck.

Finally, we turn to Rotkäppchen, which, for many, is *the* quintessential *Ost-Marke*, whose very survival became a metaphor for the east German economy in the months following the *Wende* (cf., for instance, *Der Spiegel* 1990a), and which, today, has come to be a signifier for a whole range of GDR associations, the drink of preference at *Ostalgie* parties and public events in the east, a type of shorthand for an identity (cf. Köhler 1997 and Michalsky 1997). Ironically, however, this is not the way the marketing department of Rotkäppchen sees it. When asked to define Rotkäppchen as an *Ost-Marke*, they responded, 'What is an eastern brand? Before the Second World War our company operated nationally and now it has started doing so again. There are no northern or southern brands.' Interestingly, despite this response, there is no attempt, in the promotional literature, to obliterate the period of the GDR. In contrast, Rotkäppchen gives the most in-depth account of the period in the telling of its long history. In a section entitled, '1948–1980 The Stabilization' – in itself, a far from negative summation – there are many positive things written about the fortunes of Rotkäppchen under actually existing socialism, and the story is told using words and themes with which others might feel uncomfortable:

Die nächste Umstellung wird nach Besuchen in der UdSSR fällig.
(The next adjustment became necessary after visits to the USSR.)

Bei der Errichtung des Interhotels 'Stadt Leipzig', des ersten in der DDR, wird die erste Hausmarke hergestellt. Nach dem Bau weiterer Interhotels wird die Marke 'Interhotel Halbtrocken' geschaffen und an alle Interhotels geliefert.
(The first house brand was produced to coincide with the opening of the 'Stadt Leipzig' Interhotel – the first Interhotel in the GDR. Once other Interhotels were established, the 'Interhotel medium dry brand' was created and supplied to all Interhotels.)

Zur Einsparung von Sektimporten ... wird ab 1980 eine neue Sektserie ... in bester Qualität entwickelt; auf dem zentralen Wettbewerb 'Beste Verpackung der DDR' erhalten sie den ersten Preis.
(In order to save imports of sparkling wine ... a new line of the best quality was launched in 1980; it won first prize in the 'Best Packaging in the GDR' competition.)

The next section, covering the last decade of the GDR, is entitled 'After success in the GDR, the free market' and contains the following extract, which, both in terms of vocabulary and content, speaks for itself:

Der Betrieb ist in all diesen Jahren politisch hochdekoriert und verfügt, entsprechend seiner Leitfunktion, über erhebliche soziale und kulturelle Einrichtungen – genannt seien Sportzentrum und Betriebssportgemeinschaft, Kinderkrippe, betriebs – und kombinatseigene Ferienobjekte und Errungenschaften wie etwa das Babyjahr.

(During all these years the business won many awards and much recognition from the authorities and, in accordance with its leading role, provided numerous social and cultural facilities and services for employees – for example, the sports centre and the works sports club, the creche, holiday homes, and achievements such as the 'baby year'.)

All of the prizes, all the recognition, for instance, 'Betrieb der aus-gezeichneten Qualität', (company of outstanding quality), are listed here and some are even reproduced, bearing the symbol of the GDR. As with Radeberger, there is, here too, no break in continuity, but unlike Radeberger and the other brands discussed above, the period of actu-ally existing socialism is seen as an integral, even a key part of that continuity. The approach is raw and quite unnerving in its honesty and pride in the role Rotkäppchen played in the former GDR – a role many would wish to cover up, but which Rotkäppchen wishes to trumpet. In the construction of Rotkäppchen's identity, the GDR is a foundation stone, the regime, its institutions and its culture are presented as credible sources of testimonials.

The mood of the discussion of the *Wende* and privatization, although entitled '*Wende*, privatization and the upturn', is far less cele-bratory than with the other brands discussed and we soon see why. It begins 'And then everything changed', and discusses the fall in turnover and redundancies that followed before the brand finally con-solidated and fought its way back to competitiveness. The stubborn-ness and determination to prove that this was not a 'Marke zweiter Klasse' (a second-class brand) is also evident here:

Ob nicht zuletzt Stimmen im Westen aus Rotkäppchen nach der *Wende* ein totgeborenes Kind machen wollten – der Sekt aus Freyburg an der Unstrut perlt und perlt.
(Despite voices in the west that wanted to declare Rotkäppchen dead in the water – the sparkling wine from Freyburg an der Unstrut just sparkles on and on.)

der ostdeutsche Sekt
(the east German sparkling wine)

Rotkäppchen, die prominente Marke aus dem Osten, die erfolgre-icher ist als vielerorts Westprodukte, ist ein Stück Selbstbewußtsein.

(Rotkäppchen, the prominent brand from the east, that is more successful in many places than products from the west, is a mark of self-confidence.)

This brand, more than any, seems to represent an east German, post-GDR identity, something which could only develop with a distance from the past and success in west German terms. To illustrate this point, it is interesting to note that promotional material from 1990 contains no such references. The text alludes briefly to 'the difficult times after the *Wende*', but apart from that concentrates exclusively on Rotkäppchen's historical traditions; the *Geschichte* here is not that of actually existing socialism, and there is little, if anything, to identify the brand as east German. Compare this with the promotional literature for retail outlets announcing Rotkäppchen's television advertising premiere in 1996: 'Jetzt kommt die starke Erfolgsmarke aus den neuen Bundesländern zum allerersten Mal auf den Bildschirm' (Now the strong, successful brand from the new *Länder* is appearing on television for the first time). This new confidence meant that the 'GDR-thing' did not have to be hidden any more.

But what of the marketing department's comments, that Rotkäppchen is not an *Ost-Marke* and is not marketed as such? In its latest campaign, this is certainly the case. We are told that 'Das Traditions-Sortiment hat Rotkäppchen zur erfolgreichsten deutschen Marke der letzten Jahre im Sektmarkt gemacht' (Its traditional range has made Rotkäppchen the most successful German brand in the German sparkling wine market of the last few years). Its new wine, we are told, comes 'from Germany's most northerly wine-growing region'. These subtle, but telling changes – 'German', not 'east German'; 'Germany', not 'in' or 'from the east' – added to the new emphasis on Rotkäppchen's regal and aristocratic past: for example, we are told that 'even Kaiser Wilhelm II prided himself on the fact that he introduced the sparkling wine from Freyburg to all his officers' messes because it was easy to digest'. These are all indications that Rotkäppchen is on its way to becoming a German brand, one which those being socialized into consumption now will accept as German, rather than automatically assigning it to the east German category.

The Rotkäppchen experience is almost prototypical for other east German brands that have survived unification: an initial attempt, following the *Wende*, to masquerade as west German or not-east-German; then, with the development of greater self-confidence, an exploitation of *Ostalgie* or nostalgia for the GDR; the progression to, or consolidation as, a regional brand, either within one area of the new *Länder*, or the whole region of the new *Länder*; finally, redefinition as a German brand, with or without a regional dimension, by adopting a bland, neutral identity.

Conclusion

What conclusions can we draw about these advertisements and their prescription or description of an east German identity or identities? First of all, regional identities are stronger than ever and they form a key element in advertising strategies. For many of these brands, the regional or local aspect far outweighs any pan-eastern aspect. Then there is the use of language, the lack of the expected *Fremdwörter*, the dominance of soberly constructed German words and sentences. We also have the idealizing of the countryside and its promotion as a kind of shorthand for *Heimat* and belonging. Interestingly, in these east German advertisements the countryside has also taken on some of the associations established by western advertising, such as freshness, nature, or purity. What is perhaps most interesting is that the landscape has come to be constructed as part of a neutral, safe, acceptable aspect of east German identity. Another part of this 'safe identity' is an imagined imperial or regal history: imagined, because with temporal distance, the finer points and details have been lost or blurred and the simple image that is presented provides a more attractive past into which people can buy. In terms of these two aspects in particular, the advertisements, to the outsider without the relevant cultural knowledge, appear as typical German beer advertisements.

The mythologizing of the *Wende* and unification are also aspects of an identity, although not quite as uncontested as the regal or the rural, since the period is treated differently by different parties, betraying different loyalties, experiences and views. None of these advertisements or promotional texts is particularly creative, humorous or dynamic. Instead, they are largely straightforward, literal and informative, adopting an almost anti-advertising tactic. Thus the desire among east German consumers for this type of advertising has been answered, at least by east German brands, something which, in turn, will be recycled into consumer behaviour and identity not just in the east, but also in the west as these products, particularly Radeberger and Rotkäppchen, expand. Finally, all of these aspects point to complex and contradictory constructions of identity in the texts of east German advertising, something that reflects the (at least partial) failure of attempts by western advertisers to construct an 'identikit' east German consumer.

Notes

1 The role played by advertising in the construction of identity is seen as two-fold here: on the one hand, advertisements can appeal directly to (say) national, ethnic, regional, local, gender identities and deliberately seek to create or strengthen such identities; on the other hand, as one of a variety of related and unrelated texts circulated in the public sphere of a particular country or region, advertisements inevitably contribute – in an indirect, but none the less powerful way – to a lived, shared identity, comprising common-sense assumptions, taken-for-granted knowledge about consumption, institutions, individuals, groups, language, attitudes, aspirations and so on.

2 Discourse being understood here as the meaningful, coherent interaction of text, context and participants (cf. Cook 1992).

3 For example, Sandford (1976:208) claimed that East German television was 'the most consistently socialist of the East European services', while Karl Deutsch (in Herbert and Wildenmann 1991:79) contended that its unique combination of 'Prussianism' and actually existing socialism made the GDR more communist even than the Soviet Union.

4 'Den Bundesrepublikaner, sagt Logo-Chef Vogel, könne man jederzeit "aus dem Katalog herausnehmen" ... Den DDR-Verbraucher dagegen haben die Werbefachleute erst in dürren Daten erfaßt' (*Der Spiegel* 1990b:114).

5 The notion of a life-situation was formulated in preference to the accepted concept of a lifestyle, since the latter implies a deliberate choice which is not really appropriate to the phenomenon being studied here.

References

Atkinson, Rick (1993) 'Ads cater to wary east Germans: Just the facts, please, in a world without yuppies', in *International Herald Tribune*, 28–29 August 1993, 11.

Bartram, Graham and Anthony Waine (eds) (1983) *Culture and Society in the GDR* (Lancaster: Lancaster University Press).

Berliner Morgenpost (1997) 'R4 und Kinderschokolade: Nostalgiemarken sind in', in *Berliner Morgenpost*, 10 June 1997.

Cook, Guy (1992) *The Discourse of Advertising* (London: Routledge).

Cote, Kevin (1990) 'East Germany gets new ad efforts', in *Advertising Age* 61/27 (2 July 1990), 4.

Davidson, Martin (1992) *The Consumerist Manifesto: Advertising in Postmodern Times* (London: Routledge).

Der Spiegel (1990a) 'Rotkäppchen darf nicht sterben', in *Der Spiegel* 22, 106–8.

Der Spiegel (1990b) 'Einfach lächerlich', in *Der Spiegel* 22, 114–15.

Der Spiegel (1992) 'Mehr auf der Butterseite', in *Der Spiegel* 1, 86–90.

Der Spiegel (1995) 'Spiegel-Umfrage – Viele Ostdeutsche trauern den alten Zeiten nach', in *Der Spiegel* 27, 40–7.

Durrani, Osman, Colin Good and Kevin Hilliard (eds) (1995) *The New Germany: Literature and Society after Unification* (Sheffield: Sheffield Academic Press).

Flood, John, Paul Salmon, Olive Sayce and Christopher Wells (eds) (1993) *'Das unsichtbare Band der Sprache'. Studies in German Language and Linguistic History in Memory of Leslie Seiffert* (Stuttgart: Verlag Hans-Dieter Heinz/Akademischer Verlag Stuttgart).

108   *Advertising Discourse and Constructions of Identity*

Fritsch, Barbara (1982) 'Sprachkultur in Zeitungsanzeigen', in *Sprachpflege* 31/3, 36–9.

Habermas, Jürgen (1993) 'The second life fiction of the Federal Republic: We have become "normal" again', in *New Left Review* 197 (Jan./Feb. 1993), 58–66.

Hannan, Brian (1990) 'Making the most of east Germany's media changes', in *Business Marketing Digest* 15/2 (1990), 131–7.

Harris, Ralph and Arthur Seldon (1962) *Advertising in Action* (London: The Institute for Economic Affairs/André Deutsch).

Herbert, Willi and Rudolf Wildenmann (1991) 'Deutsche Identität. Die subjektive Verfassung der Deutschen vor der Vereinigung', in Wildenmann (1991), 71–98.

Kelly, Helen (1995a) 'The discourse of post-Unification advertising', in Durrani, Good and Hilliard (1995), 167–85.

Kelly, Helen (1995b) West German Banks and East German Consumers: A Study in Intercultural Advertising Communication, PhD thesis, Aston University, Birmingham, UK.

Köhler, Regina (1997) 'Ein schaler Nachgeschmack von Honecker und Wodka', in *Berliner Morgenpost*, 14 April 1997.

Leiss, William, Stephen Kline and Sut Jhally (1990) *Social Communication in Advertising* (London: Routledge).

Lemke, Christiane (1991) *Die Ursachen des Umbruchs 1989 – Politische Sozialisation in der ehemaligen DDR* (Opladen: Westdeutscher Verlag).

McNair, Brian (1991) *Glasnost, Perestroika and the Soviet Media* (London: Routledge).

Meuschel, Sigrid (1992) *Legitimation und Parteiherrschaft – zum Paradox von Stabilität und Revolution in der DDR* (Frankfurt/Main: Suhrkamp).

Michalsky, Oliver (1997) 'Von Rache keine Spur', in *Berliner Morgenpost*, 3 January 1997.

Sandford, John (1976) *The Mass Media of the German-speaking Countries* (London: Oswald Wolff).

Schlosser, Horst Dieter (1990) *Die deutsche Sprache in der DDR, zwischen Stalinismus und Demokratie: historische, politische und kommunikative Bedingungen* (Cologne: Verlag Wissenschaft und Politik).

Stevenson, Patrick (1993) 'The German language and the construction of national identities', in Flood et al. (1993), 333–56.

Wildenmann, Rudolf (ed.) (1991) *Nation und Demokratie: Politisch-strukturelle Gestaltungsprobleme im neuen Deutschland* (Baden-Baden: Nomos-Gesellschaft).

7
Ideological Practices in East and West German Media: Reporting the Thuringian Miners' Hunger Strike

Susanne Schrabback

Introduction

The aftermath of unification was characterized by immense political, economic and social changes in east Germany, but the most crucial battle undoubtedly took place on the labour market. The transformation of the east German economy resulted in unemployment, which was unknown to east Germans. However, it was not simply unemployment that upset them, but the fact that it was accompanied by the loss of their familiar conditions of existence. Experienced in its totality, this was traumatic for many. What happened in the economic sphere was an example of the way in which unification in general was 'negotiated'. 'Es geht um Arbeit und damit um Würde' (It's about work, and therefore, about dignity) writes *Neues Deutschland* on 22 July 1993, describing the symbolic significance of one labour battle, the hunger strike of the potash miners over the impending closure of the Bischofferode mine in Thuringia in 1993. The news coverage of this strike in two daily papers, the west German *Süddeutsche Zeitung (SZ)* and the east German *Neues Deutschland (ND)*, will be the subject of this chapter.

In order to understand fully the events surrounding this hunger strike, a brief outline of what preceded them is necessary. Before unification, the West German BASF subsidiary Kali und Salz AG and the East German mines were the main competitors in the potash industry: the GDR exported twice as many potash products as West Germany, and 60 per cent went to capitalist countries. In 1990, however, it was decided to decrease the annual production in the east from 3.5 to 1.2 million tons (in the west, on the other hand, only from 2.5 to 2.0 million tons). By March 1993, 2500 miners in Thuringia had lost their jobs. At that time in the east there were four mines with 4600 – as opposed to the former figure of 30 000 – employees still working, and in the west six mines with 5200 employees. One of the east German mines to be closed was in Bischofferode, regardless of the fact that there was a prospective buyer from west Germany who had guaranteed to keep on most of the 700 employees there. As a reaction to that the miners took over the mine and kept up full production from April 1993. The protests escalated when the agreement to merge the east and west German mines was given its first reading in the Bundestag on 1 July 1993, and from then onwards the attention the media paid to the events in Bischofferode increased (see Appendix). This date is therefore the starting point for the empirical analysis.

The output

In order to establish which agendas *ND* and *SZ* set in regard to these events, their output in the months of July, August and September 1993 was analysed.

Table 7.1 illustrates how often the events in Bischofferode were in the headlines, and shows that there were far more references to them in the east German paper. This is not surprising for a number of reasons. First, the events took place in an east German region. Second, after decades of very one-sided, party-controlled GDR news reporting, the east German press for the first time was functioning as a real information source about political events (see Voltmer, Schabedoth and Schrott 1995:233). Moreover, it provided for the extended need of an eastern readership for clarification in the process of self-identification

Table 7.1   Coverage of the miners' strike in the *Süddeutsche Zeitung* and *Neues Deutschland*: number of headline references July–September 1993

	Süddeutsche Zeitung	Neues Deutschland
July 1993	23	58
Aug. 1993	6	51
Sept. 1993	3	30
Total	32	139

at a time of dramatic political change. The Bischofferode closure, with its loss of hundreds of jobs, definitely represented one of the key issues in the east, and thus gained symbolic significance. Third, although both *SZ* and *ND* aim at a target readership on the national level, this in fact is not the case: while east Germans have been increasingly buying west German papers since the fall of the Wall, east German papers are hardly read by west Germans at all (see Humphreys 1994). The relatively thin coverage of the Bischofferode events in *SZ*, however, hints at the restricted impact and significance for its (mostly western) readership that this paper attached to the events.

Headlines and actors in political discourse

The prominence of headlines makes them a useful subject for analysis. The reader decodes and interprets headlines by scanning through them, and on the basis of these processes will decide whether or not to continue reading. A headline summarizes what the article is about, it expresses its topic or, in other words, its most important semantic macrostructure. As has been shown in research on discourse comprehension (see, for example, Hartley 1982, van Dijk 1988a, 1988b, Kress and van Leeuwen 1996), it is these macrostructures that are best recalled. A headline creates in the reader a preliminary macrostructure in which the news article is constructed. This means that the headline itself will influence how the readers define what the story is about. In the following, therefore, the object of analysis will be all the headlines that appeared during the period studied.

In particular, the actors emerging in them will be focused on, as sociocultural change involves individuals, groups, institutions or countries. Such actors surface in media discourse with varied frequencies, and the description space they get also differs. This ascribes their engagement in, and responsibility for, these events in a certain way. However, it is above all the grammatical system of a language itself that facilitates the emphasis of the role news actors possess in the political process. Thus, the propositional structure may imply opinion, for instance, by placing arguments into particular semantic roles (Agent, Patient).

There are particular types of actors that appear to figure repeatedly in mass mediated political discourse. According to the sphere of society they are involved in, they fall into the following main categories: professional politicians, journalists, experts, politicians in a wider sense (for example, representatives of different movements), economic agents (for example, employers, trade unionists), and ordinary people.

Table 7.2   The actors in the headlines

Actors	Süddeutsche Zeitung		Neues Deutschland	
Professional politicans	13	(23%)	39	(20%)
Journalists	–		2	(1%)
Politicians (in wider sense)	3	(5%)	23	(12%)
Experts	–		3	(2%)
Economic agents	13	(23%)	40	(21%)
Ordinary people	27	(48%)	83	(43%)
Others	–		3	(2%)
Total	56	(100%)	193	(100%)

Note: percentages have been rounded up or down to the nearest whole number.

Table 7.2 summarizes the participants that were thematized in the news coverage on Bischofferode according to these categories.

In quantitative terms, Table 7.2 does not yield significant discrepancies regarding the categories of actors mentioned in the headlines. Protests surrounding the closure of a company which results in the loss of hundreds of jobs can be expected to emerge as a concern for groups having either a political or an economic interest, the former group mainly comprising professional politicians, the latter employers and employees. And indeed, it is these categories that appear most often as actors in the headlines: professional politicians – 23 per cent in *SZ* and 20 per cent in *ND*; economic agents – 23 per cent in *SZ* and 21 per cent in *ND*; and ordinary people (above all the miners themselves) – 48 per cent in *SZ* and 43 per cent in *ND*. Additionally, politicians in the wider sense are referred to in both papers (5 per cent in *SZ* and 12 per cent in *ND*), journalists, experts and others (in this case the police) only in *ND*, though with insignificant frequency.

If there is little difference in the frequency with which particular groups and individuals occur, how then do the papers differ in highlighting their involvement? A disparity can be observed mainly in three categories.

Professional politicians

As anticipated, the entities found in this category relate primarily to either the local level (that is, the Thuringian government), or to the central level (that is, the Federal Government in Bonn). In both papers, each level is repeatedly referred to in the headlines. Here are examples of references to political agents:

Local level	Federal level
(1) Land Thüringen (*SZ* 16.7.93) (Federal State Thuringia)	Bonn (*ND* 18.8.93) (Bonn)
(2) Thüringer Landesausschüsse (*ND* 27.7.93) (Thuringian State Council)	Bonner Kanzleramt (*ND* 26.7.93) (Bonn Office of the Federal Chancellor)
(3) Landesregierung (*ND* 30.9.93) (Thuringian State Government)	Bundestag (*ND* 8.7.93) (Lower House)
(4) Thüringer Ministerpräsident (*SZ* 12.7.93) (Thuringian Minister President)	Kanzler (*ND* 13.7.93) (Chancellor)
(5) PDS-Stadtvorsitzende (*ND* 16.8.93) (PDS City Councillor)	Bundestagspräsidentin Süssmuth (*SZ* 28.7.93) (Speaker of the Lower House Süssmuth)
(6) Vogel (*ND* 30.9.93)	Kohl (*ND* 22.7.93)

SZ and *ND* differ on the one hand in the proportion of local as opposed to central government entities, and on the other in the kinds of expressions used to refer to them. Whereas in *SZ* local and central actors occur equally often in the headlines (seven entities for local, six entities for central), this proportion clearly shifts towards the latter in *ND* where we find only eight entities on the local level but 30 referring to the central government. This steers the reader away from the local political arena, thereby labelling the events more as a matter of concern for the whole country.

Furthermore, alternative expressions are used to designate such actors. These expressions differ in their degree of individualization, and create the impression of association or detachment respectively. As illustrated in the examples above, starting from the highest degree of dissociation, these actors are referred to in terms of:

• the geographical place they are based in (example 1)
• the name of the office (examples 2 and 3)

- the occupational title (examples 4 and 5)
- the individual name (example 6)

In *ND*, we find more of the type of reference creating a sense of dissociation as far as the central government is concerned: five references to *Bonn*, two to *Bundestag* (Lower House of the Federal Parliament), one to *Bonner Kanzleramt* (Bonn Office of the Federal Chancellor). Moreover, two instances of such references possess a touch of irony, and as such create even more distance: *'die da oben'* (them up there) and *Herr Bohl* (Mister Bohl), a reference to the Thuringian Minister of Trade and Commerce. *SZ*, in contrast, more often refers to the central government by the name of individual politicians, such as *Waigel* (Minister of Finance), *Kohl* (Chancellor), and *Bundestagspräsidentin Süssmuth* (Speaker of the Lower House), thereby highlighting their distinctive engagement in the events. (References to central government politicians by name are to be found in *ND*, too, but to a much smaller extent.) The highly impersonal referent *Bonn* occurs in *SZ* only once. Another observation is that in *SZ*, to judge from the headlines, political agents exclusively from one particular party seem to be involved, namely the Christian Democrats (CDU). Given that until the elections in September 1998 this party, together with the FDP, formed the government in Germany as a whole as well as in Thuringia, it is not surprising that they are the agents immersed in the decision-making process around Bischofferode. Nevertheless, in *ND* other voices on the political spectrum also appear involved: these are representatives of the PDS in references such as *Gysi* (Chairman of the PDS party), *Fraktionschef PDS/Linke Liste, Bundestagsgruppe PDS/LL, PDS-Sachsen,* or of the SPD with references such as *Scharping, SPD-Chef Scharping, SPD.* Furthermore, apart from agents of the Thuringian and central government, other politicians are mentioned by name in *ND*. These are easterners holding posts in another east German *Bundesland*, Brandenburg, who initiated actions in that *Bundesland* expressing solidarity with the Bischofferode miners, for instance *Hildebrandt* (Minister of Labour for Brandenburg) and *Bisky* (Chairman of the PDS in Brandenburg). By using highly detached expressions in *ND* when referring to persons or parties from Bonn, an impression of 'us here' and 'them there' is created. This perception will be reinforced when we examine which actions are ascribed to these actors later on in this chapter.

Economic agents

Regarding this category, four main institutions are mentioned most often in both papers. These are:

- *Treuhand*
- Industrie-Gewerkschaft Bergbau und Energie (IGBE)
- Mitteldeutsche Kali-AG
- The European Community

The *Treuhand* Agency was set up to transform all former East German state-owned companies into competitive businesses and to privatize them. In effect, it was they who decided the fate of the potash mine in Bischofferode (Mitteldeutsche Kali-AG) by opting for a merger with the west German company (Kali und Salz AG). Once a decision was made, the private companies were left to execute this merger, and the unions to fight for the rights of the miners (as a last resort in doing so, by addressing the EC in Brussels) to prevent the unemployment that was inevitably to follow.

Furthermore, additional economic agents appear on the scene. In *ND*, the involvement of the chemical group BASF in Mannheim is highlighted as in (7).

(7) Der große Deal zwischen Treuhand und BASF (*ND* 23.7.93)
     (The big deal between Treuhand and BASF)

Since Kali und Salz AG is a subsidiary of BASF, it goes without saying that BASF itself would benefit from the merger. In *SZ*, on the other hand, this connection does not figure at all. *SZ* does stress, though, the interests of potential buyers as in (8), thereby labelling the events more as a business issue, and laying more stress on their economic aspects.

(8a) Letzte Hoffnung ist ein westdeutscher Unternehmer (*SZ* 7.7.93)
      (Last hope is a West German entrepreneur)

(8b) Interessent zieht Übernahmeangebot ab (*SZ* 17.7.93)
      (Potential buyer withdraws offer for take-over)

Ordinary people

Generally, the participants belonging to this category are either the *Kumpel*[1] themselves or their supporters. More will be said about the former category later in this chapter. Both papers express the wave of solidarity among the public. A typical headline for this is:

(9) Verzweifelt kämpft die Bevölkerung des nordthüringischen Ortes um die Arbeitsplätze von 700 Kumpeln (*SZ* 7.7.93)

(The population of the North Thuringian town desperately fights for the jobs of 700 miners)

More importantly, another significant difference between the papers is conspicuous: whereas in *SZ*, the people supporting the miners are referred to in rather general terms, *ND* describes these supporters more specifically, thereby identifying them as a particular category, as the following headlines illustrate:

(10) Kumpel erwarten 10 000 Gleichgesinnte (*ND* 31.7.93)
       (Miners expect 10 000 like-minded people)

(11) Frauen wild entschlossen, weiterzukämpfen (*ND* 6.7.93)
       (Women madly determined to continue fighting)

(12) Erste Frau im Hungerstreik (*ND* 17.7.93)
       (First woman on hunger strike)

(13) Kohlekumpel fordern: Alternative zum Reviersterben anbieten (*ND* 3.9.93)
       (Coal miners demand: offer an alternative to the death of the region)

(14) Jürgen Hensch, Hohenschönhausen, im Hungerstreik (*ND* 4.8.93)
       (Jürgen Hensch, from Hohenschönhausen, on hunger strike)

(15) Blumen für und von Jasmin aus Kassel (*ND* 25.8.93)
       (Flowers for and from Jasmin from Kassel)

(16) Britische Miners solidarisch (*ND* 15.9.93)
       (British miners in solidarity)

In example (10), the people joining in the protest demonstrations are marked as sharing the same values and aspirations as the miners by calling them *Gleichgesinnte*. The actors appearing in examples (11) to (15) accentuate the extent of the wave of solidarity in a particular fashion; they confirm that this support runs not only within the affected area of Bischofferode. Thus, in (11) to (13), on the one hand, we find women from the same potash mine who are described as determined to support their colleagues and, on the other, miners from a nearby coal mine reinforcing support. In examples (14) and (15), we encounter people from elsewhere in the country joining in the hunger strikes or making gestures of sympathy. And finally in (16), by naming fellow miners in Britain (who were on their way to Bosnia when they spontaneously decided to join their Thuringian colleagues for part of the way to Berlin), this sense of comradeship is shown even to have crossed borders. Readers are given the impression that what happens in Bischofferode has become subjectively important to a wide range of persons or groups among the population, and this is made clear to them by the example of personal signals of solidarity in the country and abroad. Individual people are easier to identify – and to identify with, as Hartley (1982) and Fowler (1991) point out – and such individualization is an expressive method of promoting feelings of empathy and understanding (or disapproval).

The actors and their semantic roles

The *Kumpel*

The people most deeply affected by the government's decision to close the potash mine, and who, as expected, appear as central actors in the articles are the miners themselves. To shed light on the question of whether they come across as the ones who are responsible for the events and determine their course, we need to examine what function they possess in the headlines: that is, whether they appear in an Agent or Patient role. This is illustrated in Table 7.3.[2]

This analysis does not reveal significant differences in the roles the *Kumpel* are given in the headlines. In both papers, they more often hold Agent than Patient position in the clause. When one has a closer look at *what* actions are attributed to the *Kumpel* in their Agent role, however, differences do emerge. In *SZ* such actions are restricted to the course of events in very general terms, referring to the fact that they are on hunger strike, or either continue with or stop it, as illustrated in

Table 7.3 The role of *Kumpel* in the headlines

	Süddeutsche Zeitung	Neues Deutschland
As Agent	8 (36%)	26 (46%)
As Patient	5 (23%)	11 (19%)
Neither	9 (41%)	20 (35%)

(17). Although the same kind of headlines occur in *ND* as well (18), they do so to a much lesser extent.

(17) Thüringer Kalikumpel im Hungerstreik (*SZ* 3.7.93)
     (Thuringian potash miners on hunger strike)

(18) Bergleute der Kaligrube von Bischofferode setzen den Hungerstreik auch am Montag fort (*ND* 6.7.93)
     (Miners from the Bischofferode potash mine continue their hunger strike on Monday)

Examples (17) and (18) refer in one way or the other to what can be called the highest level macrostructure, namely the strike itself. They do not provide information about what role the miners had in single operations, or how they contributed to, or acted upon, the course of individual events or issues to do with the strike. In the few cases where they do make such references in *SZ*, the verbs the miners are associated with are clearly negative ones:

(19) Kumpel lehnen Arbeitsplatzgarantie bis 1995 ab (*SZ* 16.7.93)
     (Miners reject guarantee of job security until 1995)

Such headlines portray the *Kumpel* as ungrateful individuals who, at a time of great job insecurity, are bold enough to refuse this generous offer by the government (who had promised the 700 miners replacement jobs for two years regardless of the closure of the mine). What more do they want? They have job security for two years. In *ND*, on the other hand, the same topic is treated quite differently (see 20); the connotation here is self-explanatory, characterizing the miners as decision-making forces rather than as spineless creatures.

(20) Kumpel erteilen Bonn Abfuhr (*ND* 17.7.93)
     (Miners send Bonn packing)

Furthermore, in *ND* we find what was mentioned earlier as lacking in *SZ*, namely the categorization of the miners through actions that acknowledge their initiative in influencing the course of events in Bischofferode. Such headlines are very frequent, as examples (21) to (29) demonstrate:

(21) Bergleute aus Bischofferode stellten vorm Landtag in Erfurt Provokateure der Polizei (*ND* 15.7.93)

(Miners from Bischofferode confronted troublemakers in the police force in front of the Thuringian Parliament in Erfurt)

(22) Kumpel beugen sich nur der EG (*ND* 19.7.93)
(Miners submit only to EC)

(23) Bergleute sind unerbittlich und zugleich realistisch (*ND* 19.7.93)
(Miners are inexorable and at the same time realistic)

(24) Bischofferoder Kumpel fordern weiter Erhalt des Werkes (*ND* 22.7.93)
(Bischofferode miners continue to demand upkeep of the mine)

(25) Betroffene Kalikumpel schütteln ihre Köpfe ... (*ND* 26.7.93)
(Affected miners shake their heads)

(26) Kalikumpel in Bischofferode sehen ihr Mißtrauen durch Fusions-Klausel bestätigt (*ND* 4.8.93)
(Potash miners see their mistrust confirmed in the merger-clause)

(27) Kumpel wollen Vertrag sehen (*ND* 6.8.93)
(Miners want to see [merger] agreement)

(28) Kali-Kumpel beharren auf Forderungen (*ND* 12.8.93)
(Potash miners insist on demands)

(29) Streikende Kumpel geben nicht auf (*ND* 25.8.93)
(Miners on strike do not give up)

With such headlines the *Kumpel* are not depicted as a naive crowd but as a responsible group trying to bring about changes as events progress. They are characterized as 'inexorable and at the same time realistic' (23), and as competent participants in the labour battle who stand up against injustice; 'they shake their heads' in reaction to the local government's unrealistic promises after the central government's decision for closure (25), or they 'see their mistrust confirmed in the merger-clause' (26) when, while fighting for the right to inspect the government's ruling on the merging of the two potash mines – 'Miners want to see [merger] agreement' (27) – they discover the existence of a clause in it which mandates the elimination of competition in the future. Headline (21) even highlights their active part in exposing vicious attempts by the local authorities to obstruct the protest strikes. Moreover, their participation is reinforced as deliberate action by verbs such as 'demand' (24) or even 'insist [on demands]' (28), 'want' (27) or 'do not give up' (29). Even the only negative action assigned to them in this paper characterizes them in somewhat heroic terms:

(30) Hungerstreikende aus Bischofferode ketteten sich in Ludwigshafen ans BASF-Tor (*ND* 30.7.93)
(Hunger strikers from Bischofferode chained themselves to the BASF-gate in Ludwigshafen)

Now a closer look will be taken at how the *Kumpel* appear in the Patient position in the headlines, and at the kind of actions to which they are subjected, and by whom. In *ND*, we find headlines in which the other economic or political powers are introduced to the reader mainly through actions which have negative connotations, and which suggest that they do not seem to consider the miners' interests, but rather act against them behind their backs, as headlines (31) to (34) show.

(31) Thüringer Landesausschüsse billigten Polizeieinsatz bei Demonstration der Kali-Kumpel (*ND* 22.7.93)
(Thuringian State Council sanctioned police intervention at demonstration of potash miners)

(32) Bonn hat nur Hohn für Kali-Kumpel in Bischofferode zu bieten (*ND* 23.7.93)
(Bonn has only scorn for potash miners from Bischofferode)

(33) Mitteldeutsche Kali-AG droht Bergleuten (*ND* 6.8.93)
(Mitteldeutsche Kali AG threatens miners)

(34) Die Meyers [DGB] fallen allen Kumpeln in den Rücken (*ND* 9.8.93)
(The Meyers [trade union organization] stab all miners in the back)

Thus, in (31) the local government has been found to be sanctioning aggressive police actions during one demonstration; the central government is shown not only not to sympathize with the fate of the miners but actually to 'scorn' them in (32); the east German potash company, instead of helping their employees, 'threaten' them in (33); and finally, the chair of the Deutscher Gewerkschaftsbund (German trade union organization) is characterized as 'stabbing the miners in the back' (34). When such agents behave favourably towards the miners, they are not directly involved in the decision-making process:

(35) Papst ermutigt pilgernde Kalikumpel (*ND* 26.8.93)
     (Pope encourages miners on pilgrimage)

One can hardly imagine the Pope's encouraging response stirring up debate in the relevant bodies in Germany. Even when such agents have a say, their positive, reassuring reaction towards the miners' actions is mitigated, as in (36). Here, the second half of the headline shows the spokesperson's positive reassurance as not having any practical consequence.

(36) Treuhandsprecher Wolf Schröde äußert Respekt für den Kampf der Bischofferoder Kalikumpel, aber bekräftigt die Fusionsentscheidung (*ND* 21.8.93)
     (*Treuhand* spokesperson Wolf Schröde expresses respect for the battle of the Bischofferode potash miners, but confirms merger decision)

In *SZ*, on the other hand, the few government members appearing in the Agent position are, indeed, depicted as taking the miners' interests seriously:

(37) Süssmuth: Kalivertrag offenlegen – dadurch kann Vertrauen bei den Kumpeln geschaffen werden (*SZ* 28.7.93)
     (Süssmuth: disclose merger agreement – this way trust can be created among the miners)

(38) Waigel bietet Kali-Kumpeln Einsicht in Fusionsverträge an (*SZ* 29.7.93)
     (Waigel offers potash miners inspection of merger agreement)

As these examples illustrate, the personal efforts of individual members of the government in resolving the conflict are underlined. The politicians are portrayed as conscientious professionals. The notion of trust in headline (37) suggests they are concerned about the miners' involvement as equals, and in (38), the miners' opportunity to inspect the merger agreement – which ought to have been a basic right for those who are affected by it in the first place, one would think – is presented as a friendly offer on the part of the Minister of Finance. The miners, on the other hand, emerge here as a group making unreasonable demands, as in (39).

(39) Auf dem Kongreß der IG Bergbau und Energie/Kalikumpeln Egoismus vorgeworfen/Gewerkschaftschef: Bischofferode hat keine Überlebenschancen (*SZ* 18.9.93)
(At the congress of the miners' union/Potash miners accused of selfishness/Union boss: Bischofferode has no chances for survival)

Professional politicians

A closer look at more headlines substantiates the observation made above regarding the role various agents on the political platform played in each paper. Above, it was stated that a polarization in the categorization of those actors takes place, and that this polarization diverges between *ND* and *SZ*.

It is a typical ideological pattern in mass mediated discourse to polarize in-groups and out-groups: that is, Us and Them. This ideological principle encourages the readers' identification with in-groups. The media present such groups in positive terms by emphasizing their positive values and characteristics, for example, by attributing positive actions to them, thereby encoding them as in-groups. Following this logic, out-groups are categorized through 'bad' properties and actions (see Herman and Chomsky 1988, van Dijk 1988a, 1988b).

For *ND* that means that the impression of dissociation from the central Government is reinforced. We find actors belonging to this group mainly with verbs that describe their involvement in negative terms:

(40) Die SPD im Ausschuss fiel mehrheitlich um (*ND* 5.7.93)
(Majority of the SPD committee members caved in)

(41) Bonn hat für Ost-Kaligruben einen 'besseren' Verwendungszweck: Kumpel raus – Giftmüll rein (*ND* 9.8.93)
(Bonn has 'better' use for Bischofferode: miners out – toxic waste in)

(42) 4 Bischofferoder Kalikumpel in Kassel: 'Wenn die da oben weiter so bescheißen, dann rappelt's auch hier' (*ND* 21.8.93)

(4 Bischofferode potash miners in Kassel: 'If them up there keep cheating, it'll stir things up here, too')

In (40) the SPD members in the committee are shown as having 'caved in' or collapsed, meaning they voted for the merger in the end. Putting it this way presupposes the existence of an original position against the merger among the party which at the end of the meeting turned out to be not so firm after all. The Federal Government's engagement is evaluated more unfavourably in example (42), where we find their part in the decisions described as a 'dirty cheat'. Headline (41) exposes the government's ulterior motives behind the closure as intending to dump toxic waste on the area of the potash mine.

Nevertheless, it is not only the Federal Government in Bonn that is categorized as an out-group in *ND*: so is the Thuringian government:

(43) Statt die Wirtschaftszerstörung in Thüringen aufzuhalten, ergeht sich die Landesregierung in Beschönigung/Bischofferoder Widerstand/Beschwichtigungen und halbe Wahrheiten à la Vogel (*ND* 30.9.93)
     (Instead of stopping the economic destruction in Thuringia, the Thuringian government indulges in euphemisms/Resistance in Bischofferode/Appeasements and half-truths à la Vogel)

They are reproached for glossing over the situation and for offering only 'appeasement' and 'half-truths'. Moreover, they are characterized as displaying unjust behaviour in a headline referred to earlier, (31), in which it is suggested that the local government has perverted the course of justice by encouraging police intervention in an otherwise peaceful protest demonstration.

If *ND* showed the local and central government in general in a negative light, we find a corresponding bias in favour of the PDS and its individual representatives. Many headlines occur which emphasize those playing an active role in supporting the miners, as illustrated in examples (44) and (45).

(44) Gysi ruft zur Solidarität auf (*ND* 7.7.93)
     (Gysi calls for solidarity)

(45) PDS fordert Widerruf der Kali-Fusion (*ND* 8.7.93)
     (PDS demands withdrawal of merger)

On the one hand, it is individual party leaders whose loyalty towards the miners is stressed and, on the other, party initiatives designed to influence the course of events to prevent the closure of the mine are emphasized.

In *SZ*, the polarization of particular actors works in the opposite direction, and creates a quite different ideological orientation from *ND*: here it is the government bodies – on the local as well as the federal level – to whom positive and loyal acts are attributed:

(46) Großzügiger Sozialplan/Thüringer Landesregierung sucht nach Ersatzarbeitsplätzen (*SZ* 15.7.93)
(Generous social plan/Thuringian government is looking for replacement jobs)

(47) Landesregierung bietet Ersatzarbeitsplätze/Kalikumpel lehnen Angebot ab (*SZ* 19.7.93)
(Thuringian State Government offers replacement jobs/Potash miners reject offer)

(48) Waigel genehmigt Fusion der Kali-Werke (*SZ* 7.7.93)
(Waigel officially approves merger of potash mines)

(49) Nach dem Angebot der Bundesregierung an die streikenden Kali-Bergleute/Kumpel lehnen Arbeitsplatzgarantie bis 1995 ab/Treuhandanstalt, IG Bergbau und Land Thüringen begrüßen dagegen den Bonner Vorschlag (*SZ* 16.7.93)
(After the offer of the Federal Government to the potash miners on strike/Miners reject job security until 1995/Treuhand, miners' union and the State of Thuringia, in contrast, welcome proposal from Bonn)

So the local government is depicted as solving the bleak situation by first looking for, (46), and then offering, replacement jobs (47). Further, their actions are described as generous in (46). The polarization of government bodies on the one hand as problem-solving agents, and the miners on the other hand as ungrateful troublemakers is carried to extremes in example (47), where we find both categorizations in the same headline. This contrast in one headline is likewise to be found in connection with proposals made by the central government in (49), which is described as an 'offer' which the miners 'refuse'. Moreover, as was observed earlier in this chapter, individual federal government politicians are depicted as making generous gestures (see again headlines (37) and (38)).

Economic agents

As was pointed out above, among the agents most frequently mentioned in the headlines are the *Treuhand*, the miners' union (IGBE) – and the EC. Again, *ND* and *SZ* differ in the way they encode these institutions. In *ND* it is suggested to the reader, as far as the miners are concerned, that the EC is the last resort in preventing the closure of the mine:

(50a) Warten auf ein Zeichen von Brüssel (*ND* 21.7.93)
       (Waiting for a sign from Brussels)

(50b) Hoffnung auf Brüssel (*ND* 27.9.93)
       ([Placing their] Hope in Brussels)

This impression is gained by describing the EC as a centre of power that might provide the long-awaited signal and as an agent on which the employees of the Bischofferode mine focus all their hopes (50). In *SZ*, by contrast, in the only occurrence of this actor (51), its sphere of influence is limited by stating the closure will go ahead irrespective of whether the EC looks into the matter.

(51) Unabhängig von EG-Prüfung/Kali-Aufsichtsrat will Bischofferode schließen (*SZ* 19.8.93)
      (Regardless of EC examination/Potash Supervisory Board wants to close Bischofferode)

With regard to the miners' union, the Industrie-Gewerkschaft Bergbau und Energie (IGBE), *ND* doubts whether it represents the interests of the miners, as headlines (52) and (53) suggest. Here, performances like 'failing' (*versagen*) and 'wriggling out' of their responsibility (*kneifen*) are attributed to the union:

(52) Solidarität mit Kalikumpeln – Gewerkschaften versagen, Gewerkschafter nicht (*ND* 31.7.93)
      (Solidarity with potash miners/Unions fail – union members do not)
(53) Wessen Interessen vertreten die Gewerkschaften/.../Doch die IG Bergbau hat gekniffen (*ND* 18.8.93)

(Whose interests do the unions represent/.../But the miners' union chickened out)

It is significant that in *SZ*, on the other hand, the union appears in the headlines exclusively with other agents. Therefore the force of their actions is enhanced precisely through opposition to (or conformity with) the other agent's behaviour. That is the case in two headlines referred to earlier, examples (49) and (39). First, in (49) the union appears together with the *Treuhand* and the local government, as well as with the central government, as taking the same position regarding the closure. By having all the institutions involved in the decision-making process lined up together as a firm front opposing the miners, the categorization of the miners as the odd ones out is reinforced. This strategy of rhetorical contrast is commonly used in news discourse, and it serves to intensify negative characterizations (see van Dijk 1998a:60). In headline (49), this contrast marks the miners as the ones who stubbornly cannot accept what apparently all the other authorities have found to be best for Bischofferode, that is, the merger. What it also discloses is that the miners have no authority in power on their side. The same instrumentalization of the miners as an out-group is achieved in (39). Here, the evaluation of the miners' behaviour in very negative terms (selfishness) in the context of the union's congress makes, by contrast, the union leader's statement seem a reasonable judgement about an inevitable situation.

The third economic agent playing a central role is the *Treuhand*. In *SZ* this institution is mentioned twice, in (54) and (49).

(54) Treuhandanstalt gerät in Kali-Streit unter Druck (*SZ* 15.7.93)
     (*Treuhand* under pressure in potash controversy)

In both cases it holds subject position in the clause. Headline (54) declares that the institution has come under pressure concerning the controversy around Bischofferode. It does not specify, though, why or how, and neither does it assign any responsibility. In (49), as pointed out earlier, all influential bodies – that is, the miner's union, the local and federal government and the *Treuhand* – present themselves as being in agreement with each other. Joining the *Treuhand* to all other powerful authorities increases the legitimation of their choice for the merger, and makes it look inescapable.

In *ND*, on the other hand, the *Treuhand* holds various semantic roles in the clause. In the Patient position it emerges as the target of the miners' protests, as illustrated in example (55).

(55) Kumpel heute vor der Treuhand (*ND* 16.9.93)
(Miners in front of *Treuhand* today)

Headlines of this kind appear repeatedly in *ND*; they imply the *Treuhand*'s responsibility in inflicting these existential fears on the miners. When we find the *Treuhand* in subject position, this paper emphazises its dubious engagement in the events:

(56) Treuhand leistet Westkonkurrenz Vorschub (*ND* 4.8.93)
(*Treuhand* panders to competitors in the west)

Such negative attributions exist in *ND* regardless of whether they appear in Agent or Patient position. Formulations like this assign this institution full accountability and control for their acts. Thus, unlike in *SZ*, where this institution is categorized as a competent authority, in *ND* it is marked as an out-group.

Conclusion

This chapter has investigated the news coverage of one of the first major industrial actions in east Germany since unification, which stirred up extensive public debate. German unification brought together two states which had developed independently of each other for 40 years, and had as a result opposing political, economic and social structures. Legislating unification meant, in effect, adapting most east German structures to western models, a process which, unsurprisingly, was accompanied by tremendous problems. Above all, it was the transformation process of the east German economy where conflicts surfaced most crucially as many companies were closed down, resulting in the loss of the basic means of subsistence for many easterners. The hunger strike of the Thuringian miners in 1993 discussed above is only one example of such conflicts deriving from Germany´s most recent past.

The focus on news coverage in two daily papers in east and west, employing a discourse analytical approach with comparisons of both papers´ headlines, revealed how differences in the involvement of certain political and economic groups were suggested to the reader.

Whereas in the west German paper various agents in power (that is, politicians, employers, trade unionists) were largely presented as dealing with issues competently and acting in the interest of the people affected, the east German paper was not only sceptical about their efforts but criticized those agents' dubious activities surrounding the events. The employees, on the other hand, were given favourable and sympathetic treatment in the latter paper but appeared as a force making unreasonable demands in the former, thereby promoting the image of the *Jammerossis* (the whingeing east Germans).

It is not new to discover that newspapers differ in the way they report the same events, and that such differences reflect their ideological practices. The hunger strike of the Bischofferode miners three years after unification is only one example of major press organs in east and west Germany encoding the same people and events in contrasting ways. However, this study has shown that there were, and still are, widely diverging discourses at work in each part of the country, which ultimately result in contrasting pictures of contemporary Germany being drawn. The media, employing the same German language within the same German state, have, since unification, reinforced rather than dismantled *Berührungsängste* (barriers) between easterners and westerners.

Appendix: synopsis of events, 1993

1.7. *Treuhand* committee in *Bundestag* vote for the merger of *Mitteldeutsche Kali AG* and *Kali und Salz AG* resulting in closure of Bischofferode mine as of 1.1.94

2.7. 14 miners start hunger strike

6.7. Federal Ministry of Finance ratifies merger

10.7. First *Solidaritätstag* in Bischofferode (on initiative of east German works and personnel committees and shop stewards); 5000 people protest against closure

13.7. 45 miners on hunger strike

17.7. *Land* and *Bund* agree on take-over of all 700 employees of the Bischofferode potash mine, and guarantee job security for them until end of 1995

20.7. *Kali und Salz AG* request examination of merger agreement at EC committee

23.7. Thuringian government sets up development agency for the region

28.7. 5000 people at demonstration in Zella-Mehlis. By end of July 300,000 DM in donations from public

1.8.   Second International *Aktionstag* in Bischofferode; 12000 people take part
12.8. Talks between works committee members and Thuringian government; outcome of talks is not disclosed
13.8. Solidarity Committee 'Five to Twelve' founded in Kassel
18.8. Birgit Breuel, chairman of *Treuhand*, requests end of mine occupation and labels it unlawful
21.8. Third International *Aktionstag* in Bischofferode – 5000 people take part
25.8. Miners' pilgrimage to Rome
27.8. 6 men and 3 women still on hunger strike
1.9.   15 miners and supporters, among them British miners and workers from Stuttgart, start protest march to *Treuhand* in Berlin
7.9.   Extraordinary meeting of *Treuhand* committee in *Bundestag*, inspection of merger agreement agreed
16.9. Protest march ends at *Treuhand* in Berlin
18.9. Demonstration of thousands of people at Berlin Alexanderplatz
20.9. Miners discontinue hunger strike until decision from Brussels

Despite the massive protests the mine in Bischofferode was closed in 1994 and its former employees faced unemployment when the promised replacement jobs did not materialize after 1995. Today, Bischofferode is marked by the exodus of its population and industry, and it faces collapse.

Notes

1 The word *Kumpel* has two connotations in German: 'miners', and 'mate' or 'pal'. This polysemy may well be the reason why this word is given preference (to its synonym *Bergarbeiter*, for instance), thereby repeatedly appealing to the reader to identify with these agents on the human rather than on the professional level.

2. Here, the categories *As Agent* and *As Patient* summarize the entities in which this role was made explicit through a verb. Another type of headline which frequently occurs in newspaper discourse is the elliptic one in which the verb has been omitted. Although a closer look at the syntactic and semantic structure underlying such headlines can reveal the same roles for certain entities, here these headlines were entered in the last category *Neither*.

References

Bell, Alan and Peter Garrett (eds) (1998) *Approaches to Media Discourse* (Oxford: Blackwell).
Fairclough, Norman (1998) 'Political discourse in the media: an analytical framework', in Bell and Garrett (1998), 142–62.
Fowler, Roger (1991) *Language in the News: Discourse and Ideology in the Press* (London: Routledge).

Hartley, John (1982) *Understanding News* (London: Routledge).

Herman, Edward S. and Noam Chomsky (1988) *Manufacturing Consent: The Political Economy of the Mass Media* (New York: Pantheon Books).

Humphreys, Peter (1994) *Media and Media Policy in Germany since 1945* (Oxford: Berg).

Klingemann, Hans-Dieter, Lutz Erbring and Nils Diederich (eds) (1995) *Zwischen Wende und Wiedervereinigung. Analysen zur politischen Kultur in West-und Ost-Berlin 1990* (Opladen: Westdeutscher Verlag).

Kress, Günter and Theo van Leeuwen (1996) *Reading Images: The Grammar of Visual Design* (London: Routledge).

van Dijk, Teun (1988a) *News Analysis. Case Studies of International and National News in the Press* (Hillsdale, NJ: Lawrence Erlbaum).

van Dijk, Teun (1998b) 'Opinions and ideologies in the press', in Bell and Garrett (1998), 21–63.

Voltmer, Katrin, Eva Schabedoth and Peter R. Schrott (1995) 'Individuelle Teilnahme an politischer Kommunikation. Zur Bedeutung von interpersonaler und massenmedialer Kommunikation im Prozess der deutschen Vereinigung', in Klingemann, Erbrings and Diederich (1995), 230–59.

8
Disgraceland GDR: Locating the Admirable amongst the Abject

John Theobald

East Germany could very well have remained a separate state. A democratised GDR would have been possible, just as the democratised Poland, Hungary and Czechoslovakia emerged out of the ashes of communism.

Staab 1998:39

'It seems to be absolutely impossible to clear up this misunderstanding in the west. There was no way in which we were trying to defend the Honecker-style GDR.' Christa Wolf, when asked by an incredulous journalist how she could have argued in autumn 1989 for the continued existence of the GDR.

Die Zeit, 14 March 1999

Introduction

The elimination of the GDR is, of course, a *fait accompli*. The prima facie evidence indicates that it went into voluntary liquidation, calling in its wealthy twin brother to wind up its affairs in the hope that the family connection would lessen or even cancel out the deficit. Statements such as those of Staab and Wolf, above, to the effect that a reformed GDR could have remained in existence are since that moment rare, and are afforded little credibility when advanced. The overwhelming consensual trend since 1990 has been to discredit the memory of the GDR and to diminish respect for all that it – and that includes its people – set out to realize in its 40 years of existence. When alternatives to this approach are advanced, they are – 'on message' with hegemonic discourse – generally dismissed as *Ostalgie* or as irrelevant and unrealistic speculation.

131

This chapter is not about *Ostalgie*, and neither is it about idle 'what if ...' fantasies. It is about restoring some balance to memory, addressing specifically some of the discursive asymmetries in unified Germany to which Habermas (see Chapter 1) has drawn attention in general, in the belief that still internally disunited eastern and western German mentalities will not live in constructive dialogue, let alone in harmony with each other, until current hierarchical perceptions of western superiority and eastern inferiority are rooted out.

The phrase 'discursive *Anschluss*' in this context may be criticized as an ill-advised use of shock tactics when applied to the process of western integration of eastern Germany in the 1990s. Yet viewed from a perspective where CDA overlaps with German Studies, it contains enough verisimilitude to justify the provocation, provided that the Nazi associations with the word *Anschluss* are left as a lesson from history, and not writ large as an alarmist parallel. Where, for example, a state has got itself into a position where support for its continuing existence has been undermined (above all from within, but also from without by a powerful neighbour) to such an extent that a majority of its population welcomes abolishing it and becoming part of the neighouring state, with its promises of prosperity and a new ideological order, to that extent the historical antecedent for using the word *Anschluss* to describe the subsequent take-over is plausible. If, following this, the new rulers make a concerted attempt to rewrite in their own terms the history, ideology, collective self-image and identity of their acquisition, from global geo-politics down to the small details of the day-to-day living context, while casting out the previous versions as if they were linguistic poison, then 'discursive *Anschluss*' is an appropriate phrase. Its use may force us to question the ease with which the world has taken the manner of German unification for granted as a desirable development and a kindness to pitiable east Germans.

At the end of the 1990s, many eastern Germans, while not wishing to turn the clock back, are in a phase where they are no longer so much in reaction against failings of the no longer existent GDR; instead, they are reacting against the more imminent ills of discovering that 'unification' really meant 'annexation', and against the accompanying cultural humiliation, and largely undifferentiated negative construction of their past by western hegemonic discourses. It is the intention here to contribute to a body of evidence and narratives which will create an antidote to the dominant western historiographical and cultural contribution to what we have called 'discursive disunity'.

Memories of resistance as confident historiography

'Memories of resistance' is one such narrative. Where a people has been oppressed by, and/or collaborated with, an authoritarian government or ideology which has then been overthrown and discredited, it is not uncommon for it to turn initially to those who courageously resisted the old regime as new models and symbols of historical respectability. One thinks, to mention just two individuals, of Vaclav Havel in the then Czechoslovak republic, or Lech Wałesa in Poland. Yet this did not happen in the GDR. There, those who resisted, suffered harassment, imprisonment and exile, and eventually played leading roles in the mass demonstrations which preceded the opening of the Berlin Wall, were rapidly marginalized as unrealistic, utopian and irrelevant as the western-sponsored and promoted discourse of unification took over from December 1989 onwards, and the state, which they wished to reform, disappeared.

Yet they, and thousands of others who resisted or who sought change in the GDR in a less prominent fashion, who worked for peace, East–West detente, nuclear disarmament, green issues, human rights, freedom of travel and expression, and a reformed GDR socialism – active individuals and groups of citizens – collectively merit recognition as positive models in a space where, up till now, few such positive models have existed. Indeed, a number of potential positive models, for example, the writers Christa Wolf and Heiner Müller, have been polemically undermined by the west-dominated media. It may be more healthy here not to construct individual symbolic icons of courage and struggle, especially since the individuals involved have moved on in very different directions; instead, collective ideas and actions will be highlighted. It is in this spirit that we may take here as an indicative example the East Berlin *samizdat*-type journal *Grenzfall* (a punning title meaning both 'borderline case', and 'the falling of borders'), produced by members of the *Initiative Frieden und Menschenrechte* (Initiative for Peace and Human Rights) between June 1986 and May 1989. It lays claim to being the GDR's first independent periodical, although many others followed it in the last three years before the opening of the Berlin Wall; these included, *Nachtgebete* (Halle), *Aufrisse* (Berlin), *fußnote 3* (Berlin), *Arche Nova* (Berlin), *Briefe der F.f.F* (Frauen für den Frieden/Women for Peace) (Berlin), *Kontext* (Berlin), *Nachdruck* (Merseburg), *Die Mücke* (Leipzig), *Umweltblätter* (Berlin) *Ostkreuz* (Berlin), and *Artikel 27* (Berlin).

Grenzfall and those involved in its production and distribution thus represent just one example of a much wider picture of reform and resistance activity in the GDR. The sources for a detailed overview of the work of groups and individuals are dispersed in small archives and private collections, and the work of cataloguing these sources is far from complete and ill-resourced (Knabe 1997:565). Such work has received no public funding, and has been left to committed individuals outside the mainstream of research activity. Publications concerning oppositional activities, such as Erhart Neubert's recent *Geschichte der Opposition in der DDR 1949–1989* (1998) have largely consisted of the writings of those who had been personally involved. Knabe reports that:

> Außenstehende haben sich dagegen bislang nur selten diesem Forschungsgebiet zugewandt, obgleich ihm für die Analyse der zweiten deutschen Diktatur in diesem Jahrhundert zweifellos eine Schlüsselrolle zukommt: wie und mit welchen Zielen haben sich Menschen gegen die Zumutungen des Parteistaates zur Wehr gesetzt? Welche Faktoren haben sie zum Widerspruch angeregt und ermutigt, welche haben sie verzweifeln lassen oder zur Anpassung veranlaßt? Wie wirksam war das mit singulärer Gründlichkeit errichtete System der umfassenden Überwachung, Steuerung und Einschüchterung eines ganzen Volkes? Fragen, die auch acht Jahre nach dem Sturz der SED-Herrschaft noch weitgehend unbeantwortet sind.
>
> (Knabe 1997:565)
>
> (Up till now, outsiders have, however, only seldom turned their attention to this research area, although it without doubt deserves to play a key role in the analysis of the second German dictatorship this century: how and with what aims did people oppose the excesses of the one-party state? What factors stimulated and encouraged them to resist, which ones drove them to despair or to conform? How efficient was the system of comprehensive surveillance, control, and intimidation of an entire people which was set up with such singular thoroughness? These are questions which remain largely unanswered eight years after the overthrow of the SED regime.)

This neglect, or sidelining of research into opposition activity stands in marked contrast to enormous interest in research into the inner workings of the GDR regime and power apparatus, and is seen by Knabe as a reflection of a lack of concern both by academics and the general public. He also sees it as an ironic curiosity of post-unification historiography that even when the subject of opposition activity is treated by researchers or publicists, the sources quoted are predominantly *Stasi* files, whose information is quoted and used in preference to that recorded by the opposition groups themselves:

> So wurde, um nur ein Beispiel zu nennen, die erste Welle der Aufarbeitungsliteratur über die unabhängigen politischen Gruppen der achtziger Jahre bis hin zu Zahlenangaben in starkem Maße von den offengelegten Unterlagen des MfS bestimmt – kaum von den Aufzeichnungen der Betroffenen.
>
> (Knabe 1997:566)

(Thus, just to give one example, the first wave of critical literature on the independent political groups of the eighties was to a large extent and including statistical material, based on the files of the Ministry for State Security that had been made public and hardly at all on the writings of those actually involved.)

One may infer from this that there has been little or no official encouragement in post-*Wende* Germany of research into oppositional activity in the GDR, and that the impetus has been strongly towards those subjects which show the GDR people in a negative light, and justify the elimination of their state. It may not be surprising that the institutions of unified Germany have shown little interest in, and given sparse publicity to, those groups in the GDR who were largely working for its continued existence within radically reformed structures, and who thus did not favour unification and westernization.

The availability of *Grenzfall* fits into this general pattern. Apart from those who kept copies of individual numbers as they appeared, or who seek the originals out in disparate archives, the only access to it is via a privately published edition of the full text of the first 15 of the 17 numbers which appeared, edited by Lev Kopelew, the exiled Soviet human rights activist, and Ralf Hirsch, one of the five GDR peace and human rights campaigners who were arrested in January 1988 (see below). Although this edition appeared in early 1989, the mode of publication is symptomatic of the continuing marginalized status of this kind of material in post-unification Germany.

Grenzfall appeared (almost) monthly from June 1986 until December 1987 (issues 1–15), then irregularly (issues 16 and 17) until May 1989. It had to be produced and distributed illicitly, and its publishers had only a typewriter, poor quality paper, and a hand-operated rotary copier. Between 800 and 1000 copies of each issue were produced, distributed and passed on from hand to hand. Regular publication ceased because on 28 January 1988, after a period in which the group's increasing public action was countered by intensified surveillance and harassment, five leading activists were arrested by the state security police, and accused of treasonable activities and of acting as enemy agents. Four of them were (as a compromise following solidarity activities from peace and human rights groups in the West, and through the agency of the Protestant Church) pushed into temporary exile in West Germany and England as an alternative to threatened long prison sentences; the fifth (Hirsch, as mentioned above), forced into a similar dilemma, went into permanent exile in the Federal Republic. Following these arrests and expulsions, with only two further editions appearing, *Grenzfall* had been effectively stifled.

Grenzfall may have been a very small-scale operation by western norms, but it was highly significant in the GDR context, and the police reaction shows how seriously it was taken. Those in temporary exile – Bärbel Bohley was the most well known of them – chose to swim against the tide and to return to the GDR when their exile time was up, arriving in time to play key roles – along with other members of the *Initiative* – in *Neues Forum* and the mass GDR reform movement of autumn 1989 prior to its take-over by unification discourse.

Such accounts of GDR state harassment of critical citizens' groups add no credit to GDR officialdom, whose rigidity and unpopularity is well known. They do, however, illuminate a social space in the GDR in which a significant will for reform of governance and structure of the system by those who had grown up and been socialized within it is apparent.

Grenzfall campaigns

An indicative quantitative listing reveals the following key preoccupations of *Grenzfall*:

- socialist democratization and internal social change (equivalents of Gorbachev's *glasnost* and *perestroika*
- environmental issues (especially Chernobyl)
- solidarity with opposition activity in neighbouring Eastern Bloc countries
- human and civil rights
- peace and disarmament
- freedom of expression and information

The theme which is conspicuous by its absence is that of German unification. The continuing existence of a radically reformed GDR is presupposed and unquestioned. The name which is way in front of all others in the number of positive references is that of Gorbachev, to the extent that there is some critical discussion in the pages of *Grenzfall* of the dangers of becoming over-reliant on him as *deus ex machina*. Here, a more detailed look will be taken at four of the six key themes identified above, and a look at the graphics used in *Grenzfall* will conclude the survey.

First, socialist democratization and internal social change, according to the Gorbachev model. *Grenzfall*'s use of Gorbachev as a lever against the relatively rigid and reactionary GDR leadership is central to its position, and exemplifies both its strength and its weakness, as well as characterizing its campaigning style. A key exemplary text comes in number six, 1987, and takes the form of a 'Letter to Gorbachev'. It is a copy of a letter, signed by prominent members of the *Initiative Frieden und Menschenrechte* – Gerd and Ulrike Poppe, Werner Fischer, Wolfgang Templin, Monika Haeger and the later discredited Ibrahim Böhme – which was delivered by hand to the Soviet Embassy on 27 May 1987 on the occasion of Gorbachev's visit to East Berlin. In its commentary, *Grenzfall* uses the tactic of driving a wedge between the GDR government and its Soviet ally and model by emphasizing that, in contrast with its subversive, even treasonable nature in the GDR, the letter was received in the embassy in full consciousness of what was going on, and met with anything but cold rejection or consternation (Hirsch and Kopelew 1989:68).

In its content too, the letter emphasizes a positive attitude to Gorbachev and his reforms as a means to undermining and isolating the GDR government in terms which it could not easily suppress without being seen to contradict the visiting Soviet leader. Thus the writers of the letter commit themselves to a socialist democratization of the GDR, to internal political change coming from the grass roots, using quotations from Gorbachev to support this. Western-style sociopolitical reform is specifically rejected. The following extracts exemplify the style. Addressing Gorbachev, the letter says:

Die wichtigen Veränderungen in der UdSSR werden von vielen Menschen in den sozialistischen Ländern mit Überraschung, Sympathie und Hoffnung aufgenommen ... Viele Ihrer Vorstellungen zur Umgestaltung der Gesellschaft in Ihrem Land berühren sich mit Forderungen der unabhängigen Friedensbewegung und der demokratischen Opposition in der DDR.

(Hirsch and Kopelew 1989:66–67)

(The important changes in the Soviet Union are greeted by many people in the socialist countries with surprise, sympathy and hope ... Many of your proposals for transforming society in your country correspond to the demands of the independent peace movement and democratic opposition in the GDR.)

Then:

Uns geht es nicht darum, bürgerliche Verhältnisse nach westlichem Muster zu übernehmen, sondern ein Gesellschaftssystem zu fördern, das die Einheit von Demokratie und Sozialismus ermöglicht.
(Hirsch and Kopelew 1989:67)
(Our desire is certainly not to take over bourgeois structures on the western model, rather to promote a social system which makes possible the unity of democracy and socialism.)

And finally:

Verehrter Michael Sergejewitsch, Ihre Politik der Umgestaltung findet bei unserer Bevölkerung deshalb so große Resonanz, weil die von Ihnen benannten Probleme uns nur allzugut bekannt sind.
(Hirsch and Kopelew 1989:67)
(Honoured Michael Sergejewitsch, your policy of restructuring finds such great resonance among our population because the problems you have identified are all too well known to us.)

The letter must be seen in the context of a broader campaign of courageous and risky critical expression and action in an oppressive society. It is on the one hand a piece of autonomous direct action, but on the other, it is by its nature and motivation an appeal for action, reform and influence from above. It takes on Gorbachev's discourse uncritically while spicing it with concepts borrowed from the western green and peace movements of the time. However, from the present perspective, it may be argued that within this text, and the phenomenon of *Grenzfall* as a whole, are to be found the beginnings of a bridge-building, alternative east–west discourse. This doubtless has strains of utopianism, and is constrained by the specific situation in which it was produced, but it deserved more attention than it got at the time, and today does not merit the neglect and selective amnesia surrounding it.

The second key theme of *Grenzfall* to be looked at here is that of the environment. Here too, the analysis will be restricted to a single representative article, this time from number 4 (1987). Typically for *Grenzfall*, this is again not just an article, but an action in the form of an appeal, an 'Offener Brief an die Regierungen aller Länder' (Open letter to the governments of all countries) (Hirsch and Kopelew 1989:50).

The readers should not merely read, but also do something, in this case sign a petition to support a campaign for a referendum (as allowed under the GDR constitution) against the continued use and expansion of nuclear energy in the GDR. The instigators were Martin Böttger, Ralf Hirsch and Gerd Poppe. This was part of the world-wide reaction to the Chernobyl catastrophe, and the style reflects this; it resembles the campaign materials of any western anti-nuclear movement and thus underlines the irrelevance of an 'iron curtain' in the nuclear age:

Wer vor Tschernobyl trotz aller Warnungen Atomanlagen errichten ließ, war ein unverantwortlicher Hasardeur. Wer aber auch nach Tschnernobyl noch an dieser Technik festhält, ist ein gefährlicher Terrorist und Verbrecher ... WEIL WIR NICHT WEITER ZUSCHAUEN WOLLEN, WIE EINE HANDVOLL VON POLITIKERN UND ATOMLOBBYISTEN UNSERE ZUKUNFT UND DAS LEBEN UNSERER KINDER AUFS SPIEL SETZEN, WEIL WIR ZU IHNEN, UNSEREN POLITIKERN, KEIN VERTRAUEN MEHR HABEN UND WEIL WIR MEINEN, DASS WO ALLE BETROFFEN SIND, AUCH ALLE ENTSCHEIDEN MÜSSEN, DESHALB FORDERN WIR, DASS DIE BEVÖLKERUNG EUROPAS SELBST ENTSCHEIDEN KÖNNEN.

(Hirsch and Kopelew 1989:50)

(Those who built nuclear power stations before Chernobyl, despite all the warnings, were irresponsible gamblers. Those who still support this technology after Chernobyl are dangerous terrorists and criminals ... BECAUSE WE NO LONGER WISH TO LOOK ON WHILE A HANDFUL OF POLITICIANS AND LOBBYISTS GAMBLE WITH OUR FUTURE AND THAT OF OUR CHILDREN, BECAUSE WE NO LONGER HAVE CONFIDENCE IN OUR POLITICIANS, BECAUSE WE BELIEVE THAT WHERE ALL ARE AFFECTED, ALL SHOULD DECIDE, WE DEMAND THAT THE PEOPLES OF EUROPE THEM-SELVES SHOULD TAKE THIS DECISION.)

Here we see the GDR opposition, courageously in that authoritarian context, acting as E.P. Thompson had exhorted active citizens to in his pamphlet *Protest and Survive*, as if the Iron Curtain did not exist. As with the letter to Gorbachev, we see the style of popular movement rhetoric rather than the phrases of politicians bearing the responsibilities of power – a mixture of utopianism and grass-roots activism within the framework of a specific campaign – but they are a manifestation of a genuine democratic impulse by people who stood to lose a lot by making public declarations of hostility to their government.

The third theme of *Grenzfall* to be examined is that of solidarity with dissident groups in neighbouring East European states, including the Soviet Union. Every issue of *Grenzfall* included sections dealing with news of groups working in Poland, Czechoslovakia, the Soviet Union and, sometimes, Romania, and expressing support for them, especially in cases of harassment or persecution. As an example, a report in number 3 (1987) illustrates how Czech dissidents were, like those in the GDR, faced with a government which wished to deny and refute the Gorbachev reforms. It expresses solidarity with VONS – the Czech committee for the defence of the politically persecuted – and its work related to the earlier arrests of Vaclav Havel, Jiri Dienstbier, and Peter Uhl. *Grenzfall* states its view that 'durch die Mobilisierung der nationalen und internationalen Öffentlichkeit soll der repressiven Praxis der Regierung im Umgang mit Andersdenkenden entgegengewirkt werden' (Hirsch and Kopelew 1989:43) (it is through the mobilization of national and international public opinion that the repressive practices of the government in its treatment of those who think differently can be resisted).

It is of interest here that in appealing to international – including Western – public opinion, the emphasis is on people's action against government, not on diplomacy or government level action. *Grenzfall* also shows here that its prime identification is with the situation in Eastern Europe, and in reform movements in neighbouring Eastern countries. There is no sense of any ethnic or national identification with West Germany whatsoever.

Expressions of solidarity with parallel groups elsewhere in Eastern Europe are frequently related to the fourth theme, that of campaigning for human and civil rights. *Grenzfall* (2/1987) contains a copy of a letter of solidarity sent by members of the *Initiative Frieden und Menschenrechte* and GDR unofficial peace activists to the Czech founders and promoters of Charta 77, on the occasion of its tenth anniversary. The letter is of interest on the one hand as a statement of solidarity, on the other as a declaration of autonomy and distinctiveness of the GDR activists. Thus, while underlining two specific common principles – those of the open and public nature of human rights work, and of the promotion of pluralism in the process of creating genuine democratization – the GDR groups also show sensitivity to the view that they are mere 'copy-cat' organizations of Charta 77: 'Dies war aufgrund unserer Voraussetzungen weder möglich, noch wollen wir es' (Hirsch and Kopelew 1989:29) (This was neither possible nor desirable because of our particular situation). They stress that human rights work in the GDR has its specific roots in being a component of the independent peace movement. One reads this not as a sign of disagreement, but as a self-confident explanation of the different profile and history of the GDR movement. An element of the distinctive character of GDR peace and human rights activity is its desire to provoke debate with – and hence its constantly rejected hope to influence – Party officialdom. This stubborn and much debated conviction that internal reform through dialogue was possible clearly made more sense to those involved in the GDR context than it did to their counterparts in neighbouring countries. It was a tough position to maintain, linked to their Gorbachev-inspired optimism, their roots in the Protestant Church, and their peace activism. A substantial part of *Grenzfall* (8/1987) was devoted to the issue. Here, contributions from the Polish reformer Adam Michnik and peace activist Jan Litynski provide a considerably more sober and reticent view of Gorbachev. Elsewhere in the same number controversy over invitations from the organizers of the 1987 END (European Nuclear Disarmament) Convention to the official GDR Peace Council to participate in the event, which *de facto* excluded the issue of travel visas to the also invited independent GDR peace activists (END's natural counterparts), reveal the influence of more disillusioned GDR voices.

Despite this, the predominantly less confrontational approach of the GDR activists, their continued critique of Western governments, and their refusal to entertain the possibility of German unification on Western terms, certainly did not enhance their public credibility once the path to unification had been taken. The account of a discussion meeting at an East Berlin youth club attended by representatives of the GDR's official Human Rights Committee in *Grenzfall* (3/1987) illustrates the most frequently expressed position on this issue. Representatives of the *Initiative Frieden und Menschenrechte* attended the meeting in the hope of involving the officials in debate. They succeeded in raising awkward questions, but received only evasive answers:

Bei den konkreten Anfragen an die praktische Arbeit des Komitees im innerstaatlichen Bereich mußte die Vertreterin, bei allem

Wohlwollen, dann auch passen. Dafür sei man nicht zuständig und die Bearbeitung von konkreten Menschenrechtsverletzungen – solche Fälle kämen in der DDR nur vereinzelt vor – würde einen für das Komitee nicht zu realisierenden Arbeitsaufwand bedeuten.

(Hirsch and Kopelew 1989:40)

(On being specifically questioned about the practical work of the Committee on internal matters, the representative, with the best will in the world, was unable to answer. One was not responsible for that area, and the taking on of specific human rights violations – of which there were only isolated cases in the GDR – would create a volume of work which was beyond the means of the Committee.)

These words, especially 'bei allem Wohlwollen' (with the best will in the world) show the writer's at least partial acceptance of the official's position, but indicate also the acceptance by officials of the existence of (albeit minimal) human rights violations in the GDR. The door to dialogue does not appear in this account to be completely closed. This position is confirmed by the final section of the report:

Vertreter der Initiative Frieden und Menschenrechte verwiesen insbesondere auf gezielte Menschenrechtsverletzungen durch zunehmenden sozialen Druck gegen politische Minderheiten. Im Arbeitsbereich bedeutete dies z.b. den Entzug von qualifizierten Arbeitsaufgaben, spezielle Beaufsichtigung und Kontrolle, weiträumige Auslegungen des Arbeitsrechtes bis hin zum Verlust des Arbeitsplatzes. Dem 'unbekannten Komitee' bot man, trotz dessen selbsterklärter Nichtzuständigkeit, eine Kontaktaufnahme an. Sollte er zustande kommen – ein nicht unproblematischer Dialog, jedenfalls was die Ausgangsposition angeht.

(Hirsch and Kopelew 1989:40)

(Representatives of the Initiative for Peace and Human Rights referred particularly to human rights violations taking the form of increasing social pressure targeted against political minorities. In the world of work this meant, for example, removal from work for which one was qualified, special surveillance and being checked up on, broad interpretations of employment law, leading to sacking. Despite its self-declared non-competence in these areas, we offered this 'unknown commitee' a further meeting. Should it come about, the dialogue will not be without its problems, at least as far as the opening positions are concerned.)

The last two sentences contain that mixture of hope – the use of the words 'contact' and 'dialogue' and the phrase 'should it come about' – and ironic/provocative scepticism (but not out-and-out rejection) shown by the use of the phrases 'unknown committee' and 'not unproblematical', which for the most part typify the group's attitude at that time to the state authorities. The episode also demonstrates, as do the contents of *Grenzfall* more generally, the uncommon readiness of the activists to be openly named and recognized, risking harassment, social exclusion or worse, in a situation where a large majority publicly conformed or accommodated.

Grenzfall graphics

The imagery of the cartoons and graphics appearing in *Grenzfall* provide visual representations of its critical perspective. Of particular interest is the change of masthead after the initial issue. The first masthead (Figure 8.1) portrays literally the falling of a closed border, represented by a wall topped by barbed wire, with *Grenz-* (border) inscribed on it in upright letters, which then turns into a pile of rubble, with *-fall* written on it in sloping letters.

The wall is clearly reminiscent of the Berlin Wall and the closed state boundary with the West. The graphic is thus implying the demolition of that boundary, and by implication, the end of German division. This was abandoned in all other issues of *Grenzfall*, doubtless due to its susceptibility to misinterpretation of the agenda of the group producing the journal, which was certainly East–West detente, but equally certainly not German unification.

The new masthead for issue two (Figure 8.2), which then remained virtually unchanged, shows a low barrier consisting of a striped wooden pole stretched between two posts. It is not drawn as a barrier

Figure 8.1   *Grenzfall* masthead 1

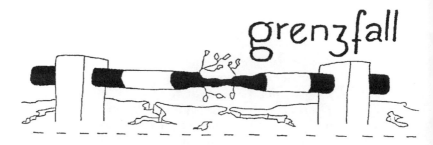

Figure 8.2   Grenzfall masthead 2

which can be raised, but is nevertheless one which is easily crossed. Moreover, the centre of the barrier has been gnawed away at, and weakened, and twigs with leaves are sprouting from that weakened central section. The ground beneath and beyond the barrier appears to be riven with crevasses, and the barrier appears to be there to prevent one from falling over the edge of a precipice. Thus, while the leaves sprouting from the dead wood appear to show new life emerging from the weakening of old barriers, the message is ambivalent since the barrier is also seen to be there as a benevolent protection against a dangerous, unstable landscape, encroaching from beyond. Eastern restrictions are subverted while to the west is danger and potential disaster – literally beyond the pale.

Cartoons break up the text of *Grenzfall* frequently in the first two issues, but are thereafter confined to one per issue on the front page. Thematically they fall into five categories: indoctrination and censorship, successful subversion and opposition, cages and imprisonment, environmental pollution, and scepticism about reform from above. Here examples will be given of the first three of these.

The front page cartoon of *Grenzfall* 4/87 (Figure 8.3) indicates the provocative cat and mouse relationship between state authorities and peace and human rights activists, and the way in which *Grenzfall* taunted those who would wish to silence or censor it. Although virtually powerless in terms of resources or equipment, it was, nevertheless, managing to distribute its message and defy official disapproval, demonstrating the power of the independent word in an authoritarian society. The rubric under the cartoon runs: 'Achtung an alle Dienststellen, ich gebe die Beschreibung der Tatwaffe durch: 35 cm mal 30cm, schwarz mit weißen Tasten, Gewicht circa 5 kg' (Attention all police stations, I will now pass on the description of the weapon used

4/87

"Achtung an alle Dienststellen, ich gebe die Beschreibung der Tatwaffe durch: 35 cm mal 30 cm, schwarz mit weißen Tasten, Gewicht circa 5 kg..."

Figure 8.3   Grenzfall 4/87: cartoon

in the crime: 35 cm by 30 cm, black with white keys, weight about 5 kg). The drawing of a uniformed policeman speaking into a microphone while looking at a large picture of a typewiter pinned to the wall in front of him portrays the authorities mockingly as perceiving the humble typewriter as a weapon used to perpetrate criminal activity, needing to be sought out, confiscated and used in evidence. They are thus shown to be both paranoid, and wishing to curtail free expression, employing their whole network of control to locate the offending object.

Cartoons in the two issues of *Grenzfall* (10/87 and 11/87) which immediately preceded the arrests of key activists around the journal and the *Initiative* show images of successful opposition to, or subver-

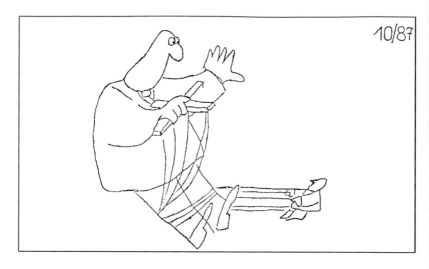

Figure 8.4   *Grenzfall* 10/87: cartoon

sion of, state authority. The first (Figure 8.4) shows a larger figure holding a marionette, whose movements he would normally be controlling, in the process of falling over since the marionette has turned on the puppet master, entwined his legs in the strings, and is in the process of pulling them tight. This variant on the David and Goliath motif portrays the overthrow of authority through action on the part of the normally passive and controlled. It empowers the powerless as the oppressor is ensnared by the very means of control that he has himself created.

The second (Figure 8.5) shows a figure gleefully turning a hand-operated duplicating machine (a reference to the group's primitive equipment) which is spewing out sheets of paper in the direction of a crowd of people consisting largely of truncheon and radio telephone-wielding policemen, and a machine gun-toting soldier. The members of the crowd appear to be prevented from advancing as the sheets of paper from the duplicating machine fly towards them. One member of the crowd in civilian dress is making a thumbs-up sign and seems to be pleased where all the others are frustrated at their inability to move in and prevent the dispersal of the papers.

Since the papers clearly represent *Grenzfall* in particular, and opposition discourse in general, this cartoon is an open provocation to the

Figure 8.5 *Grenzfall* 11–12/87: cartoon

state authorities, presented as helpless and incapable of stopping its production. It may be no coincidence that they moved in before another issue of *Grenzfall* could appear.

Three *Grenzfall* cartoons use the image of the birdcage. In the penultimate issue (1988: 1–12), and the first to appear following the arrests of key figures around *Grenzfall* and the *Initiative*, the front page shows a sad-looking parrot in a cage with its plump, bespectacled owner, hand raised and finger pointing, standing close by and saying: 'Und jetzt sprich mir nach: "Ich bin frei", "Ich bin glücklich"' (And now say after me: 'I am free', 'I am happy') (Figure 8.6). The image is self-explanatory, but its unambiguous ironic portrayal of imprisonment, authoritarian structure, imposition of discourse, and the requirement to mouth reality-denying mantras, portray the journal immediately as a provocative place in which the opposite is happening, and as a defiant space where the power to resist such processes is alive. The editorial inside the front cover reads: 'Grenzfall ist tot – ES LEBE DER GRENZFALL!' (*Grenzfall* is dead – LONG LIVE *GRENZFALL*); the message is that critical voices are not going to cave in in the face of intimidating actions.

Figure 8.6   *Grenzfall* 1–12/88: cartoon

Conclusion

While *Grenzfall* certainly does not provide us – or aim to provide us – with a picture of a reform government in waiting, any more than its equivalents did in the neighbouring countries – it is a campaigning journal, not a political manifesto or a treatise on economic reform – it does, however, indicate to us that the GDR reformers were also not less courageous, or less prepared for revolution than figures such as Lech Wałesa or Vaclav Havel, who rose to be national leaders. *Neues Forum* in the Autumn of 1989 in the GDR brought together huge regular demonstrations all over the country, and several of the people close to *Grenzfall* and the *Initiative* were involved in drafting a new constitution for the GDR in early 1990. Transposed into the Czech or Polish situation, they would have been honoured as resistance heroes, and would possibly have taken up leading positions in the new governments. In unified Germany, no such positions have been available for east German reformers. *Grenzfall* and those working around it may be seen as supporting evidence for the hypothesis that it was primarily the power of international geo-politics and Western media propaganda, rather than internal weakness, inadequacy or lack of will, as is often asserted, which led to the end of the GDR and the marginalization of its reformers, while sweeping their oppositional counterparts to power in the next-door countries. Today's Germans – east and west – have largely been deflected from these perspectives. It is nevertheless the case that their integration into unified German historiographies and mentalities would be a valuable ingredient in an eventual, more equitable German self-understanding, and in any future healing of the current persistent divide.

References

Arbeitsgruppe 'Neue Verfassung der DDR' des Runden Tisches (1990) *Entwurf. Verfassung der Deutschen Demokratischen Republik* (Berlin: BasisDruck Verlagsgesellschaft mbH; Staatsverlag der DDR).

Bohley, Bärbel *et al.* (1989) *40 Jahre DDR ... und die Bürger melden sich zu Wort* (Frankfurt/Main: Büchergilde Gutenberg).

Hahn, Hans (ed.) (1995) *Germany in the 1990s* (Amsterdam: rodopi).

Hirsch, Ralf and Lew Kopelew (1989) *Grenzfall* (Berlin: Ralph Hirsch Selbstverlag).

Knabe, Hubertus (1990) *Aufbruch in eine andere DDR. Reformer und Oppositionelle zur Zukunft ihres Landes* (Reinbek bei Hamburg: Rowohlt).

Knabe, Hubertus (1997) 'Wo liegen die Selbstzeugnisse der DDR-Opposition?', *Deutschland Archiv* 4, 565–71.

Neubert, Ehrhart (1998) *Geschichte der Opposition in der DDR 1949–1989* (Berlin: Links).

Prokop, Siegfried (ed.) (1994) *Die kurze Zeit der Utopie. Die 'zweite' DDR im vergessenen Jahr 1989–1990* (Berlin: Elefanten Press).

Staab, Andreas (1998) 'Xenophobia, Ethnicity and National Identity in Eastern Germany', *German Politics* 7/2, 31–45.

Theobald, John and Gertrud Zuber (1995) 'Who wanted Unification?', in Hahn (1995).

9
Narratives of the GDR: What Parents Tell their Children

Beth Linklater

Introduction

The wide diversity of representations of Germanness post-1989 is of vital importance as cultures are recreated in a country which lies at the heart of developments in Europe. German identities are produced through the constantly shifting interplay of nation, class, age, gender and race. Knowledge of one's own past – both private and public – has a vital role to play within this process. Such knowledge affects not only the construction of selfhood, but also relationships with others and developments on the national stage. This chapter takes as its starting point the questions that children born since the *Wende* of 1989 will ask their parents and their wider families about the past of East Germany, and the answers which they will receive.

Of course, these informal personal narratives will not be the only source of historical information to which the children have access. Within the family they will read letters and diaries, look at photo albums and hear numerous anecdotes. In the public, more formal arena media representations of all kinds will be dominant, as will school texts. In the case of the latter the influence of the teacher will play an important, and possibly contradictory, role. Literature and film from the GDR may also be available to the children, offering a fictional *Ersatz* reality which many critics have seen as more truthful than non-fictional accounts. Cultural institutions of all types, whether school, museum, gallery, monument, historical tourist site, local history group or even Parliament, will also mediate and influence the knowledge that is transferred. These institutions are often owned by the state and produce memories of which the state approves; the dominant view-point is likely to be that of the Cold War victor. Finally, the creation of history is, as Michael Bommes (1982) notes, a lucrative business, and many versions of the past will have the at least partial aim of financial profit.

Within this network of competing information the influence of the personalized spoken narrative can be especially persuasive, as the popularity of oral history shows. This form of historical research empha-sizes the story in history, bringing dry facts to apparently authentic life while offering those subjects conventionally lost to the historical records the chance to be heard. In this sense the qualitative data which forms the basis of this chapter can be seen primarily as specific and in many senses non-representative, rather than factual. This individuality – and emotionality – represents one aspect of its strength, offering a very private representation of the highly public experiment that was the GDR. Yet at the same time these tales are informed and shaped by public events, collective myths of the past, and media presentations. Their imagery and semantics offer important clues to the construction of a social consciousness. This is particularly clear where individual interviews take up the same themes, motifs and in some cases term-inology. The terms of private history have been supplied from the con-temporary public domain. In this sense the boundaries between public and private, as also between past and present, are blurred and the rel-evance of individual oral histories is thus also apparent for more general historical debates. One such debate is that of Germanness post-1989.

What will be remembered? Interviews with east Germans

The in-depth interviews analysed in this chapter were recorded in Halle an der Saale in Sachsen Anhalt in December 1997. The eight women and ten men, aged between 20 and 62, were chosen according to a process of snowballing, each person being asked to recommend others. The interviewees represent a range of backgrounds in terms of age, gender, social status and employment. The questions were intended to open up a dialogue such as would take place between child and parent, grandparent or other relative. The enthusiasm of all the interviewees to talk, often at great length, was particularly encouraging.[1] There did seem to be a sense in which a past which was being forgotten should be remembered. Not one of those asked said that they would conceal any aspect of life in the GDR, including such things as the *Stasi*, queues for bananas or waiting lists for *Trabis* (cars). Indeed these apparent and famous deprivations were reconfigured as humorous tales, elements of a national history which there was no reason to deny. The question seemed not to be what would be told, but rather what would be asked. As Tilo (aged 28), answered, 'Ich würde alles erzählen, aber das meiste wird man vergessen' (I'd talk about everything, but most of it will be forgotten) (Tape 1, A, 9.18).[2]

Like all narrated histories these accounts of the GDR are diverse and incomplete, resonant with unexplained gaps and contradictions which evince the complexity of memory. Furthermore, this very complexity is itself thematized, often exhibiting a high degree of self-reflexivity. Many recognize, for example, how their views have changed over the course of time and how much has been forgotten. Often a theme mentioned in a positive light at the beginning of an interview will have become something negative by the end. These are stories whose endings have not yet been written. Yet there are some general points to be made and some patterns which do appear, although in the search for interpretation the emphasis of certain comments has been shifted. The most striking fact about the narratives is the positive impressions of the GDR that they present. Very few, for example, emphatically answered the final question, 'Sind Sie der Meinung, daß Ihre Kinder Glück haben, weil sie nach der Wende aufwachsen?' (Do you believe your children are lucky to be growing up after the *Wende*?) with the 'yes' that had been expected. Typical was the response 'Kannst du nicht mit ja oder nein beantworten' (You can't answer that with yes or no) (Heike, Tape 1, A, 29.48). The discussions raised by this question revolved around the issues of materialism, community, work, parental responsibility and, most often, safety.

The GDR was, the children will hear from their parents, primarily a place of security, and not just in terms of practicalities such as housing and employment, but also as regards state control and personal safety. Comments such as 'Zu DDR-Zeiten war bestimmt besser gewesen, ja die Sicherheit überhaupt' (What was better in GDR times – well, everything to do with safety) (Kathrin L, Tape 1, B, 30.37), were expressed in various forms. The answers of Matthias (aged 32), and Henrik (aged 26), are typical:

> Das Leben [war] früher doch, für mich zumindest, freier gewesen. Man brauchte nicht zu gucken. Man wußte ganz genau, was man hatte ... In der heutigen Zeit muß man wirklich – man muß ständig immer alles bedenken.
>
> Matthias, Tape 1, A, 14.29,15.10

(For me, at least, life used to be freer. You didn't need to keep an eye on things. You knew exactly what you had ... Today you really have to, you really have to think about every last thing.)

Ich war nie ein überzeugter roter Fahnenträger oder so was, Blödsinn. Man hat es mitgemacht, aber nicht aus tiefstem Herzen, obwohl wir so eine Erziehung hatten. Aber wir hatten, hatten Norm, wir wußten, in welchem Rahmen wir uns bewegen durften ... und Respekt vor anderen Leuten. Das spüre ich heute überhaupt nicht mehr. Alles ist toleranter geworden. Aber das fehlt mir, *so eine gewisse Sicherheit*, die auch Kinder einfach brauchen.

Henrik, Tape 1, B, 15.26, 16.22: Author's emphasis

(I was never a convinced red flag waver or the like, rubbish. You did it, but not from the heart, although we were brought up like that. But we had norms, we knew the boundaries within which we could act ... and respect for others. I just don't get a sense of that at all any more. Everything is more tolerant. But I miss that, that safety, which children also need.)

In the first example the impersonal and general *man* (one) is used for the average person, with whom Matthias clearly associates himself and his family. He connects the organization, or indeed regulation, of life in the GDR, with freedom. This clearly shows how slippery notions such as democracy and freedom are, and how, for many, they are constructed primarily at the interface between state and individual, as experienced by the individual in his or her working life. The second answer also displays both a distancing from the state and clear identification with it. Throughout the interviews multiple identities are being constructed, whether as a member of a sports club, a single mother, a *Hallenser* (somebody from Halle), an *Ossi* (an 'eastie'), or a German. Occasionally the security of the GDR is, conversely, labelled as *langweilig* (boring) (Kathrin N, Tape 1, A, 34.09), or *trügerisch* (deceptive) (Tilo, Tape 1, A, 41.17), but more often it is depicted as *beruhigend* (comforting) and *bequem* (comfortable) (Heike, Tape 1, A, 27.27).

The theme of material security was generally extended to include physical safety. Almost without exception every person interviewed feels more worried about their safety now than they did in the GDR and this is one of the strongest emotions which will be communicated to the children. Whether this subjective feeling is based on real or anecdotal evidence, modern media reporting or lack of previous knowledge is, in respect of the overall impression, extraneous. The increase in criminal behaviour is often noted and, as in the following quotations, is repeatedly connected with a dissatisfied and restless youth population:

> Kriminalität, das ist für mich auch so ein Punkt. So schwer wie heute war das nicht. ... Und wenn ich mir das heute angucke, haben wir letztens ein paar, was weiss ich, Dreizehn-, Vierzehnjährige mit einer Schreckschußpistole durch die Stadt laufen gesehen. Da sagt doch keiner was.
>
> Jürgen, Tape 1, A, 16.05, 16.47
>
> (Criminal behaviour, that's another thing. It wasn't as bad as it is today. ... And when I look at things today, recently we saw a few, oh I don't know, thirteen or fourteen year olds running through the town centre with a blank gun. And no one says anything!)

> Ich habe wesentlich mehr Gewalterlebnisse gehabt, die mich einfach auch erschrecken. ... Und ... die Aggressivität der Jugendlichen untereinander, die ist auch viel, die ist einfach mal höher.
>
> Heike, Tape 2, B, 22.22
>
> (I've experienced a lot more violence, and that simply scares me ... And the aggression amongst the young, that's much, that's just much worse.)

Some women are now afraid to walk through the streets at night. Three people independently told of previously being able to leave prams outside shops without the fear of one's baby being abducted. Others see the fact that other countries are afraid of the Germans as further evidence of this increase in violence. It is blamed not only on a lack of future prospects for youth, but also a reduction in police presence (whereby the GDR *Abschnittsbevollmächtigte* – community police – are regarded as positive), the availability of weapons, and a significantly less effective legal system. The unquestioning adoption of East German norms (or, as some would argue, propaganda) as the basis for comparisons is particularly clear. Many complained also about the violence of the media, particularly with respect to material aimed at children:

> Die Gewalttätigkeit hat zugenommen. Die Medien üben einen außerordentlich, gelinde gesagt, unguten Einfluß auf die Massen aus. ... Muß das so sein, daß pausenlos Gewaltfilme der gesamten

Bevölkerung, fast vom Kind bis zum Greis, angeboten werden? Das hat doch mit Kultur nichts zu tun! Das kann doch nicht Auftrag sein!

Horst, Tape 3, A, 3.46, 4.31

(Violence has increased. The media have, to put it mildly, an extraordinarily negative influence on the masses … Do violent films have to be shown all the time, to the whole population, from children to old people? That's got nothing at all to do with culture, that can't be our task!)

The use of the characteristically East German term *Auftrag* (task) evinces the background from which judgements are being made. Modern comics and films are seen as representative of a culture of violence endorsed and even encouraged by an irresponsible state.

Clearly related to the theme of state control is that of education, now generally perceived as the responsibility of parents rather than the state, to the detriment of the system and the pupils. Pre-1989 'hatte jeder die gleichen Chancen' (everyone had the same chances) (Ingo, Tape 1, B, 6.09); post-1989 the situation is unfortunately not as clear cut. Many complained that kindergarten provision was now not only expensive, but also did not serve the interests of the children. Others bemoaned the three-tier system of schooling, in which money and clothes have created clear hierarchical structures. Where the GDR system of compliance, unfair advantage and boring *Staatsbürgerkunde* (citizenship classes) was mentioned it was seen largely as an accepted fact of life. Whilst interviewees knew people who had been barred from the *EOS* (the sixth form) because they were religious or had not been in the *FDJ* (the East German youth movement), they themselves did not feel that they had suffered under the GDR's polytechnical system.

The issue of equal opportunities was often raised with respect to the position of women in society. Representative was the remark 'die Achtung der Frau, da sag ich, wir sind drei Schritte zurückgegangen' (As regards respect for women, in my opinion we've taken three steps backwards), (Heike, Tape 1, A, 15.03). Those who complained were, however, careful to distance themselves from feminism, which is still understood negatively as a Western phenomenon. Many women appear to have lost the self-confidence supposedly encouraged by the GDR's policies of 'die Vereinbarung von Berufstätigkeit und Mutterschaft' (the combining of career and motherhood). They are now increasingly reliant upon a stereotypically Western version of the acquiescent female. As Kathrin O. (aged 30) so eloquently remarks:

Wenn ich die Frauen dort, wenn ich mich mit diesen Westfrauen
unterhalte, dann krieg ich manchmal so einen Hals ... Die sind
einfach anders wie wir ... Für mich kommen die Frauen da drüben
mit dem Arsch nicht hoch. ... Das beste Beispiel ist bei meiner
Freundin [in München] im Haus. Da wohnt eine, der Mann,
stockhäßlich. Stockhäßlich! So 'ne Wanne und das ist wirklich eine
zarte, zierliche Frau. Da hat sie sich die Nase operieren lassen und
das Kinn operieren lassen. Na! Für so einen Mann würde ich mich
... umoperieren lassen! Na, um Gottes willen! Ehrlich! Da hab ich
gedacht, ne, ob die auch mal ihrem Mann sagt, Mensch, wie wär es
denn mal mit ein bißchen Dauerlauf oder so ... Aber der hat bestimmt einen Haufen Geld, und damit geben sie sich eben zufrieden
... Da fehlt Power, irgendwo, bei den Frauen.

Tape 1, B, 30.36

(When I talk to the women there, those Western women, I sometimes get so angry, they are just different from us, they just can't get
off their backsides ... The best example is a woman who lives in the
same house as my friend in Munich. Her husband, he's ugly, so
ugly! A real beer belly, and she's such a delicate, petite woman. She's
had a nose job, and had her chin done. Well! For that sort of man
I'd never ... go under the knife! For God's sake! Honestly! When I
heard that I wondered if she ever says to her husband, well pal,
what about a bit of jogging ... but no doubt he's loaded, and they're
happy with that ... There's no power with those women.)

The discourse surrounding women was thus framed in terms of continued *Ossi/Wessi* stereotypes, reinforced by linguistic phrases such as
'die Frauen von da drüben' (the women from over there) or simply
Westfrauen (western women). More generally terms such as *die Leute da
drüben* (the people over there) and *Westbesuch* (a visitor from the west)
again contribute to the production of a specific east German identity.
Resentment towards bosses from the west exaggerates this effect, as
does the bitterness felt over images of the east portrayed in the media.
On a more personal level, however, most people have friends from the
west and express the hope that such negative clichés will not affect
their children:

Unsere Generation jetzt, bei uns wird immer ständig eine Zwietracht
sein, würde ich sagen, zwischen Ost und West. Ich würde auch
sagen, das verschärft sich immer mehr ... Ich habe anderthalb Jahre
in Duisburg gelebt und auch diese Feindseligkeit kam rüber. Dann

hieß es: 'Ja, jetzt macht ihr euch da hier breit und wenn ihr dann
mal alles schick habt drüben, dann kommen wir zu euch rüber.' Da
war überhaupt kein Verständnis dafür ... Aber ich würde mal sagen,
wie jetzt mein Junge mit drei Jahren die gehen da anders ran.

Sandra, Tape 1, A, 6.49

(Our generation now, there will always be divisions I'd say, between
east and west. I'd also say that it's getting worse ... I lived for a year
and a half in Duisburg and that hostility came across. You often
heard, 'Well, you behave as if you own the place now, and when
you've smartened everything up over there, then we'll come to you.'
They just didn't understand ... But I'd say that my little boy, he's
three, they'll approach it differently.)

The contradictions manifest within this statement disclose the paradoxical nature of an identity which is temporary and based in the cer-
tainties of the past rather than the uncertainties of the present. The
discourse of difference from the west thus simultaneously exists with
that of similarity to it. Many interviewees contradict themselves,
affirming difference while also expressing the wish that the next generation will be assimilated into a 'German' whole.

The west was often characterized with various forms of the adjective
kalt (cold) and compared with the former warmth of the east. Common
to many interviews was the motif of humanity or *Menschlichkeit*. Many
emphasized the recent loss of a sense of community in the face of a
dog-eat-dog society based on competition and profit, where money has
become decisive:

Der Zusammenhalt so, das, das vermiß ich jetzt so ein bißchen.
Weil, jetzt ist jeder so, macht jeder so sein Ding. Und damals haben
wir unwahrscheinlich zusammengehalten. ... Das Herzliche,
irgendwo, das war ganz anders wie jetzt. Viel mehr Wärme. Und
jetzt ist kalt. Ganz kalt.

Kathrin O, Tape 1, B, 3.16, 3.38

(The solidarity, I miss that a bit now. Everyone does his own thing
now. In the past we really stuck together ... The sincerity, somehow,
that was so different to now. Much more warmth. And now it's
cold. So very cold.)

This positive characteristic of the GDR was, though, regarded as the
result of something that was in itself negative, namely the lack of material possessions. The need to improvise and to be inventive had led to

greater appreciation of the small things that were available. Many specifically recognized the key role of the *Tauschgesellschaft* (barter society) in creating this 'humanity'. The *Arbeitskollektiv* (workers' collective) – for which there is no direct equivalent in the west – was also accorded a special meaning. These relationships appear, then, as something peculiarly East German. It is the social structures themselves, rather than simply their effects, which are seen as positive. As Karl Ulrich Mayer and Martin Diewald (1996:14) comment, the role and quality of informal ties extended far beyond a mere means of access to goods in short supply or Gaus's famed *Nischengesellschaft* (niche society):

> Sie gelten in vielfacher Weise als 'Puffer' gegen die Zumutungen und Mißstände der formalen Strukturen: als Rückzugsraum zur Ausbildung persönlicher Vertrauensbeziehungen, als Medium zur Herstellung von Öffentlichkeit und als Kanäle zur Versorgung mit denjenigen Gütern und Diensten, die ansonsten sehr schwer erhältlich waren.
> (They are valid in many different ways as a barrier against the demands and defects of the formal structures: as a space for the creation of personal relationships of trust, as a medium for the production of public discourse and as a means of provision of those goods and services which would otherwise have been difficult to obtain.)

The *Mangelsituation* (scarcity of goods) is, therefore, repeatedly described with the words *lustig* (funny) or *witzig* (comic).

Issues of democracy, freedom of speech or the freedom to travel – those subjects often portrayed as the influential factors behind the *Wende* – were mentioned comparatively rarely. Indeed they remained conspicuously absent from the reports of those who did not have *Westverwandte* (Western relatives). Young people such as Ingo (aged 23), did, however, talk of holidays and the new possibilities to study abroad:

> Das bereue ich auf keinen Fall. So wie es mir jetzt geht, wäre es mir sicher ohne die Wende nie gegangen. Ich hätte vielleicht auch studieren dürfen, damals schon. Aber, alleine wo ich jetzt schon war. Urlaubsmäßig. Oder die Möglichkeiten jetzt im Studium, woanders hinzugehen. Die ganze Freiheit. Das ist schon was.
> Tape 1, B, 14.48
> (I don't regret it in any way. My life would never have been like this without the *Wende*. I might have been allowed to study, even then.

But the places where I've already been, on holiday. Or the possibilities to study abroad. All that freedom. That's really something.)

Andreas was similarly very enthusiastic about the positive attitude towards homosexuality he had encountered in the west, which he said was something completely different from the GDR:

> In der ehemaligen DDR, da gab es Schwulsein nicht ... Das war strafbar. Und jetzt können wir uns ausleben. ... Endlich kann man das leben, was man ist, das Schwulsein. Das find ich toll.
>
> Regina/Andreas, Tape 1, B, 18.19, 20.40
>
> (In the former GDR, there was no such thing as homosexuality ... It was illegal. And now we can live our lives to the full. ... At long last we can be what we are, gay. I think that's fantastic.)

It was only in these more infrequent comments that the demands for political change voiced in the Autumn of 1989 were echoed. Yet if safety is the primary concern of the interviewees then this is no surprise, for it was in no way due to a lack of social security that the citizens of the GDR chose to leave their state or take to the streets. Not every aspect of East German society was rejected: indeed there was much that was praised, and even taken as justification for identification with the whole system, and notably with the more idealistic values of social equality and solidarity at least preached in the GDR, if not always practised. It thus appears all the more unfortunate that these elements of the system have been lost. Whether or not these positive conditions really existed, or indeed could have continued to exist if the GDR were still 'operative' today, is beyond the bounds of this discussion. Here it is important simply to register the current perspectives from which the past is being constructed and to note the effects of these constructions. Narrative consequences can frequently be more important than historical truths.

Explaining attitudes: nostalgia and narrativity

The findings of this study are by definition qualitative and make no claim to be representative. Yet when contextualized within more general statistical evidence they confirm suggestions that the citizens of the five new German states are looking back with some nostalgia for a lost past, thereby reinventing a collective GDR identity. In *Der Spiegel*'s 'first comprehensive empirical survey of GDR nostalgia' (*Der*

Spiegel 1995a:40), for example, the GDR was considered superior to the FRG in seven out of nine areas, an increase from 1990 when the figure had been three out of nine. The seven areas were mostly those of safety mentioned by my interviewees. Around 89 per cent of those interviewed believed that 'der Zusammenhalt der Menschen untereinander in der DDR stärker war als heute.' (Solidarity was stronger in the GDR than today) (1995a:49). Thomas Koch (1996) quotes a very similar survey from *Die Zeit* (1 October 1993), in which the strengths of the GDR, and by implication the weaknesses of the FRG, are again job security, child care and protection against crime.

The relationship between the general surveys which form individual opinion and the opinions that gave rise to these surveys is scrambled. As Koch (1996:190) argues, such polls do more than depict social groups: 'the latter also become aware of their being social groups through public descriptions', descriptions which, therefore, feed into what he identifies as 'the renaissance of East German group awareness and self-assurance' (1996:191). Some of the quotations used by *Der Spiegel*, for example, are echoed word for word by interviewees, who quote such surveys as evidence both for the claim that violent crime has increased by 16 per cent since the *Wende* (Heike, Tape 1, B, 3.25; Tape 2, B, 17.00) and for the fact that 'etwa jeder fünfte sich nach dieser Zeit zurücksehnt' (roughly one in five look back longingly to that past) (Heike, Tape 1, A, 12.34).

The fact that there is nostalgia for aspects of the former GDR is clear on a superficial level from the wave of products and events now marketed as specifically 'East German', from coffee, *Club Cola* and other memorabilia to *(N)ostalgie* weekend breaks (http://www.lindner.de/start-komplett.htm). *Ostalgie* parties offer music by GDR groups such as City and the Pudys, free entry to those in FDJ blue shirts or *Pionier* scarves, *Volkspolizisten* and Easty girls. Internet Honecker sites abound (see http://home.t-online.de/home/ddr/homepage.htm). Even British publications such as *The Guardian* (9 November 1993: 16) have found this topic interesting enough to warrant mention. Many interviewees talk about these forms of nostalgia: harmless, largely apolitical and, as Lothar Fritze (1995:290) suggests, 'zum Großteil "rein menschlich" verstehbar' (for the most part understandable on a purely human level), connected simply with memories of a happy childhood. Beyond this, however, nostalgia is a complicated emotion that produces very real, and more directly political, results. One could, for example, argue that the PDS captures precisely this mood of nostalgia. While the past is the object of nostalgia the cause is the present, and thus, as Fred Davis

(1979:10) notes, 'nostalgia tells us more about present moods than about past realities'. It also tells us about our own selves, being a product of the human need for stability. In transitional times of fear, discontent and uncertainty, such as the 1990s in the former GDR, nostalgic evocations of the past, whether imagined or real, offer reminders of former worth or value and ensure the 'continuity of identity' (Davis 1979:35).

Fritze (1995:276) identifies two types of nostalgia. The first, *total* nostalgia for the past, is, he says, not relevant for the GDR. This argument holds true also for my results, as does his definition of *partial* nostalgia, which, he claims, certainly does exist in the former GDR, 'bestimmte Aspekte oder Teilbereiche der DDR-Realität [werden] – auch und vielleicht gerade retrospektiv – positiv bewertet' (Certain aspects or areas of GDR reality are being positively revalued, also – and perhaps most importantly – retrospectively). These aspects include, Fritze maintains, social security (1995:280), greater social equality, the unique status of the worker figure, less competition and a specific form of solidarity or 'belonging' (1995:281).

Fritze also identifies forms of pseudo nostalgia, which he labels *Stoßseufzer-Nostalgie* (sigh nostalgia), *Trotz-Nostalgie* (defiance nostalgia) and simple *Mißverständnisse* (misunderstandings): these are irrational responses to, and criticism of, an unsatisfactory present with which one has not yet fully come to terms, rather than a real longing for the past. An unsatisfactory present might be unemployment or the fear thereof, ever increasing rents, heightened violence on the streets, complicated 'German' bureaucracy, the lack of clear political and moral orientation and indeed hope in a pluralist democracy such as the FRG, the failure of Kohl's precipitate promises of flourishing landscapes, misunderstanding of and even complete lack of interest in one's former home from *Wessi* neighbours or employers, and so on. As Heike comments, 'Es geht nicht darum, die alte DDR zurückzuhaben, so wie sie war, sondern, daß einfach alles ignoriert wird aus dieser Zeit, daß alles nur als schlecht, als grausam und einfach unmöglich dargestellt wurde' (It's not about getting the old GDR back, just as it was, it's about the fact that everything from that time is being ignored, being presented only as bad, as cruel and as simply impossible) (Tape 1, A, 13.10). These forms of nostalgia, rational or not, are clearly present in the comments of interviewees. Although specific to the timing of the interview and the personal circumstances of the interviewee at that time, wider expressions of such perspectives do appear to be having an effect on the shaping of the social fabric of eastern Germany.

For example, responses to the question 'what do you consider to be the most important events of GDR history?' clearly demonstrate the influence of partial and pseudo-nostalgia. The majority named occurrences important to them personally, rather than actual historical dates or events. Only Horst (aged 62), catalogued those text book markers such as 1949, 1953, 1956, 1961 or 1968, but even he was prompted here by his son-in-law and indeed by the interviewer. Hartmut, aged 47, remembered the building of the Berlin Wall only through the words of an old farmer about that year's bad harvest, 'die Kartoffel reichen wenn die Leute abhauen' (There will be enough potatoes to go round, if people get out) (Tape 1, B, 19.40). Others talked about FDJ parades or official holidays, such as the first of May. Here again, though, the tendency was to remember the personal form of these public events. Kathrin L, for example, remembered 1 May as her aunt's birthday rather than Labour Day. Once again the emphasis was placed upon the humorous side of these events, rather than upon their connotations of coercion. In this instance too, key words are *witzig* (comic) and *lustig* (funny):

> Irgendwie war es schon witzig immer gewesen, ja. Man hatte den Tag frei, ist schnell irgendwo hingehetzt, ist da schnell an der Tribüne vorbei, und dann schnell wieder nach Hause ... weil man den Tag eben frei hatte und das war eigentlich immer, irgendwie war das auch immer mit Festen verbunden. ... Man war eben in der Gruppe drinne, wo man alle Leute kannte, das war eben, das war irgendwie, das war Freiheit, das war so ein bißchen Freiheit gewesen. Das war echte Freiheit, ja, wirklich.
>
> Martin, Tape 1, A, 22.40, and Tape 1, B, 2.55
> (It really was all funny in a way, yes, funny. You had the day off, ran somewhere quickly, zoomed past the platform and then quickly back home ... because you had a day off and that was usually, somehow that was always connected with celebrations ... you were in a group where you knew everyone and somehow that was, that was freedom, that was a little bit of freedom. That was real freedom, yes really.)

Many referred to holidays on the Baltic coast, to sport training camps or to sporting competitions. It was these that represented freedom by offering the chance to step over fixed boundaries, a definition of freedom founded in common values rather than the politics of one specific state. Such answers reveal both a nostalgic desire to remember the good, and also an extraordinary identification of individuals with the state. Of course nostalgia, real or imagined, cannot be the sole explanation for the largely positive results of this study. Oral testimony is not just a source of information, it is also 'an event in itself' (Portelli 1990:143), a highly constructed performance which 'might better be understood in relation to narrativity than to some empiricist notion of truth' (Samuel and Thompson 1990:10). Story telling may, then, 'take us closer to past meanings and certainly to subjectivity than … the painstaking accumulation of fact' (1990:13). In twentieth-century Germany 'the stories that people … have told about their postwar country's respective origins and character' have, as Michael Frisch states, 'been part of how people in each society have coped' (1993:i). Such stories include, for example, those told in the denazification process of 1945–46, the GDR state narratives concocted by the *Stasi*, the *Protokolle* genre of writing that became popular in the GDR from the late 1970s onwards, and, more recently, the vast numbers of interviews in news articles, books and on television with GDR citizens at the time of the *Wende*. As Robin Ostow (1993:1) claims, 'By early 1992 there was reason to suspect that citizens of the former German Democratic Republic had become the world's most interviewed population', a phenomenon which Ostow (1993:4) regards both as an attempt by west Germans to understand their new fellow citizens and an opportunity for east Germans to 'confront – or at least to write – their own collective history.'

Collective memories are, therefore, as Jean Peneff (1990:44) describes, 'intoxicated' by all forms of myth, myths which come 'ready-made for adapting to our own personal situation and interpreting our own pasts'. To cope with the new one re-remembers the old. Any life story is of necessity, a form of self-justification, embodying in the telling certain values, codes, characters, fantasies, daydreams, conventions or stock incidents. The elegiac mode of story-telling, whereby the past becomes 'a kind of reverse image of the present, a time when "everyone was neighbours" and life was more secure' (Samuel and Thompson 1990:8–9), is a recognized type, to which oral history narratives are often made, consciously or otherwise, to conform. Idealization, like demonization, is a classic coping strategy. Other stories which reinforce a sense of self or a common identity can centre around common grievance or the survival of defeat or persecution. Societies undergoing rapid development and change have most obvious need of such frameworks. Thus one possible 'myth' of the GDR stylizes and adapts the more general characteristics of friendliness, safety and security. Adoption of this myth allows for loyalty to personal history, whilst endowing present identity with a meaning of which the story-teller can be proud. The function of pride as a contributory factor to the narrative is particularly relevant in the wake of the perceived take-over by the West. As Alexander von Plato (1993:73) observes, 'There is a wide consensus ... that only the people of the former GDR can judge the conditions and the quality of life in the GDR.' Perceived relations of power will have an inevitable influence on the form of the story told.

Conclusion

In an interview with *Der Spiegel*, Kindergarten teacher Brigitte Pniok claims that her pupils, 'eine ganz neue Generation von Ostdeutschen' – 'werden nicht mehr nach der DDR fragen' (an entirely new generation of east Germans – will no longer even ask about the GDR) (*Der Spiegel* 1995b:138). Fritze (1995:292) similarly trusts in the passing of time; nostalgia for the GDR will, he concludes, become simply a generation phenomenon. Yet what the children ask in the future is, perhaps, not the point, as Pniok's use of the term '*Ost*deutschen' reveals. It is the intertwining of present heterogeneous narratives of the GDR that will create the memories to come. The childrens' letters printed in the col-lection *Kinder schreiben über unser Land* (Children write about our country) (Rusch 1992), for example, display exactly the same fears and worries expressed by the adults interviewed here. The main themes of these stories are unemployment, lack of security, increased prices (despite an enhanced choice of goods and travel possibilities), nostalgia for the youth groups and the holiday camps, the destruction of the environment and anxiety about the future, themes that the children have often clearly adopted from media reports and their parents' con-versations. Yet it is important to remember, as Dorothee Wierling (1993:29) points out, that 'what is [now] experienced as a loss may later be remembered as a gain, and vice versa'. Ultimately we cannot yet know what the future relationship between narrated forms of history and the community will be. Could these memories of the GDR, with their implied elements of amnesia, offer a real political alterna-tive? Do they construct a parental past against which the children may react with a new nationalism? Or will they merely remain an idealistic but safe 'other' which ultimately maintains the status quo? Even in the post-Cold War world no dominant image of history has imposed itself. 'Der Sinn des Nachdenkens über Geschichte liegt in den Fragen und nicht in den Antworten' (The meaning of asking about history lies in the questions and not in the answers) (Wolle 1995:126).

Notes

1 I am especially grateful to Stuart Taberner and Rima Dapous for their invaluable help in the writing of this chapter. All interviewees wished to be identified by name. In this chapter, first names have been adopted. All translations from the German are my own.
2 Although my interviewees responded positively to the question 'What do you not tell your children? (Or what do you not want to tell?)', many also recognized that this was an issue that depended largely on the extent to which one had been involved in GDR state apparatus and the guilt connected with that involvement. As this guilt has in many senses been induced by Western media and comparisons with 1945, this is an issue which was felt to belong within the East/West conflict.

References

Altenhof, Ralf and Eckhard Jesse (1995) *Das wiedervereinigte Deutschland. Zwischenbilanz und Perpektiven* (Düsseldorf: Droste Verlag).
Bommes, Michael (1982) 'Gelebte Geschichte. Probleme der Oral History', in *Lili. Zeitschrift für Literatur und Linguistik*, 12/47, 75–103.
Davis, Fred (1979) *Yearning for Yesterday. A Sociology of Nostalgia* (New York: The Free Press).
Der Spiegel (1995a), 'Stolz aufs eigene Leben', 27 (3 July 1995), 40–52.
Der Spiegel (1995b), 'Rollerblades und Pittiplatsch. Was sich ostdeutsche Kinder unter der DDR vorstellen', 36 (4 September 1995), 138.
Frisch, Michael (1993) 'Introduction', in *The Oral History Review. Journal of the Oral History Association*, 21/2, i.
Fritze, Lothar (1995) 'Identifikation mit dem gelebten Leben. Gibt es Nostalgie in den neuen Bundesländern?', in Altenhof and Jesse (1995), 275–92.
Gerber, Margy (1996) *Changing Identities in East Germany. Studies in GDR Culture and Society 14/15* (Lanham: University Press of America).
Koch, Thomas (1996) 'The renaissance of East German group awareness since Unification', in Gerber (1996), 189–210.
Mayer, Karl Ulrich and Martin Diewald (1996) 'Kollektiv und Eigensinn: Die Geschichte der DDR und die Lebensverläufe ihrer Bürger', in *Aus Politik und Zeitgeschichte* 46, 8–17.
Ostow, Robin (1993) 'Restructuring our lives: National unification and German biographies', in *The Oral History Review. Journal of the Oral History Association*, 21/2, 1–8.
Peneff, Jean (1990) 'Myths in life stories', in Samuel and Thompson (1990), 36–48.
Plato, Alexander von (1993) 'The consensus against the victors: 1945 and 1990', in *The Oral History Review. Journal of the Oral History Association*, 21/2, 73–9.
Portelli, Alessandro (1990) 'Uchronic dreams. Working class memory and possible worlds', in Samuel and Thompson (1990), 143–60.
Rusch, Regina (1992) *Plötzlich ist alles ganz anders. Kinder schreiben über unser Land* (Munich: dtv).

Samuel, Raphael and Paul Thompson (1990) *The Myths we Live by* (London: Routledge)

Wierling, Dorothee (1993) 'Three generations of East German women: Four decades of the GDR and after', in *The Oral History Review. Journal of the Oral History Association*, 21/2, 19–29.

Wolle, Stefan (1995) 'Der Kampf um die Erinnerung. Vergangenheitsbewältigung im vereinigten Deutschland', in Altenhof and Jesse (1995), 99–126.

10
Changing Communicative Practices among East Germans

Peter Auer

Introduction

The current linguistic situation in Germany is undoubtedly character-ized by the adoption of west German linguistic practices in many parts of the east German speech ecology in what some call a hegemonic process. As a consequence, east Germans often combine 'old' and 'new' (eastern and western) features in their language – unless, of course, they follow the west German usage completely. In this context, the most interesting research questions are where the appropriation of west German practices has occurred most rapidly (and, conversely, where it has not occurred at all), and how this appropriation has occurred. This chapter presents some tentative answers to these questions.

The first part presents some results of a contrastive study of com-municative performances of east and west Germans in (authentic) job interviews, a communicative genre in which pressure to accom-modate to the western style can be expected to be high. In the second part of the chapter, the job interview data (collected in 1994/5) will be reconsidered from a diachronic point of view and compared to similar materials collected shortly after the *Wende* and in the GDR, respectively. The aim here is to establish whether typical GDR stylistic features disappeared abruptly after the fall of the East German regime, or whether they have survived political unification.

A genre-based approach to the study of communicative practices

Linguistic research on east Germany in the first years after the *Wende* focused on the reconstruction of political language characteristic of the periods before and during the *Wende* and on post-*Wende* vocabulary changes. Although some writers voiced their suspicion that more is involved, empirical investigations of interactional language use were extremely scarce. Arguments about the 'Fortbestehen unterschwelliger Sprachhaltungen, Stile, Redeweisen' (survival of an undercurrent of language attitudes, styles, ways of speaking), leading to 'bestimmten Kommunikationsstörungen' (certain communication disturbances) (Müller 1994:131), or about the possibility of 'kommunikative Havarien' (communicative accidents) due to 'tieferliegende Unterschiede ... z.B. im Bereich des Informationstransfers, der Gesprächs- und Argumentationsstrategien und der Bewertungsmuster für kommunikatives Handeln' (deeper differences, ... such as in the area of information transfer, conversational and argumentative strategies and evaluation patterns for communication) (Fraas and Steyer 1992:176) generally remained at the level of speculation or individual experiences and anecdotal recollections.

Dissatisfied with this situation, a group of researchers at the Universities of Halle, Leipzig and Hamburg (including the present writer) have been trying to fill the gaps since 1993. This has meant (a) taking into account not (only) 'official' language use, but also linguistic practices of 'ordinary' east Germans in salient social contexts, (b) working (above all) with spoken language data, (c) working on a sound empirical basis, and (d) providing some kind of theoretical background, particularly from an interpretive and interactional point of view.

One of the starting points for this research was the contention that any attempt to investigate communicative or linguistic differences between east and west Germans as such (or, for that matter, between men and women, Blacks and Whites, or any other category pair) is bound to get one into methodological difficulties. What is required instead is a level of analysis mediating between these social categories and the verbal behaviour of their members, such as implied in the notion of 'activity types' (in the sense of Levinson 1992), 'text genres' (the notion used by Fix 1994) or 'communicative genres' (a notion developed by Thomas Luckmann: cf. Luckmann 1986, 1988; Günthner and Knoblauch 1995, and used in the Hamburg project on job interviews). Following Luckmann, we understand communicative genres as typified verbal structures of a certain complexity which are historically evolved sedimentations of solutions to routine social problems in a community. A genre approach to differences between eastern and western Germany implies looking at (a) the inventory of communicative genres salient in the community/communities, and (b) the rules and regularities which govern language use and communication within particular genres.

Differences are by no means difficult to find. Hellmann (1989) and Lerchner (1992a:311f) were probably the first to point out that a number of what they call 'kommunikative Situationen' used to be either highly incompatible in East and West Germany before 1989, or restricted to one of the two countries. Some of these genres (mainly written ones) have already been investigated in detail, such as *Arbeitszeugnisse* (references) (Kühn 1995), called *Beurteilungen* (assessments) in the GDR (cf. Fix 1995, 1994:135ff), *Stellengesuche* (job-seeking advertisements: cf. Barz 1997), as well as some exclusively East German genres such as political *Losungen* (slogans: cf. Fix 1992:137ff) and ritual texts in the *Jugendweihe* (the ceremony in which 14 year-olds were given adult status: Kauke 1997). Yet most of the speech ecology of the GDR, particularly the oral genres, remains to be explored.

The job interview is one of those oral communicative genres which was scarcely known in the GDR. The analytical problem in an empirical investigation of this genre in contemporary east Germany is therefore not reconstructive (as in the case of the GDR-typical genres listed above); rather we need to show how participants who have been brought up in a 'communicative culture' in which the respective genre knowledge was not necessary and therefore could not be acquired, deal with genre-specific roles and the tasks they imply today, in times when the genre is vital for professional careers in a shrinking job market. There are various possibilities. One is that since 1989, east Germans have acquired the knowledge necessary to perform in such a genre just as west Germans would;[1] this implies a complete adoption of the western communicative practice. The other possibility is that western genre knowledge has been acquired only selectively, if at all, either through a lack of opportunity (for instance, lack of exposure to the genre), or through lack of motivation. East Germans who have not (fully) acquired the western model will have to use other resources when taking part in a job interview. Obviously, one is common sense; if the routine provisions of the genre are not made use of, participants will have to find *ad hoc* solutions to the communicative problems for which these routines have been developed. 'Common sense', however, may not provide the same solutions for east and west Germans. Another resource is similar communicative genres of the GDR, with which participants in the job interview are already familiar as a result of their linguistic socialization (cf. Auer 1998 for such intertextual transfer).

East and west German applicants in job interviews

The following results from our study are to a large degree based on the empirical work by my collaborators Karin Birkner and Friederike Kern (cf. also Birkner 1998, Kern 1998, Birkner and Kern, forthcoming) and their analysis of a corpus of 20 east–west and 20 west–west job interviews, most of them for relatively senior posts. The east German applicants always had to deal with west German interviewers or personnel managers, so the institutionally more powerful position was occupied by the western participant.

Job interviews present a difficult situation for applicants, not so much because of their overt sequential and topical structure, but rather because of what has been called the 'hidden agenda' of the interview, which invests many seemingly 'innocent' verbal activities (questions in particular) with a second, underlying meaning (cf. Roberts 1985, Roberts and Sayers 1987, Adelswård 1988, Sarangi 1994, Roberts and Sarangi 1995). The casualness with which these central questions are often phrased may also be misleading; interviewers try to create an informal atmosphere, which conceals the actual relationship of power and the roles of the examiner and the examined. For the applicant, the most important task is therefore to look beneath the surface of the interviewer's questions and to answer them in such a way as to make sure that their status on, and relevance to, the hidden agenda is adequately dealt with.

There is a considerable degree of incongruity between these genre expectations and those of everyday talk. To give a very simple example, positive self-assessments may be seen as self-praise, a dispreferred activity in everyday conversations. Yet in job interviews, not being willing to talk about one's own abilities and personal strengths not only means that a chance for positive self-presentation goes unused, it may even be perceived by the interviewers as an attempt to conceal negative aspects of one's personality or professional past.

Our results suggest that at least an important subgroup of east Germans are less able (or, perhaps, in some cases less willing) to recognize and deal with this hidden agenda than most west Germans of a comparable background and in applications for comparable jobs. These east Germans tend to transfer everyday structures of conversational organization and face-work into the job interview in cases where a more genre-specific behaviour would have been more appropriate, at least according to the western ways of 'playing the game'. In the following, I will give some examples.

Consider, for instance, this first example where the east German applicant has to deal with the standard interview question 'What are your strengths and weaknesses?' The applicant appears to be deeply puzzled by this question; much to his west German interviewers' amusement, he expresses his surprise at such an extraordinary and clever question by his *DES is=aber ne frage* ('what a question!').

(1) (N.2)²

> *I1*: WO liegen ihre STÄRken? (–) und wo meinen sie liegen ihre SCHWÄChen.
> –>*B*: <pp> DES is=aber ne frage;
> *I1*: das=ne FRAge. STIMMT=S, die is ihnen noch NIE begegnet.
> ((general amusement))
> *I1*: und dann kriegen sie sie HIER in IXberg zum erschten mal. (–) zu hören.
> *B*: nu ja. (was will mer) (–) darauf SAgen.
> *Interviewer 1*: What are your strengths? And what do you think are your weaknesses?
> *Applicant*: What a question!
> *Interviewer 1*: What a question, I know, you've never come across it before.
> ((General amusement among the interviewers.))
> And now you get to hear it for the first time ((here)) in X-Berg.
> *Applicant*: Well. (what can) you say.

If they do not have a stock of standard answers to standard questions such as this one at their disposal, interviewees may run into trouble when they formulate their answers spontaneously. For instance, the above applicant finally mentions as his main weakness the fact that he finds it hard to see a project through to a successful conclusion, which is a negative blow for his application:

(2) (N.2)

> *B*: es is manchmal (–) die mangelnde kontinuiTÄT. WÜRD ich mal sagen.=also daß man (–) sich EINfach mal (–) LÄNger; über

ne LÄNgere zeit; (2.5) dann (–) wenn also was' (.) was ANsteht;
dass man da nich intenSIV (–) auch TÄGlich sondern daß man
irgendwann mal noch mal ne PAUse einschiebt, das würd ich
SCHON sagen das is schon (eine schwäche)
Applicant: Sometimes there is a lack of continuity. That's what I
would say. That you ((=I)) just (keep working) longer, for a longer
period of time, in case something needs to be done. That you
(don't) intensively (–) also daily but that you have a break now and
then, well I would say this is certainly (a weak point).

Compare this with a west German applicant´s answer to the same
question by the same interviewer. He brings into play a personality
trait which is only relevant in his private sphere, thereby neutralizing
its potential to be used against him in the job interview:

(3) (N.3)

I1: <acc> haben sie auch SCHWÄChen?
B: (1.5) SCHWÄChen?
I1: <pp> mhm.
B: (ich) bin (.) ab und ZU etwas LAUnisch.
  ((general laughter))
Interviewer 1: Do you have any weaknesses?
Applicant: Weaknesses?
Interviewer 1: mhm
Applicant: Sometimes (I) am a little moody.
  ((general laughter))

A similar problem occurs in the following interview in response to
another standard question: 'What do you find particularly appealing
about the job you are applying for?' 'Playing the game' of the interview
requires an answer to this question which explains why the applicant
would love to work in this particular position for this particular
company, even though his/her only interest may be to get back into
employment. But only east German applicants express such a mis-
match between their true aims and the interviewer's question, as in the
following example:

(4) (VERSAND 4)

I3: was macht ihnen denn SPASS am verkaufen;
B: (1) tja (.) SPASS (.) hm (–) .h was macht mir SPASS; .h

I3: (1) weil sie grade SACHten das ! MÖCHT! ich ja auch (irgendwo).
B: ja ich will ja GELD verdienen; ja, (.) also wem=man GELD verdienen (will mußte ja) irgendwo: [was (.
I3:   ] ick kann ja
                                                        [mhm,
B: nich [daHIN] gehen, und (mich daHINstellen) und SAgen,
I1:   [mhm,]
B: (–) also LEUte ich mach das mal aus lauter SPA:SS. (–) [das mach
                                                            [mhm,
B: ich ja nu=NICH. e:h eh NUR (.) aus spaß. ich möcht ja och wat verDIEnen. .h
Interviewer 3: What do you like about selling? [literally: what makes selling fun for you?]
Applicant: Well, what do I like (–) hm (–) what do I like ...
Interviewer 3: Because you just said I would like to do it (somehow).
Applicant: Yes, I want to earn money you see? If you (want) to earn money, you (have to) somehow [what (–) I can't go [there and (be stood there) and say,
Interviewer 3:   [mhm
Interviewer 1:   [mhm
Applicant: well guys I'm doing this just for fun. [I wouldn't do that, just for fun
Interviewer 3:   [mhm
Applicant: I want to earn some money, don't I.

In her answers, the applicant does not operate in accordance with the regularities and structures of the job interview, but rather with those of everyday talk. Her answer is honest instead of strategic, but none the less fails to give the interviewer the kind of information he is after: he wants to find out what and how strong the applicant´s motivation for the job is. This may be due to the east German's lack of familiarity with the genre, but alternatively, it may also be a consequence of a lack of willingness to comply with it.

In the following extract, the interviewer again asks a standard question, which implies a complex play with perspectives. The interviewee is asked to speculate on how her colleagues would assess her professional abilities.

(5) (VERSAND 2)

I2: was würden die ((i.e., your colleagues)) SAgen, wenn wir sie FRAgen würden, was sie besonders an ihnen SCHÄTzen?

> B: h: joa. (0.5) das is=ne gute FRAge. (1) ((clicks tongue)) man muß
> EIGNtlich, wie jesacht, wie alle andern AUCH, PÜNKTlich sein,
> man muß na[türlich, .h (–) wie
> I2: [<pp>m:hm,
> B: jeSACHT, weil ja auch jeder seine arbeit HAT, seine KUNden,
> daß man dran intresSIERT is, diese alle ANzurufen, und .h (–) es
> hat ja JEder sein festes AUFgabengebiet. ne,
> ((omission))
> es is auch würklich:, (–) ne=tolle TEAMarbeit; MUSS ich sagen.
> also JEder [probiert da wirklich JEden zu helfen.
> I2: [<p>mhm, <p>mhm.
> *Interviewer 2*: What would they ((viz., your colleagues)) say if we
> asked them what they admire in you?
> *Applicant*: Well, that's a good question. ((clicks tongue)) As I said
> before, you have to be, well, on time, as all the others have to be
> too, of course you have [to be, as I said before,
> *Interviewer 2*: [mhm
> *Applicant*: because each of us has her own job, her own customers,
> so that you have an interest of your own in ringing them all up, and
> each of us has her specific area of work, you see.
> ((omission))
> It really is a good team, I have to say. Everybody [tries to help every-
> body, really.
> *Interviewer 2*: [mhm, mhm

The applicant is asked what her colleagues at work would say they
particularly appreciate in her work if asked. The purpose of the question is to elicit details about the applicant's personality and social
character by providing her with an opportunity to talk about herself
indirectly, thereby avoiding direct self-praise. Yet, in her answer, the
applicant seems to avoid taking the proposed perspective, referring
instead to qualities of the team as a whole, of which she is a part:
punctuality, reliability, the fact that everybody helps everybody else,
and so on. Of course, the interviewer is not satisfied with this reply. In
the following minutes of the interview (not reproduced here), he
insists on his original question, reformulating it several times and
trying to get the applicant to provide a satisfactory answer which
would focus on herself, not on the team, but all these attempts fail. To
him, at least, the problem was due to the east German interviewee's

lack of familiarity with the genre: after the job interview proper, he initiated a teaching sequence in which he explained to the applicant the status of the question in extract (5) on the hidden agenda of the interview.

In the examples discussed so far, lack of genre knowledge is certainly important, but it may not be the whole issue. Looking once more at the way in which the applicant in the last example fails to adopt the perspective suggested by the interviewer, it may be argued that in addition, a 'cultural' issue is involved. In fact, the applicant uses a topos which we regularly found in east Germans' answers of this kind. The answer is given in such a way as not to foreground the individual, but rather the team ('collective') of which the speaker was or is a part. The topos of mutual help and solidarity in the team indirectly answers the questions of the merits of the individual as well: his or her quality as an employee is not defined by her individual weaknesses and strengths, but rather by the very fact of fitting into the team, of sharing its aims and aspirations. This, in turn, was an extremely important part of East German work ethics before the *Wende*. (On this issue and the uses of the topos 'fits into the collective', cf. Keßler 1997.)

Cultural differences certainly are involved in extract (4), in which the (western) topos 'fun at work' (*Spaß bei der Arbeit*) is explicitly rejected by the East German applicant as not applicable to the economic sphere (for details, see Auer, Birkner and Kern 1997; Birkner forthcoming). The applicant indicates that the materialistic basis of work as an employee would only be camouflaged by the notion of 'fun'. Recourse to the materialistic basis of society is a vulgarized element of Marxist theory, which seems to have made its way into the everyday culture of the GDR.

The list of inconsistencies between the western definition of the genre (represented by the interviewers) and the east Germans' performances is of course not complete. What I wanted to demonstrate on the basis of only a handful of examples is that east German performances sometimes conform more with everyday rules of conversational conduct (dispreference for self-praise, dispreference for disagreement, particularly in hierarchical contexts) than with those of the genre in question. In addition, more general features of the east German life-world, of the applicants' experiences in their previous, pre-*Wende* careers, and even of the *Weltanschauung* of the GDR in general may have an influence on their verbal performance in the job interview.

The diachrony of change

Focusing on differences and problems, as we did in the previous section, suggests that there are no commonalities between east and west Germans. Of course, this is not true. Communicative differences between east and west Germans are minor in many areas of the speech ecology, and a great amount of conversational work involving east and west Germans, in non-institutional but also in institutional encounters, is perfectly unproblematic. This leads to the question of the location of change within this ecology: which of the east Germans' communicative practices have undergone change in recent years, and which have remained the same? Some suggestions will be presented in this section, based on a comparison of semi-official genres before and after the *Wende*: that is, genres that are not part of everyone's daily life, but not strictly beyond the reach of 'the normal citizen' either (such as political speeches or media performances). I will restrict myself to stylistic issues in the more narrow sense of the term; in other words, the selection of linguistic structures.

If we take the job interviews (certainly a semi-official genre in this sense) as the most recent state of affairs (representing the year 1994/5), the problem is to find older comparable data from the time shortly after and before the *Wende*. As to the former, I will compare the authentic job interviews with role-played job interviews recorded in eastern Germany three years earlier (in 1992). It is not only the year of the recordings which makes this data different from the authentic material: the role-playing speakers, who participated in a training programme, were unemployed former 'leading cadres'; they were, on average, older than those in the authentic data; and they had had hardly any contact with west Germany, let alone lived there for some time (as was the case with some of the authentic applicants). Of course, they had not been pre-selected on the basis of written records for the training programme either, which obviously was the case with the authentic interviews. For many reasons, language use in the role-played interviews can therefore be expected to be less convergent with west German practices and to reflect more strongly pre-*Wende* features.

The more severe problem is to document language use in the times before the *Wende*, since published authentic speech data is very rare. There is, however, an important (though not completely unproblematic) data source: the book *Reise nach Rostock, DDR* compiled by Erika Runge, a West German journalist and writer, in 1971.[3] Herself a member of the West German Communist Party, Runge was allowed to travel to Rostock in 1970, and to talk to and record citizens of the GDR who, although carefully selected for her by the SED, came from very different parts of East German society. Since the stylistic level seems to have been edited very little, the book is an excellent document of semi-official language use in the GDR.

In the following discussion, I shall give an unsystematic and selective list of some particularly striking stylistic features in Runge's interviews, which clearly set them apart from West German language use in similar situations. State-and-party-language in the strict sense of the word (political vocabulary and idioms) is of course not considered.[4]

Selected stylistic features in Runge's interviews

First of all, there is widespread use of the first person plural possessive pronoun *unser* (our) with nouns denoting institutions, concepts and social organizations (claimed to be typical) of the GDR (including, of course, references to the state itself), such as in extract (6) (and also in extract (7)):

(6)

daß Sie sich hier vor einem Gesellschaftlichen Gericht befinden, das gemäß Artikel 92 *unserer* Verfassung von den Bürgern *unseres* Staates, speziell von den Bürgern *unserer* Stadt, vorgeschlagen und vom Stadtparlament gewählt wurde ... Wir stellen hohe Anforderungen an *unsere* Jugend.

(Chairman of the mediation committee/Schiedsgericht, addressing a delinquent, p. 155)

(that you are here before a Social Court which in accordance with paragraph 92 of *our* constitution has been proposed by the citizens of *our* state, particularly by the citizens of *our* city, and elected by the city parliament ... We place high demands on *our* youth.)

This pervasive usage of the first person plural possessive pronoun was a well-known feature of official language use in the GDR (cf. Bergmann 1992:136), taken from the corresponding style of Russian used in the Soviet Union. Its typical East German flavour derives from the fact that it makes explicit and underscores a relation of ownership which is contextually determined anyway and does not actually need to be stated.

Second, routine formulae containing the modal verbs *können* (can) or *mögen* (would like to) plus the infinitive *sagen* (say) are frequently employed to introduce or structure speakers' turns:

(7)

> Wir haben in unserer Republik noch einen großen Mittelstand … *Und ich möchte sagen,* die Aufgabe der Liberal-Demokratischen Partei ist es, den Mittelstand mit einzubeziehen in den Aufbau, also in den Aufbau des Sozialismus. (owner of a furniture factory, p. 75)
> (We still have a large middle class in our republic … *And I would like to say,* the duty of the Liberal Democratic Party is to include the middle class in the building, well, the building of socialism.)

These routines are semantically empty, but in addition to structuring turns, their conversational function may also be related to processes of planning. At the same time (and possibly for the same reason), they add to the speaker's turn a connotation of institutional talk, suitable for recording directly in the minutes of a meeting.

Third, another striking feature is the avoidance of the feminine suffix *-in* in names of professions when reference is made to a woman:

(8)

> Meine Frau ist *Wirtschaftsleiter* beim RDGB-Feriendienst (city mayor, p. 119)
> (instead of West German *Wirtschaftsleiterin*)
> (My wife is a manager at the RDGB (= a trade union) holiday service)

This difference between East and West German language use was perhaps more pronounced in mundane talk than in the official jargon of the GDR. Nevertheless, it is based on a certain *Weltanschauung* linked to the GDR, according to which the non-use of the feminine suffix is a consequence of equal rights granted to men and women in socialist society, and indicates that gender does not matter (cf. Sobotta 1997).

Fourth, as part of the somewhat baroque style of the official jargon, rhetorical doublets (more or less synonymous pairs of adjectives, nouns, verbs or adverbs, conjoined by *und*) occurred frequently. These doublets are amply documented in written and spoken GDR documents of a political and non-political nature, and they also appear in the Runge interviews (for further comments and bibliographical references, see Birkner and Kern 1996:9ff):

(9)

> [Die Sektionsräte] haben die Aufgabe, den Sektionsdirektor in seiner Arbeit *zu beraten und zu unterstützen* und setzen sich aus Angehörigen

der Sektion und aus bewährten Vertretern der Praxis, der jeweiligen entsprechenden Praxis zusammen, um auch hier den Einfluß der Gesellschaft *sichtbar und deutlich* zu machen (university professor, p. 323).
(The section councils have the task of *advising and supporting* the director of the section in his activities and are composed of members of the section and of reliable representatives of the practical domain, of the relevant domain of practice, in order to make the influence of society *visible and clear* here too.)

Fifth, the format *den Beruf des ...*/*die Funktion eines X haben/ausüben* (to have or carry out the job or function of X) instead of simply *X sein* (to be an X), was widely used to refer to occupations and social functions. The main stylistic effect is the same as in the rhetorical doublets: amplification through material not necessary on grammatical or semantic grounds:

(10)

> seitdem bin ich hier auf der Werft und lerne *den Beruf* als Rohrleitungsmonteur (apprentice, p. 66)
> (since then I have been here in the shipyard and have been learning *the trade* of a pipe fitter

Sixth, simple syntactic forms were avoided and replaced by more complex ones, with the result that utterances sound more momentous, even pompous. An example is the use of so-called *Funktionsverbgefüge*, a complex predicate, where simple verbs would also be available:

(11)

> dieser Hafen hat ... einen Umschlag von 8,2 Tonnen *vollzogen*
> (secretary of the Rat des Bezirks [city council], p. 13)
> (instead of: *hat 8,2 Tonnen umgeschlagen*, handled 8.2 tons)
> (This harbour has ... completed handling a volume of traffic of 8.2 tons)

Seventh, syntactic complexity (and formality) was also achieved through nominalizations. In all official written documents of the GDR, these nominalizations abounded, but the Runge interviews are full of examples, too:

(12)

> wird die gegenseitige Hilfe und Zusammenarbeit aller Bürger durch den Wohnbezirksausschuß als wichtige Aufgabe in Angriff genom-

men, um neue *Impulse zur Entfaltung der sozialistischen Gemeinschaft
zu geben.* (employee, p. 215; note also the further examples of a
rhetorical doublet and a complex predicate)
(mutual support and cooperation of all citizens will be taken on
board as an important task by the district housing committee,
in order to give a new *impetus to the development of the socialist
community.*)

As a consequence of this rather convoluted, stiff and pretentious way
of speaking, and as a result of the attempt to attain a hyperformal
stylistic level, solecisms and verbal derailments are unavoidable.

Stylistic features in role-played job interviews

In the role-played job interviews (which were also recorded in
Rostock), most of these features persist, although some of them are less
frequent than in Runge's *Reise nach Rostock.*

First of all, the excessive usage of the first person plural possessive
pronoun for GDR institutions must be seen in the context of the
themes of Runge´s interviews. Often her interviewees talked about the
institutions of their state which they explained to the western interviewer. In the role-played job interviews, this was not the case. The
'East German' possessive pronoun occurred only once in our data, and
it was immediately self-repaired by the speaker (which may indicate
the relatively conscious status of this feature and its out-of-place use):

(13) (Ros II 6m)
I1: <<pp> mhm> ja=also (.) eh (–) die sozialen: LEIStungen bestehen
halt darin daß wir: (–) eine beTRIEBSeigene (–) TAgesstätte
haben, (.) für *unsere* KINder, also nicht für UNsere kinder
sondern für die kinder der ANgestellten?
(*Interviewer 1*: OK, um, our social benefits are that we have a day care
centre of our own, for *our* children, well not for our children but for
the employees' children.)

Second, in a few cases, the *ich möchte/kann sagen* routine occurred:

(14) (Ros II.4)
B: eh (–) *ich möchte EIgentlich SAgen* daß: (.) gerade diese strecke[5] mir
LIEgen würde weil ich eigentlich GERne auch mit (.) ÄLteren
MENschen (.) umgeh; (1) eh (–) DA (.) sehe ich (.) von meiner
seite aus keine proBLEme.

(*Applicant*: Um *I would like to say* that it is precisely this kind of work that would suit me because, you see, I like dealing with older people; um, I don't see any problem there as far as I am concerned.)

Third, references to functions and jobs using expressions such as *der Beruf des .../die Funktion eines* occur on various occasions:

(15) (Ros II.6m)

B: eh=habe bei der deutsche SEEreederei, (.) geLERNT? (.) *den beRUF eines* maSCHInenbetriebsschlossers, (–) mith (–) abiTUR?

(*Applicant*: At the German Sea Shipping Company I learned *the trade* of industrial machine fitter with a grammar school diploma.)

Fourth, simple syntactic expressions are avoided wherever possible (cf. the detailed investigation of this point in Auer 1998). Consider, for example, the complex verbal predicate in this extract:

(16) (Ros. I.2)

B: ich habe: ehm (–) schon während meiner BUNdeswehrzeit? (.) *ins auge gefaßt?* (.) ehm; (–) mit meiner frau mich SELBStändig zu machen?

(instead of: *ich wollte* ... 'I wanted to ...')

(*Applicant*: During my time in the army I um already had my sights on um (–) becoming self-employed with my wife.)

Fifth, nominal style predominates and leads to a high level of formality; self-repairs of less complex (nominalized, formal) expressions by substituting more complex (nominalized, formal) ones indicate that speakers quite consciously aim at reaching a 'high' stylistic level (cf. again Auer 1998 for details):

(17) (Ros II.9k)

B: JA:. (–) zu meinen STÄRken, (.) zähl ich EIgentlich; (–) eh proBLEme; (.) systeMAtisch. (–) anzugehn, (.) (ich sag mal,) (–) UND; (–) eh (.) *NACH; AUFfinden (.) von geeigneten LÖsungen diese dann auch konsequent (–) DURCHzusetzen.*

(*Applicant*: OK, as one of my strong points I would consider approaching problems in a systematic way, (let me say) and um, after finding suitable solutions, implementing them systematically.)

And as in the Runge interviews, this excessive formality may lead to malapropisms and derailments.

All in all, stylistic convergence towards a West German style seems to be moderate in the Rostock interviews. An explanation of this small degree of accommodation would require a more detailed discussion than is possible here (cf. Auer 1998), but several issues can be identified. First of all, as mentioned above, most participants in the training programme had had little exposure to Western semi-formal genres and the verbal styles they require. Second, the persistence of features which are in some way or other related to formality suggests that the hierarchical character of the job interview is reflected directly in the east Germans' way of speaking. Third, there is evidence that in selecting style features appropriate for hierarchical situations, the east Germans draw upon resources imported from other, neighbouring genres which they are familiar with from pre-*Wende* times (that is, of the GDR state-and-party discourse).

Stylistic features in authentic job interviews

Finally, let us have a look at the authentic job interviews. Here important changes have occurred.

1 The typically East German usage of the possessive pronoun is absent.
2 The *ich möchte sagen* routine is also lacking completely.
3 Female speakers normally use feminine forms to refer to themselves; this is remarkable and indicates the hegemonic character of the job interview, since in everyday conversations east German women often continue to use the 'old' form. Only one example of the 'East German masculine form' was found, and was self-repaired by the speaker shortly afterwards (concealed by a repair on the content level):

(18) (Versand 4)

> B: geLERNT hab i:ch *texTILfacharbeiter-* (1) in CE-stadt
>   ((omission of ca. 10 lines))
>   !NEIN!; (–) enTSCHULjin sie bitte- (–) das muß ich n=biß
>   [chen zuRÜCK
> I3: [MACHT nix
> B: <<acc>ich war> (.) *texTILverkäuferin. verKÄUferin* war ich. .hh
> I2:   mhm,
> (*Applicant*: I was trained as a *skilled textile worker*, in C-town
>   ((omission))
> No! I´m sorry, now I have to go [back a little.
> *Interviewer 3*:   [never mind.

Applicant: I was a *textile saleswoman*. I was a *saleswoman*.
Interviewer 2: mhm.)

4 Rhetorical doublets have disappeared entirely.

5 The frame *der Beruf/die Position des X* is only used (twice) by one of
the 20 East German applicants:

(19) (V&W 4)

B: <<acc,mf> ich ging drei jahre nach schweRIN,> (.) erlernte dort
den beruf des (.) MAUrers, .h (.) und legte gleichzeitig mein abiTUR
ab?
(1.0)
((schluckt))
I1: wie kommen sie (zu) zum MAUrerberuf?
(*Applicant*: I went to Schwerin for three years. There I learned *the
trade of bricklayer*, and at the same time, I took my grammar school
exams.
((gulps))
Interviewer: How did you come to be a bricklayer?)
[Note the reformulation in the interviewer´s follow-up question:
Beruf des Mauers becomes *Maurerberuf*.]

6 Only in a small subgroup of applicants in the authentic interviews
(three out of 20) does the tendency to replace simple expressions by
more complex ones continue to feature. Consider the following
example of a *Funktionsverbgefüge*:

(20) (V & W 4)

B: ((...)) wo[rauf eh] ich immer
I1:   [((clears throat))]
B: immer noch beSTREBT war, war !NEBen! dem studium, (1,5)
doch=*en gewissen PRAxis;(.)bezug; (–) HERzustellen?*
(instead of: *mich auf die Praxis zu beziehen, praktisch tätig zu sein*)
(*Applicant*: What continued to be my aspiration was to establish a
link to practical issues alongside of my studies.)

7 Only with these same speakers do we also find the trend towards
hyper-formal, nominalized expressions. For example:

(21) (Log 3)

> *B*: und das heißt also WEM=man dann: eh; wenn die zeit (.)
> ABgelaufen <<cresc>WÄre-> eh (.) gibt es dann ANdre
> *möglichkeiten eines EINsatzes in dieser firma?*
> (*Applicant*: so this means when you would um (–) when the time ran
> out, would there be another possibility of employment in your
> company?)

Comparison of the three sources

By way of summary, Table 10.1 gives an overview of the East German
stylistic features found in the Runge interviews, the use of these same
features in the 1992 role-played job interviews, and their use in the
authentic interviews of 1994/95.

The overview shows that the loss of typical East German stylistic features certainly did not occur abruptly in 1989/1990, and certainly not in

Table 10.1   Frequency of occurrence of 'East German' stylistic features in three
sources

	Runge interviews 1970	Role plays 1992	Job interviews 1994/1995
1st person pl. poss. pronoun	very frequent	rare (?)	absent (?)
ich kann/möchte sagen-routine	very frequent	occasionally used	absent
masc. forms for names of professions used by female speakers	very frequent	very frequent	rare
rhetorical doublets	very frequent	frequent	absent
der Beruf/die Funktion des/der ... formula	very frequent	occasionally used	rare
complex syntax: *Funktionsverbgefüge*	frequent	very frequent	in only 3 out of 20 speakers
complex syntax: nominalizations	frequent	very frequent	in only 3 out of 20 speakers

the speech of all east Germans to the same degree. While the 1992 role-played job interviews are similar to the pre-*Wende* data in many respects, the 1995 job interviews show a completely different picture; most of the East German features have disappeared or only appear very infrequently.

Conclusion

We began with the questions of where, to what degree, and how the appropriation of western verbal practices has been taking place in speakers brought up in East Germany. Is there anything like an East German linguistic identity left? Or have all East German traits been given up in favour of the linguistic practices of the west, and/or in favour of new regional features (such as the regional varieties of Saxony, Mecklenburg, and so on)? Insofar as our investigations of (job) interviews with east and west Germans permit us to answer these questions, the results suggest that important differences continue to exist in certain parts of the east German speech ecology, some of which have to do with a lack of specific genre knowledge, others with stylistic resources taken over from pre-*Wende* GDR verbal practices and their 'cultural' underpinnings. But there is also evidence that these pre-*Wende* practices – in particular those on the stylistic level (in the narrow sense) – are being lost, at least in those parts of east German society in which hegemonic pressure from the west is strongest.

Notes

1   Of course, not every west German knows how to act as an applicant in a job interview equally well. In fact, performance in the job interview is subject to explicit teaching and training, and perfection is hard to achieve.
2   All transcriptions follow the GAT-conventions ('Gesprächsanalytisches Transkriptionssytem', cf. Selting *et al.* 1998). Symbols used here:

(2.5)	2.5 seconds pause
(–)	short pause
(.)	very short pause
EINfach	loud, heavily stressed syllable
!MÖCHT!	very heavily stressed syllable
<pp>	very quiet passage
=	running words together
[was	words spoken simultaneously
[mhm	
(ich glaube)	unclear; likely wording
<acc>	becoming faster
.h	breathing in

English translations are simplified

3 Runge became famous in West Germany in the late sixties as the author of the *Bottroper Protokolle,* the best-known example of the so-called protocol literature: a technique of interviewing people in a certain social field and editing and arranging their (mostly autobiographical) answers while treating their way of presenting themselves with due respect ('ihre Selbstdarstellungen zu respektieren': Runge 1971:7).
4 Runge's method of editing her texts is described in Schröder (1995). There is no reason to believe that she added East German stylistic features to her data, which was after all intended to be read by West Germans. (The book was not published or available in the GDR.) She may have omitted some of the most bureaucratic-sounding passages, however.
5 A GDR word for *Aufgabe* (task) or *Tätigkeitsfeld* (professional field).

References

Adelswård,Viveka (1988) 'Styles of Success', PhD Thesis, University of Linköping.

Apfelbaum, Birgit and Helga Kotthoff (eds) (forthcoming) *Kultur(en) im Gespräch* (Opladen: Westdeutscher Verlag).

Apfelbaum, Birgit and Herrmann Müller (eds) (1998) *Fremde im Gespräch* (Frankfurt/Main: Verlag für Interkulturelle Kommunikation).

Auer, Peter (1998) 'Learning how to play the game. An investigation of role-played job interviews in East Germany', in *Text* 18/1, 7–38.

Auer, Peter, Karin Birkner and Friederike Kern (1997) 'Wörter – Formeln – Argumente. Was in Bewerbungsgesprächen 'Spaß' macht', in Barz and Fix (1997), 213–32.

Barz, Irmhild (1997) 'Was ich kann und wie ich bin. Individualitätsgewinn und Identitätsverlust beim Umgang mit Berufen und ihren Bezeichnungen', in Barz and Fix (1997), 75–91.

Barz, Irmhild and Ulla Fix (eds) (1997) *Deutsch-deutsche Kommunikationserfahrungen im arbeitsweltlichen Alltag* (Heidelberg: Winter).

Bergmann, Christian (1992) 'Parteisprache und Parteidenken. Zum Sprachgebrauch des ZK der SED', in Lerchner (1992b), 101–65.

Birkner, Karin (1998) '"Normalerweise sagt man da ...". Gattungsnormen im Bewerbungsgespräch', in Apfelbaum and Müller (1998), 241–62.

Birkner, Karin (forthcoming) 'Ost- und Westdeutsche im Bewerbungsgespräch: Ein Fall von Interkultureller Kommunikation?', in Apfelbaum and Kotthoff (forthcoming).

Birkner, Karin and Friederike Kern (1996) 'Deutsch-deutsche Reparaturversuche. Alltagsrhetorische Gestaltungsverfahren ostdeutscher Sprecherinnen und Sprecher im westdeutschen Aktivitätstyp "Bewerbungsgespräch"', in *GAL-Bulletin. Zeitschrift für angewandte Linguistik* 25, 53–76.

Birkner, Karin and Friederike Kern (forthcoming) 'Impression management in east and west German job interviews', in Spencer-Oatey (forthcoming).

Drew, Paul and John C. Heritage (eds) (1992) *Talk at Work. Interaction in Institutional Settings* (Cambridge: Cambridge University Press).

Fix, Ulla (1992) 'Rituelle Kommunikation im öffentlichen Sprachgebrauch der DDR und ihre Begleitumstände', in Lerchner (1992b), 3–85.

Fix, Ulla (1994) 'Sprache vor und nach der "Wende". "Gewendete" Texte – "gewendete" Textsorten', in Heringer *et al.* (1994), 131–48.

Fix, Ulla (1995) 'Texte mit doppeltem Boden? Diskursanalytische Untersuchung inklusiver und exklusiver personenbeurteilender Texte im Kommunikationskontext der DDR', in Wodak and Kirsch (1995), 71–92.

Fraas, Claudia and Kathrin Steyer (1992) 'Sprache der Wende – Wende der Sprache? Beharrungsvermögen und Dynamik von Strukturen im öffentlichen Sprachgebrauch', in *Deutsche Sprache* 2, 172–84.

Günthner, Susanne and Hubert Knoblauch (1995) 'Culturally patterned speaking practices – the analysis of communicative genres', in *Pragmatics* 5/1, 1–32.

Hellmann, Manfred (1989) 'Zwei Gesellschaften – zwei Sprachkulturen? Acht Thesen zur öffentlichen Sprache in der Bundesrepublik Deutschland und in der Deutschen Demokratischen Republik', in *Forum für interdisziplinäre Forschung* 2/2, 27–38.

Heringer, Hans Jürgen, Gunhild Samson, Michel Kauffmann and Wolfgang Bader (eds), (1994) *Tendenzen der deutschen Gegenwartssprache* (Tübingen: Niemeyer).

Kauke, Wilma (1997) 'Politische Rituale als Spiegelbild des Gesellschaftlichen. Die Kommunikationskonstellation des Rituals 'Jugendweihe' in der DDR und seine Entwicklung nach der Wende', in Barz and Fix (1997), 367–78.

Kern, Friederike (1998) '"Kultur im Gespräch" – Lebensläufe in Bewerbungsgesprächen', in Apfelbaum and Müller, 219–40.

Keßler, Christine (1997) '"...und fügt sich gut ins Kollektiv ein" – Muster personenbeurteilender Texte in der DDR', in Barz and Fix (1997), 303–14.

Knapp, Karlfried, Werner Enninger and Annelie Knapp-Potthoff (eds) (1987) *Analyzing Intercultural Communication* (Berlin: Mouton de Gruyter).

Kühn, Ingrid (1995) 'Alltagssprachliche Textsortenstile', in Stickel (1995), 328–54.

Lerchner, Gotthard (1992a) 'Broiler, Plast(e) und Datsche machen noch nicht den Unterschied. Fremdheit und Toleranz in einer plurizentrischen deutschen Kommunikationskultur', in Lerchner (1992b), 297–332.

Lerchner, Gotthard (ed.) (1992b) *Sprachgebrauch im Wandel. Anmerkungen zur Kommunikationskultur in der DDR vor und nach der Wende* (Frankfurt/Main: Lang).

Levinson, Stephen C. (1992) 'Activity types and language', in Drew and Heritage (1992), 66–100.

Luckmann, Thomas (1986) 'Grundformen der gesellschaftlichen Vermittlung des Wissens: Kommunikative Gattungen', in *Kölner Zeitschrift für Soziologie und Sozialpsychologie* 27, 191–211.

Luckmann, Thomas (1988) 'Kommunikative Gattungen im kommunikativen "Haushalt" einer Gesellschaft', in Smolka-Koerdt, Spangenberg and Tillmann-Bartylla (1988), 279–88.

Müller, Gerhard (1994) 'Der 'Besserwessi' und die innere Mauer', in *Muttersprache* 2, 118–36.

Roberts, Celia (1985) *The Interview Game and How It´s Played* (London: BBC).

Roberts, Celia and Srikant Sarangi (1995) '"But are they one of us?": Managing and evaluating identities in work-related contexts', in *Multilingua* 14/4, 363–90.

Roberts, Celia and Pete Sayers (1987) 'Keeping the gate: how judgements are made in intercultural interviews', in Knapp, Enninger and Knapp-Potthoff (1987), 111–35.

Runge, Erika (1971) *Reise nach Rostock*, DDR (Frankfurt/Main: Suhrkamp).

Sarangi, Srikant (1994) 'Accounting for mismatches in intercultural selection interviews', in *Multilingua* 13, 1/2, 163–94.

Schröder, Hans Joachim (1995) 'Interviewliteratur zum Leben in der DDR', in *Internationales Archiv für Sozialgeschichte der deutschen Literatur*, 20/1, 67–115.

Selting, Margret *et al.* (1998) 'Gesprächsanalytisches Transkriptionssystem', in *Linguistische Berichte* 34/173, 91–122.

Smolka-Koerdt, G., Peter M. Spangenberg and Dagmar Tillmann-Bartylla (eds) (1988) *Der Ursprung der Literatur* (Munich: Fink).

Sobotta, Kirsten (1997) 'Texte über Frauen in der Köthener Tageszeitung der 80er Jahre', in Barz and Fix (1997), 173–80.

Spencer-Oatey, Helen (ed.) (forthcoming) *Culturally Speaking: Managing Relations in Talk across Cultures* (London: Cassell).

Stickel, Gerhard (ed.) (1995) *Stilfragen* (Berlin, New York: de Gruyter).

Wodak, Ruth and Fritz Peter Kirsch (eds) (1995), *Totalitäre Sprache – Langue de bois – Language of Dictatorship* (Vienna: Passagen Verlag).

11
Arriving at Identities: Positioning of Speakers in German Television Talk Shows[1]

Grit Liebscher

Introduction

This chapter focuses on Germanness as the social space emergent in conversation through the intersection of personal and national identities. I argue along with Bakhtin that the utterance is a promising site for an analysis of national identity because '[t]he very problem of the national and the individual in language is basically the problem of the utterance' (1986:63). My chapter is based on an analysis of interactions among eastern and western Germans on talk shows in eastern and western Germany between 1989 and 1995. The aim of this analysis is to aid our understanding of German identities and their changes since the fall of the Wall in 1989.

In these interactions, certain lexico-grammatical entities, namely *deictics*, position speaker and audience in regard to concepts of German national identities. Deictics (for example, *we* and *here*) are a group of words whose referents always change with the setting. While deictics appear in all kinds of speech events, the deictics I will discuss can be more narrowly defined as a linguistic inventory in reference to political and cultural social spaces. This inventory is a resource with which speakers of any national community can refer to their communities. Through use in daily interactions, the relationship between these deictics and their referents becomes naturalized for speakers of a community and sets these speakers apart from members of other communities referred to as *they* and *there*. Deictics take on 'relative meanings', that is, meanings which are motivated for the speakers of a community.

The deictics I will discuss in this chapter are pronouns (for example, *we*), adverbs (for example, *here*) and verbs of motion (for example, *go over there*). Before the fall of the Wall, people of the GDR and the Federal Republic used the same pronoun *wir* (we) and the same adverb *hier* (here) to name their respective communities. Prior to 1989, the 'mirror-image' or 'moiety' relationship between the two countries (Borneman 1992) nurtured contexts when *sie* (they) and *drüben* (over there) were used to mean only the other German state, rather than any other foreign country. One of these contexts was talk about arrivals of individuals in the two states, in which the motion verbs *rübergehen* (to go over there) and *rüberkommen* (to come over here) were employed in describing these arrivals. Going from the GDR to the Federal Republic had different connotations from going in the other direction, namely from the Federal Republic to the GDR. The first direction often implied an immigration process while the latter did not.

I argue that, while these arrivals took place before 1989, talk about them after 1989 constructs eastern and western social spaces. This is the case because individual speakers project the past through their identities onto the present utterance. Deictic pronouns, adverbs and motion verbs receive double meanings of past and present social spaces through the speaker and the location of the talk. The first point of my argument is that deictics position speakers of eastern and western Germany in talk in relation to social spaces because these deictics inhibit 'relative meanings' of past communities. In talk, these relative meanings appear as 'perspectives', defined by Sandig (1996:37) as 'Repräsentation von etwas für jemanden von einer gegebenen Position aus' (representation of something for somebody from a certain perspective: my translation). Perspectives in my data are realized as different kinds of 'Germanness'; they result from speakers identifying themselves in relation to German identities.

The second point of my argument concerns the referential aspect of these deictics. *Here* and *there* are called locative-deictic adverbs in linguistic theory, thus stressing their reference to place. Based on evidence from my data, I argue that these adverbs can lose their anchoring in geographic location. Instead, these deictic adverbs can refer to conceptual social spaces indexing different concepts of German identity. Similarly, motion verbs can denote moves between social spaces: that is, conceptual arrivals as opposed to physical arrivals. The former are moves in time rather than space, of which the change into a unified Germany is an example.

While the unification of Germany in October 1990 marks a historical date, this was neither the beginning nor the end of the process of unifying the people from eastern and western Germany, and the arrivals documented in talk present a more differentiated picture about the kinds of social spaces conceptualized as 'Germanness'.

Data

German television talk show data turned out to be fascinating material for investigating the intersection between personal and national identity, and specifically the shaping of new German national identities starting in 1989. After 1989, talk show culture in the Federal Republic radically changed by starting to be produced in and broadcast from cities in the GDR and later eastern Germany. As a result, the talk show community changed. Though the production team was still almost exclusively from western Germany, people from eastern Germany were invited as panel guests and partially or fully formed the studio audience, depending on the city chosen as the production site. The audience watching western German television programmes had always included people in eastern Germany, even before 1989. This audience, which television stations in the Federal Republic were able to treat as 'overhearers' from another country before 1989, received an active status after 1989 when the thematic focus of talk shows was predominantly on the future of the two German states and thus also on people in the eastern German community.

Among the talk shows recorded between 1989 and 1990, only a handful were produced by the two GDR television stations Fernsehen DDR 1 and Fernsehen DDR 2. One such talk show was *elf 99*, which grew out of a show with the same title intended for young people and produced and broadcast in the GDR before 1989. With German unification in October 1990, the television landscape in eastern Germany changed as the GDR stations ceased to exist. MDR was founded as a new station serving the southern area of eastern Germany, and my data include talk shows produced by MDR in Dresden, a city in Saxony, eastern Germany, between 1992 and 1994. On these talk shows, studio and television audiences are predominantly from eastern Germany, while equal numbers of panel guests are from western and eastern Germany. The most interesting participants for my analysis, however, are talk show hosts from western Germany hired by MDR. As I will demonstrate in the analysis later, their physical location in eastern Germany conflicts with their 'habitus', a term introduced by Bourdieu (1977, 1991), which can be defined as the 'dynamic intersection of structure and action, society and individual' (Postone, LiPuma and Calhoun 1993b:4).

Methodology

My analysis of talk is strongly influenced by conversation analysis (Schegloff, Sacks and Jefferson, among others). This method was begun by analysts who observed audio- and videotaped material of talk as the exchange of utterances between two or more speakers. In search of systematic structures in the organization of talk, conversation analysts pay close attention to pauses, overlaps between speakers, gesture and eye gaze, as well as the selection of lexical items and grammatical structures from a set of alternatives available to the speaker.[2]

In the following analysis, I pay attention to conversational details because I believe they allow us to understand the relationship between the individual and the social world. I subscribe to a recent trend among conversation analysts who are interested in the social meaning of talk (Goodwin 1990, Keating 1998). This trend is subject to an understanding of talk as social activity where speakers' knowledge about the social world is 'contextualized' in talk.[3] If talk is contextualized by the speakers themselves, the context necessarily becomes part of the interaction, and an analysis of talk reveals which aspects of context become relevant to participants.

As I am first and foremost interested in this contextualized talk, my analysis will focus on who says what to whom, when and where, and how speakers define themselves with regard to their audience and location. For each of the data segments presented in the next section of this chapter, I will therefore include information on the place and date of the show, the kind of audience(s), participants, and information on the social context at the time of speaking. I make this information part of my analysis because I can assume that this knowledge is also available to the speakers themselves. In the analysis, I will also pay attention to the times that speakers talk about, which is reflected grammatically in the tenses they use in their utterances.

Data analysis

Introduction

In this part of the chapter, I discuss several data segments from some of the German talk shows described above. These segments are in chronological order starting with 1989 and ending with 1995 in order to better identify the directions of change in conceptualizing Germanness. The common element in all data segments is the motif of *arrival* in talk. Besides arrival as a focus in talk, arrivals of speakers at the setting, in other words their physical relocation, contextualize this talk.

Speakers' positions and change of relative meanings

Data segment 1 is from the N3 talk show *III nach 9* from 10 November 1989, one day after the fall of the Wall. The major point I want to discuss is that the talk show host from the Federal Republic positions himself figuratively in the GDR. The segment is also evidence of changing 'relative meanings' of lexical items since 1989.

The talk show takes place in Bremen in the Federal Republic. The talk show host speaks to two panel guests, Wolfgang Lippert, a singer from the GDR, and Kirsten Lippert, his wife. Lippert was already in the Federal Republic for the production of the show, and the fall of the Wall took him by surprise. His wife was then invited to come on the show, now that travel to the Federal Republic was possible. The segment contains a narrative account about the previous night when the Wall was opened for travel from the GDR to the Federal Republic.

Data segment 1:[4] N3 *III nach 9*, 10 November 1989

TS1	talk show host (Giovanni di Lorenzo, from the Federal Republic)
L	Wolfgang Lippert (singer, from the GDR)
K	Kirsten Lippert (Lippert's wife, from the GDR)

1 L: ja ich habe heute – ich war ja eigentlich zufällig *hier*
       yes I did today – I just happened to be *here*
2   und eh (0.1) wie gesagt deswegen tuts mir auch leid,
       and uh (0.1) as I said that's why I really regret
3   ich wäre lieber *zuhause* mitten im gewühl wo frauen in
       I would rather be *at home* in the middle of it all where
       women in
4   unter-eh in eh   [in (0.1) nachthemden an der grenze stehen
       underw-uh in uh   [in (0.1) nightgowns stand at the border
5 K: [nachthemden
                        [nightgowns
6 TS1: und wärst *rüber*gegangen
       and you would have gone *across* [the border]
7 L: un eh ich wär *rüber*gegangen auch un *hin und her* und hätte
       an uh I would have gone across the border and *back and forth*
8   mich irgendwo hingesetzt und zugeguckt
       and would have sat somewhere and watched

In lines 1–3, Lippert sets up a dichotomy of places: *hier* (here) and *zuhause* (at home). The place formulation *zuhause* is not simply a reference to place but also describes the relationship between L and the place: L identifies himself as a person from the GDR. Although *here*, the Federal Republic as the place of speaking, is geographically closer, L positions himself emotionally closer to *there*, the GDR as his *zuhause* (home). The 'point of view' or 'empathy structure' (Kuno 1987)[5] positions L in the GDR.

The same 'point of view' is employed by the talk show host TS1 in line 6: *und wärst rübergegangen* (and you would have gone across), describing in the subjunctive L's hypothetical crossing the border from the GDR into the Federal Republic. The verb *rübergehen* (to go across) positions TS1 in the social space of the GDR because *gehen* (to go) highlights the departure from the GDR. By taking L's point of view, TS1 does not adhere to the perspective of his audience in Bremen, for whom *rüberkommen* (come across) would highlight the arrival in the Federal Republic, which would also position him, someone from the Federal Republic, in the social space Federal Republic. Instead, he adjusts his point of view to the GDR perspective.

Considering that TS1 is the talk show host and L is the guest, TS1 adopts the perspective of his guest, which can be seen as a 'positive face strategy' (Brown and Levinson 1987). Scollon and Scollon (1995:36) define this strategy as 'involvement': 'One shows involvement by taking the point of view of other participants.' TS1 accommodates his guest by selecting vocabulary which positions him in the same space with his guest, thus making the guest feel more at home and reducing the distance between them.[6] This positioning also correlates with the fact that TS1 addresses L with *du* (you, informal) as opposed to *Sie* (you, formal). In anticipation of a later example I want to draw attention to the fact that the talk show takes place in the Federal Republic, the community where TS1 is at home.

A last point I want to make about data segment 1 is that of changing 'relative meanings'. The speakers talk about the day of the opening of the Wall, which is the day before the talk show. At the time of the show, the Wall was open and it was all of a sudden possible for people to go *hin und her* (back and forth), line 7, between the GDR and the Federal Republic. For a person from the GDR, 'arrival' in the Federal Republic from the GDR was not, as previously associated with *rübergehen* (go over there), the permanent arrival in the Federal Republic, but could now mean a coming and going (*hin und her*). What this suggests is that words, such as *rübergehen*, would change the meaning they had possessed during 40 years of division.

'Outsiderness' and social spaces in flux

Data segment 2 is from an MDR show in Dresden in eastern Germany which was aired on 23 April 1993. The studio audience is almost exclusively from the local area, eastern Germany, and the show is produced to be shown on MDR, which has its television audience in southeastern Germany. The talk show host is from the former Federal Republic. He is confronted with a similar situation to that of TS1, which is to address a person from the former GDR and talk about how that person left the GDR to go to the Federal Republic. This second host addresses the actress Marijam Agischewa, who had left the GDR in the summer of 1989. At that time, the talk show host was still living in the Federal Republic. In the data segment, he positions himself as an outsider to eastern Germans. This 'outsiderness' is made in reference to the time talked about, the time before 1989. However, it carries over into the time of speaking and could be understood as discursively constructing differences between present social spaces in Germany.

Data segment 2: MDR talk show, 23 April 1993

> *TS2* Talk show host (Jan Hofer, former Federal Republic)
> *MA* Marijam Agischewa (eastern German, escaped GDR in summer 1989)

> 1 *TS2*: sie waren eines der ganz grossen talente der ddr und 1989
> you were one of the big talents in the gdr and in 1989
> 2   haben sie sich dann trotzdem entschlossen (0.2)
>   *rüberzumachen*
>   you nevertheless decided to (0.2) *go across*
> 3   (0.1) sind sie *in den westen gegangen*, hat ihnen das gut getan
>   (0.1) you *went* (or: *moved*) *to the west*, was that good for you
> 4 *MA*: ja das hat mir glaube ich sehr gut getan
>   yes I believe that was good for me

For the GDR audience, *rüberzumachen* (to go across) and *in den westen gegangen* (went – or moved – to the Federal Republic) evoke a familiar perspective because the GDR point of view is taken. The point of departure is 'home', the GDR, and the point of arrival is the other state, the Federal Republic. The unfamiliar perspective for the audience, that which would display Federal Republic identification, would have been if the speaker had positioned himself in the former Federal Republic using *rüberkommen* (to come across) and *in den westen kommen* (to come or move to the Federal Republic). Since the speaker is in the GDR, the former perspective might be considered more natural for the geographic setting. However, segment 1 exemplified how speakers can employ perspectives independent of geographic locations. As in segment 1, it can be argued that TS2 employs the perspective of his guest, which diminishes social distance between himself and his guest. In contrast to segment 1, however, both his guest and most of his audience are eastern Germans, so TS2's positive face strategy is effective not only for his guest but also for his audience.

By selecting *rüberzumachen* and *rübergegangen*, TS2 positions himself in the social space of the GDR at a time when he still lived in the Federal Republic. This word selection could be understood as claiming experience in the GDR which he does not have, which is not part of his 'habitus'. However, TS2 finds a way to indicate that he does not count himself as part of the GDR community: he brackets his talk, that is, he pauses before the word *rüberzumachen*[7] and produces a smile while he says *rüberzumachen* (0.1) *sind in den westen gegangen* (go across (0.1) you went [or: moved] to the west). Thus, although he positions himself through his words in the social space GDR, he displays through the bracketing that he was an outsider to the GDR at that time in the past. This 'outsiderness' is carried over into the present, evoking the countries GDR and Federal Republic as different. In the speaker's utterance, individual experience and past and present social spaces intersect. Thus, while the speaker distances himself in relation to the past, he also keeps a distance in the present through his utterance. It is therefore possible that the bracketing indexes an apology for evoking the division into GDR and Federal Republic through words such as *rüberzumachen*, for the awkwardness of using these words from the past. After all, the Wall, that element which created the 'relative meanings' of these words, is not there any more.

So far, I have shown that speakers' language may index 'involvement', precisely because different points of view are pragmatically indexed with motion verbs in a particular speech situation. TS2 indicates his awareness of the limitations in projecting a point of view of the previously other community, while TS1 does not. Among the variables which are different for TS1's and TS2's speech situation is the fact that the conversation for TS1 takes place in western Germany, while TS2 talks in eastern Germany to an eastern German audience. Moreover, while the date for TS1's talk show is November 1989, the talk show for TS2 takes place in April 1993, a time at which eastern and western Germans were past the brief euphoria after the opening of the Wall.

Data segment 3 follows after the previous segment in the same talk show. This segment shows that, when speakers formulate places of arrival, ambiguities arise with the social space in flux and that once again social conditions in Germany are important variables. As in data segment 2, the host again employs the GDR perspective while indicating his outsiderness.

Data segment 3: MDR talk show, 23 April 1993

```
1 TS2: hatten sie eigentlich probleme wieder zurückzukommen
         did you have any problems coming back
2        in ihre alte heimat
         to your old home/homeland
```

The return which TS2 addresses happened after 1989, when the social space referred to as *ihre alte heimat* (your old home/homeland) was already in flux. MA's home used to be the GDR but by then unification had made eastern Germany part of a new social space by joining western Germany. The ambiguity arises because the referent is diffuse for reasons of social change: TS2's question addresses a return to a place that no longer exists though it is still MA's *alte heimat* of the past.

So far, I have argued that *ihre alte heimat* (your old home/homeland) is heard as returning to the social space which used to be GDR, but it could also denote the local geographical space, for example the town or *Land* (federal state) where the talk show takes place. The reason why the social space GDR comes to mind first as the referent is because *rübergehen* (go over there) earlier in the conversation (see data segment 2) evoked leaving the GDR and going to the Federal Republic, while *zurückzukommen* in this segment denotes the opposite movement. It is likely that the verb couple *rübergehen* and *zurückkommen,* which was used during the times of a divided Germany before 1989 to denote opposite movements (and perspectives), influences the understanding that these verbs are attached to the social spaces of eastern and western Germany even after unification. MA's following response to TS2's question is evidence that *alte heimat* (old home) is heard as referring to the social space of eastern Germany after unification:

```
3 MA: naja (.) probleme kann ich nich sagen, aber es war schon
         well (.) not really problems, but it was definitely
4        anders, (.2) s war ja ne menge passiert und ich war nich
         different, (.2) a lot had happened and I did not
5        dabei und die menschen haben sich auch verändert
         witness it and the people have changed too
```

I now want to consider how TS2 employs the GDR perspective while indicating his outsiderness in data segment 3. By saying *zurückzukommen* (to come back), TS2 positions himself in eastern Germany as the social space of arrival. He employs the GDR perspective as opposed to the alternative *zurückzugehen* (to go back). When formulating the space, he excludes himself by using *your* instead of *our home*. Though he positions himself in that local space by *zurückzukommen*, he does not claim membership with the community of that space before 1989, thus indexing his origins in the Federal Republic.

The examples so far have demonstrated the high degree to which national identification is embedded in language. Speakers can position themselves in conversations towards one or the other community because linguistic resources are tied to a certain perspective. Thus, they can indicate empathy with the 'other' group while indexing non-belonging at the same time.

Overlapping spaces and slips of the tongue

Data segment 4 is from another MDR talk show aired on 5 March 1993. The talk show host from the former Federal Republic addresses a guest who had left the GDR before 1989 and escaped to the Federal Republic. This talk show host uses place formulations as if she were in the former Federal Republic. Since the talk show takes place in the former GDR, her usage of place formulations is incorrect for the given context; however, it does signify that the speaker is from the former Federal Republic. For the studio and television audiences, who are mostly eastern Germans, her usage of place formulations is unfamiliar. Therefore, this host positions herself, intentionally or not, in opposition to the audiences.

Data segment 4: MDR talk show, 5 March 1993

Hick   Peter Hick (escaped from the GDR before 1989)
TS3   talk show host (Christel Cohn-Vossen, from the former Federal Republic)

```
1  TS3:   aber sie kommen ja aus der ex-ddr
           but you come from the former gdr
2  Hick:  richtig
           that's right
3  TS3:   sie sind auf ziemlich schwierigem wege hierher gekommen
           you came here by a difficult route
4          >wie war das,<
           what happened
```

5 *Hick*: ich bin bei irgendeiner produktion mal *abgehauen* weil
   I *escaped* during some production or other because

6   ich einfach mal die nase voll hatte
         I'd just had enough

In line 1, TS3 employs the linguistic structure commonly used to formulate origin, *you come from x*, which can be understood as formulating Hick's original identity as *aus der ex-ddr* (from the ex-GDR). At the
same time, *you come from x* formulates a movement whereby *ex-ddr* is
the place of departure. This movement is obviously associated in line
3 when the place of arrival is formulated as *hierher* and the perfect
tense *sind gekommen* is used in reference to a past event. Since the
show takes place in eastern Germany, the logical assumption would
be that this point of arrival is eastern Germany. However, from a
point earlier in the conversation we know that, before 1989, Hick
had escaped from the GDR and moved to the Federal Republic. If this
knowledge is applied as a 'contextualization cue' (Gumperz 1982),
hierher would refer to the Federal Republic and be a slip of the
tongue.

Considering that TS3 had lived most of her life in the Federal
Republic, it seems likely that *hierher* is a slip of the tongue by the talk
show host from western Germany hired by MDR. Her habitual ways
of conceptualizing the Federal Republic as 'here' and the GDR as
'there' may be reflected in her use of *sind ... hierher gekommen* (came
here). Thus, while physically moving herself from western to eastern
Germany, namely speaking on an MDR talk show in Dresden, she
uses the deictic she is familiar with from having lived in the Federal
Republic. This interpretation assumes a mental time frame in which
the event is seen as one in the past without relation to the present.
An alternative interpretation, however, is based on a frame in which
the speaker conceptualizes unification as western Germany extended
to include eastern Germany. In that case, the place at which Hick
originally arrived at the moment of speaking is the present location of
the speaker. The social space of Germany at the time of speaking
overrides the status of eastern Germany at the time when the event
occurred.

It is curious that the ongoing conversation is not hindered because
of the inherent ambiguity of the adverb's referents. Hick does not ask
for any clarification. This suggests that the contextualization cues from
the social context are sufficient to clarify the references. Such cues are,
for example, the prototypical arrival of people from the GDR in the

Federal Republic. Also, Hick as well as TS3 may find himself conceptualizing social spaces independent of the place of speaking; the geographical coordinates of *here* (eastern Germany) and *there* (western Germany) may be irrelevant for both participants in their interaction. What the locative-deictic adverbs refer to are rather relations between groups in the social space, whereby the relations at the time of speaking may override the ones at the time of the event.

This argument can be supported with an analysis of the conversation that occurs two minutes later in the same show. The talk show host (TS3) still refers to the GDR as *there*, and Hick in his answer refers to an ambiguous space of the present as *here*.

Data segment 5: MDR talk show, 5 March 1993

1 *TS3*:   aber sie hatten ja auch *dort* schon einen beruf, wie
           but you also had a profession *there*, how
2   sind sie zum stuntman geworden ich meine das war ja
           did you become a stuntman, i mean that was
3   *in der ddr* nun nicht alltäglich
           not common *in the gdr*
4 *Hick*: nun is *hier* vielleicht auch nich
           well it isn't common *here* either

The *dort* (there) in TS3's turn (line 1) is obviously referring to the GDR, based on previous talk and contextualization cues within the same turn, namely the *in der ddr* (in the GDR) in line 3, which has the same referent as *dort*. *Dort* denotes the GDR of the past because the sentence is in past tense (*war*, was). It refers temporally back to the place (or social space) of the GDR. Hick's *hier* (here) refers, by use of the present tense, to a present social space. This space is the unified Germany. However, the *dort-hier* dichotomy denoting eastern and western spaces gives rise to an understanding of *hier* as the space of western Germany, in that case revealing once more the disjunction between place of speaking and changing social spaces. As with the previous segment, *hier* could be the Federal Republic, if Hick is making a slip of the tongue imagining himself located in western Germany. On the other hand, if one feels that the present social space overrides the past one, *hier* could be referring to the unified Germany where *hier* is used synonymously for the western Germany of the past and unified Germany.

Arriving at identity?

In the previous sections, I discussed different perspectives of deictics and motion verbs in the context of arrivals. I focused on how these perspectives emerge in post-1989 interactions about the past. I argued that these perspectives by way of deictic usage can be employed to demonstrate empathy with the audiences but also that they impose constraints on speakers in terms of claiming in- and outsiderness. Discussing data segments from 1993, I then demonstrated that deictics formulating social spaces of the past, in particular points of arrival, receive an ambiguity because speakers map present social spaces on to past ones.

The discussion of the following segment focuses on another aspect of *hier* (here). I argue that *hier* disguises hierarchies within the social space because of the locative-deictic component of this adverb. This segment is drawn from a talk show aired on 25 August 1995 by N3, a western German television station. The speakers are Ellis Huber from the former Federal Republic and Horst Grunert from the former GDR. By their selection of place formulations, they project different groups and relationships between these groups in the social space at the time of speaking, 1995.

I discuss this segment at the end of the chapter because it addresses once more the larger question concerning the arrival of the German community at a unified national identity. In this instance, arrival is explicitly used as a metaphor for the change into a new social space, the unified Germany, referred to as *hier* (here) by the first speaker in the segment. The speaker makes it a precondition for this arrival to dissolve the PDS, the legal successor of the SED, the ruling Communist Party in the GDR. I focus on the way that speakers denote these political social spaces through the deictic-locative adverb *hier* as opposed to a formulation with a pronoun *bei uns* (here where we are).

Data segment 6: N3 talk show 'III nach 9', 25 August 1995

> *Hub*   Ellis Huber, President of the Ärztekammer Berlin (Berlin medical board)
> *Grun*   Horst Grunert, former Ambassador from the GDR
>
> 1 *Hub*:   dann löst doch endlich die pds auf und *kommt hier an*
>   well then dissolve the pds and *come here*
> 2 *Grun*:   *zu ihnen* meinen sie?
>   *to you* you mean?

3 *Hub*:   *nein zu- in dieses land*
         no to- to this country
4 *Grun*: oh
         oh
5 *Hub*:   *diese nostalgie die sie mittragen die hilft ja nicht weiter*
         this nostalgia which you carry doesn't get us anywhere

The verb *ankommen* (to arrive) again frames a move of people: however, this time not to arrive at a physical location but at the German national identity. Since Huber makes *dissolving the PDS* a prerequisite for this arrival, a shift from eastern identification is required before 'entering' *hier* (here), entering the German national identity. *Hier*, though a deictic-locative adverb, refers to the social space at the time of speaking with the political order of western Germany and a group of people who are *hier* already, including the speaker from western Germany. While the locative adverb *hier* does not explicitly state the relationships between groups in the social space, Grunert in his question makes them explicit by using personal pronouns: *zu ihnen meinen sie* ([come] to you you mean), identifying Huber as being part of that group which is already *hier*. In his answer, Huber starts out with *zu–* (to-), projecting the personal pronoun *uns* (us), but then resorts to a place formulation: *in dieses land* (to this country). As with *hier*, Huber thus manages to avoid the hierarchical implications of *we* versus *you*, where *you* (the PDS as a possible metaphor for anything eastern German) have not arrived yet at the present location, while *we* are already part of this new national identity. *We* could be heard as implying the social space of western Germany, the community where the speaker is originally from.

In this last segment, the social space as the referent for *here* is conceptualized in terms of an unfinished arrival. Points of departure and arrival, as well as the moving subjects and those who have already arrived, echo the arrival movement discussed at the beginning of this chapter: the point of departure is in the eastern German community, while the point of arrival is the western German community now extended to a unified Germany. Instead of a *we* incorporating all Germans, there is still a *they* which is presented as outside the social space of Germany at the time of speaking. Germanness is here still conceptualized in terms of the relationship between eastern and western communities as hierarchical and incompatible within one social space.

The arrival metaphor has survived in conceptualizing the relationships between social spaces in a unified Germany. This is the case to a large extent because deictics and motion verbs with 'relative meanings' from a divided Germany echo these meanings in talk about the past. By positioning speakers in the social spaces of eastern and western Germany in post-*Wende* conversations about the past, these meanings survive through the speakers in present utterances. So it is difficult, it seems, to express a unified Germany using a language which refers to past social spaces at the same time.

Conclusion

In this chapter, I have focused on Germanness as emerging in interactions. I have argued that deictics with relative meanings from before 1989 position speakers and audiences in the social spaces of eastern and western Germany in talk after 1989. Specifically, I have shown that opposite perspectives of adverbs, pronouns and motion verbs in the utterance can be used by speakers to show empathy with a person or a group of people including audiences. If speakers are physically located in the 'other' place, adverbs or motion verbs reveal a disjunction between the speakers' physical location and the social spaces denoted by the deictics. Another interpretation of these deictics suggests that social spaces at the time of speaking get mapped on to social spaces of the past, referred to by the same deictic forms. The last segment in particular showed how past social spaces can be made present by other parties in the conversation drawing on the speaker's 'habitus' as a contextualization cue. The discussion in this chapter has therefore demonstrated that the east–west relationship in Germany is still present in speakers' use of those deictics referring to national communities, and reveals how these deictics refer to social spaces, including social relationships within these spaces, rather than geographic locations.

Notes

1 I would like to thank everyone who has contributed comments towards the final version of this chapter, especially Peter Auer, Kit Belgum, Patrick Stevenson, Jürgen Streeck, and Barbara Wolbert.
2 When I discuss the selection of words and phrases by speakers, I do not imply that speakers make these selections consciously.
3 My approach in making context part of the analysis has been strongly influenced by Gumperz's (1982) and Auer's (1996) works on contextualization.

4 Transcription notations:

    (.2)   seconds pause according to speech rhythm
    ,   falling intonation
    [overlap between speakers
    > < talk within these spaces is spoken faster
    italic my discussion focus

5 Motion verbs imply a direction which Kuno (1987) calls 'camera perspective' or 'point of view', and which was also noted by Bühler (1965). These directions figuratively position the speaker using *go there* at the point of departure and *come here* at the point of arrival. Since *here* denotes the 'familiar', while *there* denotes the 'other' or 'unfamiliar', *come here* implies that the speaker is closer to the point of arrival (*here*), while *go there* implies that the speaker is closer to the point of departure (*there*).

6 Since L uses *zuhause* in reference to the point of departure and TS1 positions himself in the same social space, this distance is even more decreased. It is almost as if TS1 claimed they both had the same *zuhause*, which interestingly removes the border between the two social spaces GDR and Federal Republic and makes them one social space. It is not unlikely that the perturbation *un eh* (an uh) at the beginning of L's next turn, line 7, indicates L's difficulties in readjusting the perspectives.

7 It was brought to my attention by colleagues from western Germany that *rübermachen* was used in the Federal Republic in reference to the move from the GDR to the Federal Republic for a person from the GDR, thus evoking the voice of a person from the GDR. I would consider this a special case of perspective in which the direction of the move (east to west) is opposed to the 'direction' of the perspective (west to east).

References

Auer, Peter (1996) 'From context to contextualization', in *Links & Letters* 3, 11–28.

Bakhtin, Mikhail (1986) *Speech Genres & Other Late Essays* (Austin: University of Texas Press).

Borneman, John (1992) *Belonging in the Two Berlins. Kin, State, Nation* (Cambridge: Cambridge University Press).

Bourdieu, Pierre (1977) 'The economics of linguistic exchanges', in *Social Science Information/Information sur les sciences sociales* 16/6, 645–68.

Bourdieu, Pierre (1991) *Language and Symbolic Power* (Cambridge, MA: Harvard University Press).

Brown, Penelope and Stephen Levinson (1987) *Politeness. Some Universals in Language Use* (Cambridge: Cambridge University Press).

Bühler, Karl (1965) *Sprachtheorie* (Stuttgart: Gustav Fischer Verlag).

Goodwin, Marjorie H. (1990) *He-said-she-said: Talk as Social Organization among Black Children* (Bloomington: Indiana University Press).

Gumperz, John J. (1982) *Discourse Strategies* (Cambridge: Cambridge University Press).

Keating, Elizabeth (1998) *Power Sharing: Language, Rank, Gender and Social Space in Pohnpei, Micronesia* (Oxford: Oxford University Press).

Kuno, Susumu (1987) *Functional Syntax. Anaphora, Discourse and Empathy* (Chicago, IL: University of Chicago Press).

Postone, Moishe, Edward LiPuma, and Craig Calhoun (eds) (1993a) *Bourdieu: Critical Perspectives* (Cambridge: Polity Press).

Postone, Moishe, Edward LiPuma and Craig Calhoun (1993b) 'Introduction: Bourdieu and social theory', in Postone, LiPuma and Calhoun (1993a), 2–16.

Sacks, Harvey, Emanuel A. Schegloff and Gail Jefferson (1974) 'A simplest systematics for the organization of turn-taking for conversation', in *Language* 50/4, 696–735.

Sandig, Barbara (1996) 'Sprachliche Perspektivierung and perspektivierende Stile', in *Zeitschrift für Literaturwissenschaft und Linguistik* 102, 36–63.

Schegloff, Emanuel A. (1972) 'Notes on a conversational practice: formulating place', in Sudnow (1972), 75–119.

Scollon, Ron and Suzanne Wong Scollon (1995) *Intercultural Communication. A Discourse Approach* (Oxford: Blackwell).

Sudnow, D. (ed.) (1972) *Studies in Social Interaction* (New York: Free Press).

12

'Es ist so; jedenfalls erscheint es mir so': Markers of Uncertainty and Vagueness in Speeches of East and West German Politicians

Stephan Elspaß

Introduction

It has been argued that people in East Germany mastered two registers, one 'public' and one 'private', and could easily switch between the two (Reséndiz 1992:136, Thierse 1993:123, Fix 1996:40). Whereas the private register seems to have remained almost unaffected by the *Wende* and the associated socio-economic changes, in many areas of public life people had to adapt linguistically to a new style of discourse: business talks (Ylönen 1992), round-table discussions, talk shows (Kreutz 1997a; Liebscher, Chapter 11, this volume), or job interviews (Auer, Chapter 10, this volume) presented new communicative fields, new contexts, even new text types in which noticeable differences between the 'everyday rhetoric' (to use Peter Auer's term) of east and west emerged.

However, the public language of political discourse in post-*Wende* Germany has scarcely been analysed. Many current assumptions about linguistic differences between east and west German politicians are based on impressions rather than on empirical research. Differences in the language used by politicians are mostly identified by a few examples on the lexico-semantic level. An example illustrating just such an impressionistic approach can be found in a recent article in the daily *Kölner Stadt-Anzeiger*, which reveals many of the stereotypes about east German politicians:

Man merkt es nicht nur am Dialekt. Wenn im Bundestag ein Abgeordneter die Umstehenden reihenweise mit Handschlag begrüßt, von 'Zielstellung', 'Nachhol[e]bedarf' und seiner Bonner 'Zwei-Raum-Wohnung' spricht, dann besteht kein Zweifel: So einer stammt aus den neuen Bundesländern – und gilt häufig noch als belächelter Sonderling, als ostdeutscher Satellit im westdeutschen Polit-Kosmos.

Loreck 1998

(You can spot them not just by their dialect. If an MP greets everyone with a handshake and talks about 'objectives', 'catching up' and his 'two-room-flat' in Bonn, then there can be no doubt that this MP is from the new *Länder* in the east – and as such he is often derided as an outsider, as an east German satellite in the west German political cosmos.)

The author suggests that even today – more than eight years after the first MPs from east Germany moved into the German Bundestag – east German politicians can be distinguished from their west German colleagues not only by their regional accent, but also by their use of certain words and expressions ('Zielstellung', 'Nachhol[e]bedarf',[1] 'Zwei-Raum-Wohnung'; the west German equivalents would read 'Ziel', 'Nachholbedarf', 'Zwei-Zimmer-Wohnung') and even rituals of politeness (such as excessive handshaking). Moreover, according to the author, the careful observer can spot them by these shibboleths.

The post-*Wende* discourse was, of course, a new linguistic experience for *both* east and west Germans in that they met for the first time in 40 years in a common German Parliament. The starting position of the newly elected east German MPs in the twelfth Bundestag (1990), however, differed considerably from that of their west German colleagues. Whereas 71 per cent of the west Germans had been members of the previous Parliament, only half of the east German MPs had been representatives in the tenth and last Volkskammer (GDR Parliament) that lasted from April to October 1990 (Scholz 1993:273). Most could not claim any prior parliamentary experience. Even the newcomers among the west German MPs often had the advantage of some training in public speaking or experience in local or *Länder* (federal state) parliaments. East Germans, on the other hand, had to adapt to the new communicative field of western-style parliamentary discourse.

Against this background, evidence of communicative differences between east and west German MPs in Parliament can be expected. The scant linguistic research on east and west political language, however, does not present a homogeneous picture. Most authors, like Loreck, maintain that communicative and linguistic differences do still exist. For example, in his analysis of an east German political discussion programme on television, Läzer (1996:167, 169) found that the discourse behaviour of east German politicians is 'agreement-orientated' and thus fundamentally different from that of west German politicians.[2] The data from a Halle University thesis (*Diplomarbeit*) from 1995, however, seem rather to suggest a correlation between the performance of a speaker in Parliament and his or her lack of experience as a public speaker; only MPs with a career as priests or teachers in the former GDR appear more confident and practised (Biege and Bose 1997:124). There is some empirical evidence to support the characterization of east German inhibition or insecurity as opposed to west German self-assurance and confidence, but it has been observed primarily in the speech of young people (Reséndiz 1992, Kreutz 1997a, 1997b). Analysts of political language are therefore faced with the following questions: do these observations on 'communicative uncertainty' (Kreutz) in the speech of east Germans also hold true for east German MPs as compared to their west German counterparts? Or rather, are such differences the result of oratorical (in)experience? And finally, if that is the case, is there any evidence of change over the years?

This chapter will concentrate on the notion of uncertainty and vagueness and its linguistic representation. It will investigate linguistic markers which have often, particularly in feminist linguistics (Günthner 1992) and in the text genre 'academic writing' (Meyer 1997), served to show such sometimes different notions as 'soft-spokenness', politeness, indirectness, mitigation, vagueness or understatement. Key questions will therefore be: (1) whether significant differences can be established between east and west German politicians in their use of such markers as a reflection of 'uncertainty' or even 'insecurity', and (2) whether these differences have changed in recent years, leading to a convergence of what has previously been labelled 'two cultures of communication'.

Linguistic markers of uncertainty and vagueness

The following brief overview of the most prominent markers of uncertainty and vagueness is based on an exposition by Johannes Erben (1994) and will serve as a basis for the analysis:

• 'verba dicendi/sentiendi' in the first person	*ich glaube/nehme an/denke/ finde, daß ...* [I believe/assume/think/find that ...]; *wir halten ... für* [we consider sb/sth ... to be]
(– with additional modal verb:)	*ich möchte annehmen, daß ...* [I would assume/presume that ...]
• verbal phrases with a similar function	*es scheint/wir hatten den Eindruck/ es sieht so aus* [it seems/we had the impression that/it looks as if]
(– with additional modal verb:)	*es mag ... erscheinen, daß ...* [it may seem that ...]
• modal adverbs	*vielleicht, wahrscheinlich, gut und gern, im Grunde, eigentlich* [maybe, probably, easily, basically, actually]
• adverbial phrases expressing modality	*meines Erachtens, nach meinem Dafürhalten, meiner Meinung nach* [in my opinion]
• conditional clauses	*wenn ich recht sehe, ...* [if I'm right/correct, ...]
• subjunctive II/conditional	*Das könnte so sein.* [That could be the case.]
• 'futurum exactum' (putative statement)	*Er wird nicht zu Hause sein.* [He won't be at home.]
• modal particles	*fast/beinahe, etwa, bis zu, jedenfalls, wohl, kaum* [almost, roughly, up to, anyway, surely, hardly]
• certain patterns of word formation	*Fast-, Beinahe-, Quasi-Aufwertung* [quasi- ...]

According to Erben, the German language contains a set of linguistic expressions that can be identified as indicating a speaker's uncertainty and vagueness about his or her own proposition (1994:7). He demonstrates that such markers have become increasingly prominent in the German language, with many having only emerged in the modern period (1994:16–21).

Uncertain and vague speech styles of east and west German politicians

In the following, a passage from the Volkskammer debate of 1990 on the Reunification Treaty will be analysed. The analysis is based on the premise that the new discourse situation in the tenth and last Volkskammer,[3] which was the first to be freely elected and lasted from March to October 1990, presented a change in the socio-communicative framework of the new MPs and their role within this framework. The speech is made by a member of the Social Democrats, Richard Schröder, and contains, apart from the lexical shibboleth *Nachholebedarf* (see above), some linguistic elements which would have been highly unusual in a Bundestag speech at that time. His display of uncertainty and vagueness is particularly noticeable:

> *Zwischenfrage*: Herr Abgeordneter, ich hätte die Zwischenfrage: Ist Ihnen bekannt, wer jetzt die 55 Millionen Auslandseinnahmen kassiert, die von den Betrieben erwirtschaftet werden?
> *Schröder (SPD)*: *Das würde ich Ihnen gern sagen, wenn ich es wüßte. Ich denke*, das ist eine Frage der Ermittlungsbehörden, festzustellen, was aus diesen Geldern geworden ist.
> (Beifall bei allen Fraktionen)
> Es fällt uns Sozialdemokraten nicht leicht, die Schließung einer ganzen Reihe von Betrieben voraussagen zu müssen; denn das heißt – wir wissen das – Arbeitsplatzverlust und Arbeitslosigkeit. *Wir hoffen und denken, daß* gesagt werden kann:
> Erstens: Es werden Arbeitsplätze verlorengehen, es werden auch neue entstehen. Es gibt in der DDR *ungefähr* 600 Betriebe mit bis zu 100 Angestellten und in der Bundesrepublik 26 000. Hier ist ein großer Nachholebedarf, und dort werden *zweifellos* Arbeitsplätze entstehen.
> Zweitens: *Wir rechnen nicht mit* Dauerarbeitslosigkeit, sondern mit einer Arbeitslosigkeit der verlängerten Arbeitsplatzsuche.
> (Gelächter bei PDS und Bündnis 90/Grüne)
> Da brauchen Sie nicht zu lachen, das *wird* so sein.
> Und drittens: Kein Arbeitsloser wird mittellos dastehen.
>
> Einigungsvertrag 1990. *Zur Sache*: 30–1
> (*Question*: ... Do you know who gets the 55 million that our businesses make from foreign trade?
> *Schröder (SPD)*: *I would gladly tell you that, if only I knew. I think* that it is up to the committee of inquiry to find out what happened to the money.

(Approval from all parties)
It is not easy for us Social Democrats to have to predict the closure of a lot of businesses because it means – and we all know that – a loss of jobs and unemployment. *We hope and think* that we will be able to say:
Firstly, jobs will be lost, but some new jobs will be created. In the GDR, there are *roughly* 600 businesses with up to 100 employees, compared to 26 000 in the Federal Republic. We have a lot of catching up to do, and *undoubtedly* new jobs will be created there.
Secondly, *we do not expect* that there will be long-term unemployment, but rather only temporary unemployment with people having to spend longer looking for jobs.
(Laughter from the *PDS* and Bündnis 90/Grüne)
There is no need for laughter. *This will be the case.*
And thirdly, no unemployed citizen will be without means.)

Here, Schröder does something which would normally have been avoided by experienced speakers in the West. When asked about the whereabouts of DM 55 million, he openly admits that he does not know where the money went (*Das würde ich Ihnen gern sagen, wenn ich es wüßte/*I would gladly tell you that, if only I knew). He can only express his hope and presumption that new jobs will be created (*Wir hoffen und denken, daß ...*/We hope and think that ...; *... und dort werden zweifellos Arbeitsplätze entstehen/...*and undoubtedly new jobs will be created there), and he foresees only temporary unemployment (*Wir rechnen nicht mit Dauerarbeitslosigkeit ...*/We do not expect that there will be long-term unemployment ...), which must sound like wishful thinking as it is immediately derided by the opposition. Even his protesting *das wird so sein* (that will be the case) could be interpreted as uncertainty (the periphrastic form with *wird* as a putative statement).
The speeches in the tenth Volkskammer differ considerably from the former state rhetoric. Erhard Eppler, a former West German cabinet minister, remarks on the official GDR rhetoric:

Im SED-Staat wurde abgelesen, auch wenn nur ein paar Grußworte oder Glückwünsche zu einer Ordensverleihung angesagt waren. Freie Rede war nicht nur unüblich, sie war auch suspekt. Allzu leicht konnte die Sprecherin oder der Sprecher vom rechten Wege abkommen. Wer in der Volkskammer frei gesprochen hätte, wäre wohl rasch in den Verdacht des 'bürgerlichen Subjektivismus' geraten.

Was öffentlich gesagt wurde, mußte 'stimmen', es mußte im Einklang stehen mit den sprachlichen Vorgaben der SED, meist auch ihres letzten Parteitages. Davon abweichen und also frei sprechen konnten nur Leute, die nicht auf die parteiamtlich verordnete Sprache verpflichtet waren. Und das waren, zumindest in der Öffentlichkeit, allein die Kirchenleute.

Eppler 1992:36

(In the former SED state it was common practice to read from notes, even if it was only a short address or a congratulatory message. To speak extempore was not only uncommon, but also suspicious. All too easily the speaker could wander from the straight and narrow. Anyone who had extemporized in the Volkskammer would immediately have been suspected of 'bourgeois subjectivism'. Everything that was said in public had to 'fit in', it had to be in line with the linguistic directives of the SED, in most instances also with the resolutions of the last party congress. Only people who were not obliged to stick to the official party rhetoric could deviate and thus speak extempore. And these were, at least in public, only churchmen.)

Not surprisingly, markers of uncertainty and vagueness appear in abundance in post-*Wende* speeches of East German politicians in the tenth Volkskammer and later in the Bundestag. However, putative statements, subjectivism and conjecture are not what the electorate wants to hear from their MPs. In this respect, the West German tradition of political rhetoric is probably best summarized in a statement by the late political scientist, Thomas Ellwein (cited in Erben 1994:22): 'Aber unter den Politikern bevorzugen wir bisher den Typ, der sich hinstellt und sagt: Es ist so, und das und das müssen wir tun' (We have always tended to prefer the kind of politician who stands up and says: the situation is like this, and we have to do this and that). The dilemma for politicians is that on the one hand they know, for example, about the vagueness of forecasts, yet on the other hand they are prevented from admitting this by common rhetorical practice. This was obviously not the case in the last Volkskammer, which has been characterized in retrospect as being much more of a '*Redeparlament*' (a real debating chamber) than the Bundestag (Scholz 1993:277; see also Burkhardt 1992)[4].

West German politicians, especially male ones, have always been anxious to make sure that they do not appear 'soft-spoken' in public. For example, it is common practice to have markers of uncertainty and vagueness changed or simply deleted from the printed version of a speech. Consider the following transcriptions of a speech by Wolfgang Bötsch with the corresponding passages in the stenographic report, in which the 'verba dicendi/sentiendi' *ich glaube* (I believe/I think), *ich meine* (I think), and *ich sage nur* (I can only say) are missing:

Transcription	Stenographic Report
Und *ich meine*, wenn die Vorfelddebatte ...	Ich möchte mir erlauben, einiges zum Verlauf der heutigen Debatte zu sagen. Wenn die Vorfelddebatte ...
Und *ich glaube*, wir haben das heute fair getan, und ich will ... *ich sage nur*: Im Vorfeld war das leider nicht immer der Fall.	Wir haben die heutige Debatte fair geführt. Im Vorfeld war das leider nicht immer der Fall.
Und *ich glaube*, es hat sich heute auch gezeigt, wie richtig es war ...	Heute hat sich auch gezeigt, wie richtig es war ...
(And *I think* if the preliminary debate ...	Hauptstadt 1991:2788A-B I would like to say a few things about the way today's debate has gone. If the preliminary debate...
And *I think* we have done that fairly today, and I want to ... *I would just say*: in the run-up to the debate that was unfortunately not always the case.	We have conducted the debate fairly today. In the run-up to the debate that was unfortunately not always the case.
And *I think* we have seen today how right it was ...	We have seen today how right it was ...)

The questions now arise as to whether the difference between east and west German politicians in their use of such markers as a reflection of 'uncertainty' or 'vagueness' also emerged in the post-*Wende* Bundestag, and then whether this difference has changed in recent years. To explore these questions, I carried out a quantitative analysis based on a corpus of 20 speeches by female MPs from 1991 and 20 from 1997, in each case ten by east German and ten by west German MPs. The 1991 speeches are exclusively taken from a debate on the 'situation of crèches and kindergartens in the new *Länder*' and the famous *Hauptstadtdebatte*, in which the Bundestag decided to move the parliament and the governmental institutions to Berlin. Most of the 1997 speeches are taken from a debate in February on the government's policy on women in the wake of the International Women's Conference in Beijing. Transcriptions of the video-taped debates were also considered in the case of noticeable discrepancies between the stenographic reports and the spoken version.

There are two methodological restrictions:

1 For the quantitative analysis, only four types of markers were considered: (1) verba dicendi/sentiendi, (2) verbal phrases, (3) modal adverbs, and (4) adverbial phrases expressing modality. It goes without saying that only those linguistic items were taken into account which were seen as indicating uncertainty and vagueness in the respective contexts.
2 In the research on 'hedges', the question of whether gender has an influence on the use of hedges is highly controversial (Günthner 1992, Markkanen and Schröder 1997: 8–9). Thus, to rule out gender-related differences, only speeches by female MPs were analysed.

Table 12.1 shows the data of the quantitative analysis.

Table 12.1   Some markers of uncertainty and vagueness in speeches by east and west German female MPs

	1991 speeches		1997 speeches	
	West MPs	*East MPs*	*West MPs*	*East MPs*
Total length of speeches (number of words)	7000	9200	14 700	13 500
Markers of uncertainty and vagueness				
1. verba dicendi/verba sentiendi	22 (32.4)	23 (25.0)	28 (19.0)	11 (8.1)
2. verbal phrases	8 (11.4)	4 (4.3)	9 (6.1)	5 (3.7)
3. modal adverbs	4 (5.7)	17 (18.5)	14 (9.5)	11 (8.1)
4. adverbial phrases expressing modality	5 (7.1)	5 (5.4)	5 (3.4)	8 (5.9)
Total	39 (56.6)	49 (53.2)	56 (38.0)	35 (25.8)

Note: Numbers in brackets show the number of markers of uncertainty/vagueness per 10 000 words.

In view of the relatively small sample, the results cannot, of course, be fully representative, but a few noticeable tendencies may be pointed out and serve as a basis for further considerations:

1 There appears to be no empirical evidence for concluding that east German MPs use more markers of uncertainty and vagueness than west German MPs (except for 'modal adverbs' in 1991).
2 The decrease in the overall use of markers of uncertainty and vagueness from the 1991 to the 1997 debates is more noticeable in the speeches of east German MPs (about 50 per cent fewer compared to a third fewer in the speeches of west German MPs).
3 The use of verba dicendi/sentiendi and modal adverbs in particular has declined in the speeches of east German MPs.
4 West German MPs still use remarkably more verba dicendi/sentiendi than their east German colleagues. This is, as will be discussed later, dependent on the type of speaker.

The relatively high number of markers for both east and west German MPs in 1991 can be attributed to the fact that most of them were parliamentary newcomers (six out of the ten 'west MPs' and five 'east MPs' – with the other five having been members of the short-lived last Volkskammer – compared to only three new 'west MPs' and one new 'east MP' in 1997). This may serve to support the hypothesis mentioned earlier that the performance of a speaker correlates significantly with his or her oratorical experience. For a more adequate picture of the individual style and the similarities between certain speakers, a detailed discussion of some examples is necessary. According to the frequency of markers of uncertainty and vagueness in their speeches, the speakers can be classified into three types – Type A, Type B and Type C – irrespective of their east or west German origin.

Type A is identified by a virtual absence of markers of uncertainty and vagueness. Most of the more experienced MPs are in this category. It appears, however, that some of the parliamentary newcomers, from both east and west, also make an effort to adapt instantly to what they see as western-style political rhetoric. The speech by Sigrid Semper in the *Hauptstadtdebatte* 1991, for example, does not contain a single marker. A metalinguistic comment at the beginning of her speech may serve to indicate her attempt not to appear 'soft-spoken' or emotional:

Sigrid Semper (FDP): Gerade als Abgeordnete aus einem der neuen Bundesländer bewegt mich die Debatte um den Regierungssitz

Berlin sehr stark. *Trotzdem möchte ich heute keine gefühlsbetonte Rede halten,* sondern vielmehr Sachargumente nennen, die leider in den vergangenen Wochen und Monaten oftmals so stark in den Hintergrund gedrängt wurden.

Hauptstadt 1991:2787A

(*Sigrid Semper (FDP):* Being an MP from one of the new *Länder*, this debate about Berlin as the seat of the government affects me personally a great deal. *However, I do not want to make an emotional speech,* but rather present arguments, which have unfortunately been neglected in the last few weeks and months.)

Some of the speakers only manage to avoid displaying their lack of oratorical experience or routine by sticking to their manuscript. Intralingual or extralingual interruption, however, can cause speakers to lose their thread. In Parliament, this is most evident in the case of interventions, questions or heckling, which usually turn speeches into short dialogues.

Vizepräsidentin Dr Antje Vollmer: Frau Ministerin, gestatten Sie eine Zwischenfrage der Kollegin Niehuis?
Claudia Nolte, Bundesministerin für Familie, Senioren, Frauen und Jugend: Wie könnte ich das verwehren?
Dr Edith Niehuis (SPD): Ich bedanke mich. – Sie haben die Bundesländer gelobt, die ihre Vorschläge nach der Weltfrauenkonferenz bei Ihnen eingereicht haben. Bei den bayerischen Vorschlägen steht, daß Bayern von jetzt ab plant, in die Verfassung aufzunehmen, daß Säuglingskurse für Mädchen Pflicht werden.
(Heiterkeit bei Abgeordneten der SPD)
Halten Sie das im Sinne der Weltfrauenkonferenz für sinnvoll?
Claudia Nolte: Mir ist, *ehrlich gesagt,* dieser Punkt bei der Aufnahme in die Aktionsplattform *so* nicht aufgefallen.
(*Christel Hanewinckel [SPD]:* So steht es in Ihrem Bericht!)
Ich hatte den Eindruck, daß Bayern genau diesen Punkt in der Verfassung ändern will, Frau Niehuis. Da *würde* ich noch einmal genau nachschauen.
(*Maria Eichhorn [CDU/CSU]:* So ist es!)
Im Grundsatz ändert das nichts an der Tatsache, daß ich mir gewünscht hätte, daß auch andere Länder, die von sich sagen, daß sie sehr fortschrittlich sind und viel gemacht haben, ihre Zuarbeit geleistet hätten, so daß wir sie hätten aufnehmen können und sie sich auch hätten präsentieren können.

(Beifall bei der CDU/CSU und der FDP. – Dr Uwe Küster [SPD]:
Das war eine ganz klare Antwort auf eine ganz klare Frage!)

Frauen 1997:14371D/14372A

(Deputy Speaker Dr Antje Vollmer: Will you allow a question from
colleague Niehuis?

Claudia Nolte, Minister for Families, Pensioners, Women and Youth:
How could I say no?

Dr Edith Niehuis (SPD): Thank you. – You just praised the federal
Länder which have handed in their proposals after the International
Women's Conference. The Bavarian proposals include a plan to incor-
porate compulsory courses in baby-care for girls into the constitution.

(Laughter among members of the SPD)
Do you consider this useful in the spirit of the International
Women's Conference?

Claudia Nolte: I was, *actually/to be honest*, not aware of such a
proposal for the action platform.

(Christel Hanewinckel [SPD]: That's what your report says!)

I was under the impression that Bavaria was actually going to change
this point in the constitution, Ms Niehuis, I *would* look this up again.

(Maria Eichhorn [CDU/CSU]: Exactly, you are right!)

Basically, this does not affect the fact that I would have wished that
some other *Länder*, which consider themselves progressive and to
have done a lot, had made their contribution so that we could have
allowed them to join and so that they could have presented themselves.

(Approval from the CDU/CSU and the FDP. – Dr Uwe Küster
[SPD]: That was a very clear response to a very clear question!))

The question by Niehuis causes a disruption of Nolte's otherwise self-
confident and complacent speech. She is slightly confused by the reference to an alleged motion by the Bavarian government. (Note the
concessive expression *ehrlich gesagt*/to be honest, and the modal parti-
cle *so*.) In the course of the debate, it emerges that she remembered
correctly that the article in question was to be abolished; Niehuis later
apologises for her error (14294C). Nevertheless, Nolte's momentary
doubts are very obvious. Although she remembers the relevant passage,
she uses markers of uncertainty and vagueness (such as the verbal
phrase *ich hatte den Eindruck*/I was under the impression, or the subjunctive II forms) which put her in a position from which she can
withdraw from her statement should the need arise. She then also
changes the subject (*Im Grundsatz...*/Basically, ...). As the sarcastic

comment by Uwe Küster MP on the lack of clarity in Nolte's response shows, vagueness is immediately pointed out and exposed as a weakness in a speech, a fact which makes it quite clear that it is not tolerated in the Bundestag.

Type B is characterized by a 'moderate' use of markers of uncertainty and vagueness. Most of the speakers could be subsumed within this type. It is again noticeable that markers of uncertainty and vagueness occur especially when speakers show signs of doubts or insecurity after questions or heckling:

> *Dr Ursula Fischer (PDS/Linke Liste):* Hinzu kommt, daß bei jeder passenden und unpassenden Gelegenheit den Frauen eingeredet werden soll, daß sie nur am Kochtopf gute Mütter sein können.
> *(Gerhard Reddemann [CDU/CSU]:* Wer erzählt denn so etwas?)
> – Das erzählen Sie *irgendwann vielleicht* in abgewandelter Form auch.
> – Diese Auffassung hat doch wohl das Leben längst widerlegt.
> *(Gerhard Reddemann [CDU/CSU]:* Sie bauen doch Pappkameraden auf!)
> – Meine Redezeit ist sehr kurz; ich möchte das jetzt zu Ende bringen.
> Kinderkrippen 1991:2449B
> *(Dr Ursula Fischer (PDS/Linke Liste):* In addition, women are told at every possible opportunity that they can only be good mothers when slaving away over a hot stove all day.
> *(Gerhard Reddemann [CDU/CSU]:* Who says that?)
> – You *might be* saying this *one day* in a similar way, as well.
> – Life has shown that this is not the case.
> *(Gerhard Reddemann [CDU/CSU]:* You are just making it up!)
> – I have only a little time to speak. I would like to come to a conclusion.)

Only a few MPs can be categorized as Type C speakers, frequently using markers of uncertainty and vagueness. While examining some prominent examples of such speakers, it will be worth looking more closely at the specific function of such markers and at possible developments over the years.

Careful wording, or 'soft-spokenness', characterizes the first speech in the 1991 debate on kindergartens by Christel Hanewinckel MP. Her inexperience as a parliamentary speaker becomes evident not only in her use of markers of uncertainty and vagueness, but also in an ingenuous proposal for the funding of crèches and kindergartens:

Christel Hanewinckel (SPD): Ich habe auch einen Finanzierungsvorschlag, nur hat die Fraktion der SPD dieses Geld schon ausgegeben; *ich bin hier erst neu.* Mein Vorschlag *wäre* nämlich *gewesen,* das Geld für das Fahrwerk des Jäger 90 z. B. dafür auszugeben. Aber das wird nun *wohl* nicht mehr funktionieren, *wie mir gesagt wurde.* *Ich denke,* trotzdem ist es nötig, sich mit den Verteidigungshaushältern zusammenzusetzen … .

Kinderkrippen 1991:2443C/D

(Christel Hanewinckel (SPD): I also have a proposal for how to fund this, only the SPD has already spent the money; *I'm new here.* My proposal *would have been* to spend the money for the undercarriage of the Jäger 90 for crèches instead, for example. But this *probably* won't work anymore, *I've been told.* It is, nevertheless, necessary, *I think,* to sit down with the people who work out the defence budget … .)

Almost apologetically, she refers to her status as a newcomer in the Bundestag *(ich bin hier erst neu*/I'm new here). This is followed by a number of markers of uncertainty and vagueness (subjunctive *wäre … gewesen*/would have been, adverb *wohl*/here: probably, verbum sentiendi *ich denke*/I think, phrase *wie mir gesagt wurde*/I've been told). Seven years after her maiden speech, however, Hanewinckel appears much more confident, even argumentative. Particularly in her response to a short intervention she is quite self-assured:

Christel Hanewinckel (SPD): Herr Kollege Geißler, ich bin etwas überrascht über Ihre Wortwahl. Sie sagten, Sie hätten das Ganze 1986 initiiert und durchgesetzt. *Das dürfte ja* bei den damals herrschenden Mehrheitsverhältnissen *nicht ganz so schwergefallen sein.* Aber Sie haben ja eigentlich etwas anderes gefragt. *Ich denke,* Sie wissen genausogut wie ich, daß in den letzten Wochen mehrfach durch die Presse gegangen ist, daß verschiedentlich von Kolleginnen und Kollegen von Ihrer Stelle genau andersherum argumentiert worden ist.

Frauen 1997:14397D

(Christel Hanewinckel (SPD): Mr Geißler, I am slightly surprised by your choice of words. You said that you initiated and accomplished all this in 1986. With your majority back then *that would hardly have posed a problem for you.* But, actually, you asked something else. *I think* you know as well as I do that in the last few weeks it was in the papers that on various

occasions your party colleagues have used quite contrary arguments.)

Though markers of uncertainty and vagueness have not disappeared from her speech entirely, their number (compared to her speech in 1991) has indeed dropped by a half. In terms of numbers, she could now be more aptly characterized as a Type B speaker. Moreover, it is worth noting that what might appear as a marker of uncertainty and vagueness, like the subjunctive II in *dürfte ja ... nicht ganz so schwergefallen sein* (that would have hardly posed a problem for you), turns out to be polemic irony. Hanewinckel's growing confidence, of which the decrease in the number of markers of uncertainty and vagueness may serve as an indicator, can be considered as an example of 'successful' assimilation to the new communicative situation in which she was immersed after the *Wende*.

Other Type C speakers, however, have hardly changed at all over the years. Compare Hanewinckel's development as a speaker with the following passage from a speech by Angela Merkel. A response to a question in the 1991 debate reads as follows:

Dr Angela Merkel, Bundesministerin für Frauen und Jugend: Herr Schmidt, *ich sage immer*, daß es mir, wenn ich durch die Kommunen in den alten Bundesländern fahre und sehe, daß es so viele schöne Festhallen, so viele schöne Schwimmhallen und so viele schöne Fußgängerzonen gibt, wirklich schwer klarzumachen ist, daß diese Kommunen es nicht geschafft haben, ein bedarfsgerechtes Angebot an Kindertagesstättenplätzen zu erreichen.

(Beifall bei der CDU/CSU und der FDP – Wilhelm Schmidt [Salzgitter] [SPD]: Aber Sie wollen doch den Anspruch durchsetzen!) *Es ist so; jedenfalls erscheint es mir so.* Das gilt für alle Kommunen. *Ich kann nur sagen:* Wenn es vor zehn, vor 15 oder vor 20 Jahren politisch wichtig gewesen wäre, dann wäre es auch machbar gewesen.

(Beifall bei der CDU/CSU und der FDP)

Kinderkrippen 1991:2452D/2453A

(*Dr Angela Merkel, Minister for Women and Youth:* Mr Schmidt, *I keep saying* this: whenever I travel through the districts in the old *Länder* and see that there are so many nice festival halls, so many nice public indoor pools and so many nice pedestrian precincts, I can hardly understand that the local authorities have failed to offer sufficient places in crèches to meet the demand.

(Approval from the CDU/CSU and FDP – Wilhelm Schmidt (SPD): It is you who wants to implement this right!) That is the situation; *or at least that is my impression.* The same holds for local authorities. *I can only say*: if it had been an important political issue ten, 15 or 20 years ago, then it would have been possible to put it into practice.)

Particularly at the beginning of her career, Merkel was known for her 'soft-spokenness' in speeches and interviews. Typical of this is her use of verba dicendi/sentiendi and hedged performatives (*ich sage immer*/I keep saying, *Ich kann nur sagen*/I can only say) and numerous other markers in this speech. Most revealing, though, is her immediate reaction to the heckling: *Es ist so; jedenfalls erscheint es mir so* (That is the situation; or at least that is my impression). Most speakers would have stopped after *Es ist so*. Merkel, however, is 'honest' enough to concede that her statement is based on impressions (*jedenfalls erscheint es mir so*), impressions of which she has given a detailed account earlier (*daß es mir ...*). In contrast to Hanewinckel, therefore, Merkel has hardly changed her style. Her recent speeches still contain as many markers of uncertainty and vagueness as her earlier speeches. Nevertheless, she does appear more confident and has gained respect for her detailed knowledge and diligence.

The very calculated use of markers of uncertainty and vagueness in the last two examples shows quite clearly that a typology of speakers which is based solely on frequency of such markers does not do justice to the various functions they can have and that have to be considered in the analysis of political speeches and other text types. As already mentioned earlier, markers of uncertainty and vagueness are typical of certain text types, as in, for example, academic discourse. The use of markers of uncertainty and vagueness in the sense of signals (and not symptoms) of uncertainty and vagueness can then be explained as demonstrating 'academic' caution regarding distance from a proposition. Peter von Polenz, who maintains that the modern style of argumentation can be regarded as a legacy of the Enlightenment, points out the use of hedged performatives (performatives in combination with modal verbs and other modal expressions) which he calls the *ich-würde-meinen* (I would think) style. He considers this 'coyness' a means of promoting the image of the speaker by a feigned down-toning of a statement (1988:187–8). It may then be argued that speakers such as Angela Merkel cultivate the use of markers of uncertainty and vagueness as rhetorical devices (or 'hedging strategies') to reduce, for example, the distance between the political speaker and the public, to mitigate what might otherwise seem too forceful or to steal the opposition's thunder.

Summary and conclusion

The linguistic markers analysed here in post-*Wende* speeches can be considered symptoms of 'communicative uncertainty' as well as signals of a speaker's attitude towards a proposition. In the first sense, the use of such markers cannot be attributed to any defined social group (such as 'east Germans'), but rather to the type of speaker, the communicative background and the discourse situation. In the latter sense, such markers can serve as a rhetorical device.

Markers of uncertainty and vagueness are not a common feature in speeches by east German MPs in the post-*Wende* Bundestag. The speeches in the short-lived tenth Volkskammer were characterized by a high frequency of such markers as opposed to the (pre- and post-1990) Bundestag. In post-1990 speeches, there is a perceptible tendency towards a general avoidance of markers of uncertainty and vagueness. The extent to which east German MPs have ceased to employ such markers may be interpreted as the degree to which they have already adapted to western-style parliamentary discourse. Three different types of speakers can be distinguished according to their rare, moderate or frequent use of markers of uncertainty and vagueness. An occasionally salient employment of such markers which is noticeable immediately after the *Wende* is attributed to the oratorical inexperience of a certain type of speaker from the east German *Länder*. (It must be remembered, however, that this affects most parliamentary newcomers.) As in the case of Christel Hanewinckel MP, most such speakers – in displaying their increasing confidence – have assimilated over the years to the 'traditional' West German style of speaking, which can be observed in the decreasing occurrence of markers of uncertainty and vagueness.

A few female east German and even west German MPs have, however, retained a style of 'soft-spokenness', a style which can be interpreted as a specific technique of political rhetoric. It remains to be investigated, however, to what extent the respect and popularity these politicians have gained is related to their style of speaking and in particular to the way they employ markers of uncertainty and vagueness.

In any case, the particular manner of speaking which especially east German MPs brought into the post-*Wende* Bundestag introduced into the parliamentary battlefield a form of respect, politeness and reduction in tension. When one considers that the Bundestag had to find (or rather, had an opportunity to find) a new language after the *Wende* – just as the first democratic German Parliament had to find its own language in 1848, and the new German parliaments had to regain their language after the fall of the Third Reich – it is remarkable that little has remained of the style of discourse in the last GDR Volkskammer, the 'Redeparlament' of 1990. Rather than a convergence of the two formerly separated 'cultures of communication', we have experienced in the language of the Bundestag what could only be called another form of west German linguistic hegemony.

Notes

1 This is a misprint, since the 'typical' East German version should read *Nachholebedarf*; this was confirmed by the author in a private conversation. See the example in the first extract, p. 210.
2 A weakness of this otherwise thorough case study is, however, that only representatives of the SPD, PDS and BÜNDNIS 90 in Brandenburg, but no members of the CDU and the FDP, took part in the discussion.
3 The elections took place on 18 March 1990.
4 It should be noted that the stenographic report of the Volkskammer in this particular period reflects much more authentically the spoken language of the speeches than the stenographic reports of the Bundestag.

References

Biege, Angela and Ines Bose (1997) 'Untersuchungen zur Redeweise in Landtagen', in *Deutsche Sprache* 2, 123–31.
Born, Joachim and Gerhard Stickel (eds) (1993) *Deutsch als Verkehrssprache in Europa* (IDS Jahrbuch 1992) (Berlin, New York: de Gruyter).
Burkhardt, Armin (1992) 'Ein Parlament sucht(e) seine Sprache. Zur Sprache der Volkskammer', in Burkhard and Fritzsche (1992), 155–97.
Burkhardt, Armin and K. Peter Fritzsche (eds) (1992) *Sprache im Umbruch. Politischer Sprachwandel im Zeichen von 'Wende' und 'Vereinigung'* (Berlin, New York: de Gruyter).
Eppler, Erhard (1992) *Kavalleriepferde beim Hornsignal. Die Krise der Politik im Spiegel der Sprache* (Frankfurt/Main: Suhrkamp).
Erben, Johannes (1994) *Sprachliche Signale zur Markierung der Unsicherheit oder Unschärfe von Aussagen im Neuhochdeutschen* (Sitzungsberichte der Sächsischen Akademie der Wissenschaften zu Leipzig, Philologisch-historische Klasse, 134/3) (Berlin: Akademie Verlag).
Fix, Ulla (1996) 'Rituelle Kommunikation im öffentlichen Sprachgebrauch der DDR und ihre Begleitumstände: Möglichkeiten und Grenzen der selbstbe-

stimmten und mitbestimmenden Kommunikation in der DDR', in Lerchner (1996), 11–63.

Günthner, Susanne (1992) 'Sprache und Geschlecht: Ist Kommunikation zwischen Männern und Frauen interkulturelle Kommunikation?', in *Linguistische Berichte* 138, 124–43.

Herzog, Dieter, Hilke Rebenstorf and Bernhard Weßels (eds) (1993) *Parlament und Gesellschaft. Eine Funktionsanalyse der repräsentativen Demokratie* (Opladen: Westdeutscher Verlag).

Klein, Josef and Hajo Diekmannshenke (eds) (1996) *Sprachstrategien und Dialogblockaden. Linguistische und politikwissenschaftliche Studien zur politischen Kommunikation* (Berlin, New York: de Gruyter).

Kreutz, Heinz (1997a) 'Aspects of communicative uncertainty in the language of young East Germans during the Wende', in *Monash University Linguistics Papers* 1, 11–23.

Kreutz, Heinz (1997b) 'Some observations on hedging phenomena and modifying devices as regional markers in the speech of young east Germans', in Markkanen and Schröder (1997), 208–31.

Läzer, Rüdiger (1996) '"sie könn' das inzwischen wie ein westdeutscher politiker". Metakommunikative Situationsbearbeitung und thematische Steuerung in einer ostdeutschen "Elefantenrunde"', in Klein and Diekmannshenke (1996), 165–90.

Lerchner, Gotthard (ed.) (1996) *Sprachgebrauch im Wandel. Anmerkungen zur Kommunikationskultur in der DDR vor und nach der Wende*, 2nd edn (Frankfurt/Main: Lang).

Loreck, Ortwin (1998) 'Ochsentour in der Bonner Kälte. Sie tun sich schwer in der geölten Polit-Maschinerie und gelten als Sonderlinge, die Bundestagsabgeordneten der Abteilung Ost – aber sie bringen auch Begabungen hervor', in *Kölner Stadt-Anzeiger,* 14/15 March 1998, 4.

Markkanen, Raija and Hartmut Schröder (eds) (1997) *Hedging and Discourse. Approaches to the Analysis of a Pragmatic Phenomenon in Academic Texts* (Berlin, New York: de Gruyter).

Meyer, Paul Georg (1997) 'Hedging strategies in written academic discourse: strengthening the argument by weakening the claim', in Markkanen and Schröder (1997), 21–41.

Munske, Horst Haider, Peter von Polenz, Oskar Reichmann and Reiner Hildebrandt (eds) (1988) *Deutscher Wortschatz. Lexikologische Studien. Ludwig Erich Schmitt zum 80. Geburtstag von seinen Marburger Schülern* (Berlin, New York: de Gruyter).

Polenz, Peter von (1988) 'Argumentationswörter. Sprachgeschichtliche Stichproben bei Müntzer und Forster, Thomasius und Wolff', in Munske et al. (1988), 181–99.

Reséndiz, Julia Liebe (1992) 'Woran erkennen sich Ost- und Westdeutsche? Eine Spracheinstellungsstudie am Beispiel von Rundfunksendungen', in Welke et al. (1992), 127–40.

Scholz, Bettina (1993) 'Bundestag und Volkskammer. Meinungsprofile von Abgeordneten im Vergleich', in Herzog, Rebenstorf and Weßels (1993), 272–99.

Thierse, Wolfgang (1993) '"Sprich, damit ich dich sehe". Beobachtungen zum Verhältnis von Sprache und Politik in der DDR-Vergangenheit', in Born and Stickel (1993), 114–26.

Welke, Klaus, Wolfgang W. Sauer and Helmut Glück (eds) (1992), *Die deutsche Sprache nach der Wende* (Germanistische Linguistik 110–1) (Hildesheim, Zurich, New York: Olms).

Ylönen, Sabine (1992) 'Probleme deutsch-deutscher Kommunikation. Unterschiede im kommunikativen Verhalten zwischen Alt- und Neu-Bundesbürgern', in *Sprachreport* 2–3, 17–20.

Primary sources

'Einigungsvertrag' (1990), in *Zur Sache. Themen parlamentarischer Beratung: Auf dem Weg zur deutschen Einheit III. Deutschlandpolitische Debatten im Deutschen Bundestag vom 23. Mai bis zum 21. Juni 1990 mit Beratungen der Volkskammer der DDR zum Staatsvertrag über die Schaffung einer Währungs-, Wirtschafts- und Sozialunion und zur polnischen Westgrenze* (Bonn: Dt. Bundestag, Referat Öffentlichkeitsarbeit).

'Kinderkrippen' (1991), in *Verhandlungen des Deutschen Bundestages, 12. Wahlperiode, Stenographische Berichte,* vol. 157 (Bonn: Nomos).

'Hauptstadtdebatte' (1991), in *Verhandlungen des Deutschen Bundestages, 12. Wahlperiode, Stenographische Berichte,* vol. 157 (Bonn: Nomos).

'Frauen' (1997), in *Verhandlungen des Deutschen Bundestages, 13. Wahlperiode, Stenographische Berichte,* vol. 187,2 (Bonn:Nomos).

13
The Influence of Attitudes and Social Networks on Long-Term Linguistic Accommodation in Germany

Birgit Barden

Introduction

During or shortly after the collapse of the GDR, many East Germans left their country and settled in West Germany for political and/or economic reasons. This migration prompted us[1] to analyse the social and linguistic integration of newcomers from Saxony into the southwest of Germany. The linguistic differences between the newcomers and the residents of the new region are relatively small, and they do not have to learn a new language to communicate. However, differences between the dialects can indicate social and cultural differences, which can lead to problems: people from Saxony are recognized very easily as 'people from the east' because of their striking dialect. After the first euphoria of reunification had subsided, the situation for the newcomers became worse. On the one hand, newcomers may start to hide their different dialect by accommodation and try to develop a more western identity. On the other hand, they may choose to use the Saxon dialect to maintain their old identity and identification as coming from the east, and not change their language.

We were interested in the question of how the process of integration developed, the process of accommodation to the new area, and the convergence towards or divergence from the new language over two years. Our aim was to analyse how the informants represent themselves (linguistically and socially) in interviews, and to use these self-representations to explain the differences in terms of actual language change with the help of the concepts of social networks and attitudes towards social surroundings. In a longitudinal study, 56 people aged from 12 to 52, who had moved from east to west Germany, were interviewed eight times. The interviews were conducted by speakers of standard German over a two-year period between 1990 and 1992. Our informants came from the new federal state of Saxony, most of them from Dresden or Leipzig, some from Chemnitz or from smaller cities; they had grown up there and lived there during the last year before their migration. At the beginning of our investigation, they should not have lived in west Germany for longer than one year.

We selected two receiving dialect regions: the city of Constance in the south-west of Germany (an Alemannic-speaking, Upper German dialect area) and the city of Saarbrücken in the westernmost part of Germany (a mixed Rheinpfälzisch/Moselle-Franconian, that is Middle German dialect area). As the traditionally very low prestige of Upper Saxon Vernacular (USV) is well known (Bausinger 1972, Sauerborn and Baur 1975, 'Wiener' 1991, Allensbacher Berichte 1998), a high degree of pressure to accommodate to either the local dialect of the receiving area or the standard variety of German (as a kind of neutral way of speaking) was expected. This pressure may be reinforced by the 'out-group' interview situation, in which the interviewer came from west Germany and used the standard German variety.[2]

USV is a regional dialect koine easily described and recognized by 12 phonological features. (For further details on USV, see Becker and Bergmann 1969; Barden and Großkopf 1998:43–7.) Our methodology involved investigating changes in language production on the basis of these 12 variables, whose non-standard realizations are considered to be distinctive features of USV. For these 12 variables, indices were calculated referring to the percentage of non-standard realizations in the interview data. An overall index refers to all non-standard realizations. Some of the variables are gradual; therefore, we can distinguish between forms which are very close to the standard (intermediate realizations) and forms which are very different from the standard (strong realizations). Because of these different possible realizations of the vernacular, we calculated a subset of the USV non-standard forms, which we called 'strong realizations'. Thus, we distinguish between four possible categories: standard forms, all non-standard forms, and the two sub-categories of the latter (intermediate and strong realizations).

Figure 13.1 shows the development of the linguistic changes for the whole group over the two years of investigations. The points of refer-

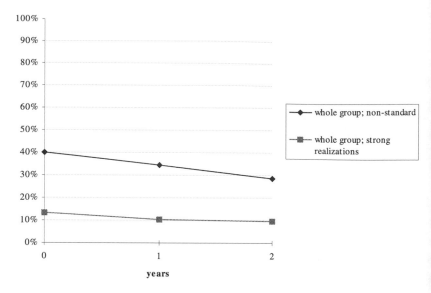

Figure 13.1   Whole group: mean values of (a) all non-standard and (b) strong realizations for all variables

ence are the data from the first interview, the fifth (after one year), and the eighth (after two years). The upper line represents the reduction of all non-standard forms: on average, there is an absolute loss of USV of 11 per cent (from 40 per cent to 29 per cent) over the two years, 6 per cent in the first, and 5 per cent in the second year. The bottom line shows the strong realizations that are reduced by only about 5 per cent (from 14 per cent to 9 per cent): 3 per cent in the first and 2 per cent in the second year. So an average person continuously reduced his or her USV over the two years.

Sociolinguistic explanations

The aim of the project was to focus on possible sociolinguistic explanations for the loss of USV realizations such as was found in our group of speakers. In our case, the social integration of the migrants in the new, west German social environment had to be investigated, and, in addition, the way in which this integration was perceived by the migrants themselves had to be taken into account; that is, we used the concepts of social networks and attitudes to explain linguistic accommodation.[3]

Social networks

Information on informants' social networks was gathered in the interviews by a special technique: they were asked to draw a diagram of their network by placing circles at various distances from their *ego*, with the distances indicating the emotional stance the informant took *vis-à-vis* the network contact (the more distance = the less affection) and with the sizes of the circles indicating the (reported) frequency of contacts. The informants were also asked to identify the origins of the people in the network: that is, whether they were from Saxony, locals of the new place of residence, or from other parts of Germany. This technique revealed how informants themselves perceived and described their networks. This special enquiry was carried out after one year of investigation and a second time after two years of investigation. In addition, informants were asked at every interview whether they had made new acquaintances or whether old ones had been broken off. With this combination of methods, we gained significant insights into the development of social contacts, whether they remained stable or involved change.

Figure 13.2 shows a complex network and illustrates the aspects of density, emotional distance, and the intensity of the contacts. The analysis of network structure was based on three dimensions:

- the (reported) density of the network was estimated according to the number of network contacts listed, the clusters within the network, and the multiplexity of the contacts;[4]
- the proportion of Saxon versus local contacts in the network;
- the informants' subjective satisfaction with their network.

The possible combinations of these three dimensions (density, importance of Saxon contacts, satisfaction with contacts) are summarized in Figure 13.3.

However, not all of these items occurred in our data. Rather, the largest number of informants belonged to network type 3 (informants satisfied with a dense network of contacts including few Saxons), followed by types 7 and 8 (loose networks with few Saxons), and by types 5 and 6 (loose networks with important Saxon contacts); only one informant was a representative of network type 1 (satisfied with a dense network in which Saxons play an important role). The subjective feeling of integration was articulated in a pronounced way by informants of type 3, followed by the persons of type 7. Although persons of type 7 have a loose network, they are satisfied with this. As one such informant said:

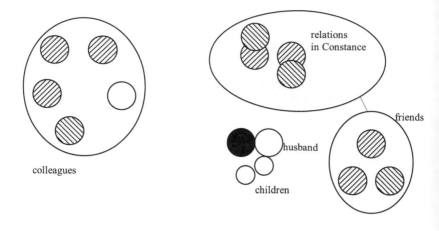

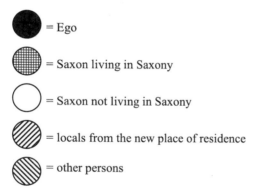

friends   ⊕

The origin of the persons in the network is symbolized by the hatching:

● = Ego

⊞ = Saxon living in Saxony

○ = Saxon not living in Saxony

◆ = locals from the new place of residence

◆ = other persons

The lines around the small circles symbolize a cluster: the persons within a cluster know each other.

Figure 13.2   Example of a social network

> Zu meinen früheren Kollegen oder Freunden in Dresden habe ich keinen Kontakt mehr. Hier in Konstanz kenne ich nicht viele Leute, aber das ist mir egal und das brauche ich auch nicht. Die Abende oder die Wochenenden möchte ich mit meiner Frau verbringen.
>
> (K19, VII)

(I don't have any contact any more with my former friends or colleagues in Dresden. Here in Constance, I don't know many people,

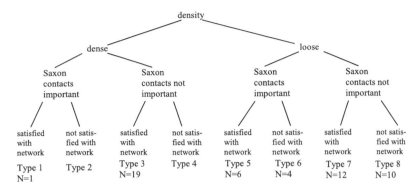

Figure 13.3   Possible combinations of networks

but I don't care, and I don't need it. In the evening or at weekends, I want to be with my wife.)

In contrast, informants of type 8 had experienced a great sense of dissatisfaction with their new circumstances, for example:

Ich werde Chemnitz meinen Kumpels aus Konstanz zeigen, damit sie mal sehen, was wirkliche Freunde sind. Hier werde ich nie einen richtigen Freund finden, dem ich auch wirklich vertrauen kann.

(K17,VII)

(I will show Chemnitz to my friends from Constance, so they can see what real friends are like. Here I will never find a real friend that I can really trust.).

Attitudes

To analyse attitudes we tried to develop a picture of the everyday life of the informants and to reconstruct processes of identification with the old and new social environment, socially and linguistically. For this reason, we again took the interviews as the basis of our investigation, because we wanted to know how the informants themselves perceived and evaluated the success of their migration. For example, topics such as what the informants experienced in the GDR and in the new place of residence, or what their opinions were about the different social systems, were important. This also includes their different attitudes towards the varieties of German in the old and new surroundings. Finally, the two main aspects shown in Table 13.1 were differentiated.

The first dimension refers to the informants' attitudes towards the new and the old region. Under this heading, three types of loyalty to the region (*Ortsbezogenheit*) were distinguished: (1) a positive attitude towards the receiving region (that is Saarbrücken and Constance) – these people play down their feelings towards, and their contacts with, Saxony and feel close to the new place of residence; (2) a neutral stance, which we named 'cosmopolitan' – these informants claimed that, for them, loyalty to the region was not important at all; indeed, they claimed to be able to live anywhere; (3) a positive attitude towards the region of origin (Saxony) – these people maintain their contacts in Saxony and still preserve a strong identification with it.

The second dimension refers to the way in which the informants came to terms with their individual migration and how they evaluated its success. Again three types were distinguished, representing proto-typical patterns of assimilation. The first prototype we called the 'cheerful soul'. These informants emphasize the positive experiences and ignore the negative ones. They are highly satisfied with their new living conditions in the west, and they look upon their migration as a success throughout, even in cases where 'objectively speaking' this evaluation is not evident in any straightforward way. For example:

> Ich habe keine schlechten Erfahrungen gemacht. Nein, überhaupt nicht. Alle Leute, die ich bisher kennengelernt habe, sind wirklich nett. Bei der Arbeit machen sie häufig Witze über unseren Dialekt, über unsere Aussprache und über die Tatsache, dass wir aus dem Osten kommen, aber das finde ich witzig, das stört mich nicht.
>
> (K11, I)
>
> (I haven't had any bad experiences. No, not at all. All the people I've met so far are really great. At work, they often crack jokes about our dialect, about our pronunciation, and about the fact that we have come from the 'east', but that's funny, it doesn't bother me.)

Table 13.1 Regional affiliation and evaluation of migration

	Loyalty towards receiving region	No regional loyalty (cosmopolitans)	Loyalty towards the region of origin
the 'cheerful soul' (*die Frohnatur*)	11	5	0
the 'laid back type' (*der Gelassene*)	7	11	5
the 'fighter' (*der Kämpfer*)	7	3	3

The second prototype, called the 'laid back type', has a rather distant way of perceiving and describing his or her experiences in the new environment. The usual attitude is that 'things will turn out all right' without much active intervention on the part of the informant. Negative experiences of migration are seen but do not result in a negative overall view of life. Mostly persons of this type see the advantages and disadvantages of life in the east and west very clearly. In the interviews, this view leads to detailed reflections, which, however, do not seem to affect the person very deeply. For example:

Wir haben hier noch keine Freunde. Aber wenn wir mehr Zeit haben, finden wir sicher welche. Im Moment ist der Job wichtiger und das ist auch o.k. so. (S21, II)
(We don't have any friends yet. But when there's more time, we'll find some all right. At the moment, the job is more important, and that's okay.)

The third prototype, the 'fighter', is highly dissatisfied with his or her life after migration. Negative experiences are underlined, and positive ones are seldom mentioned. But unlike the 'laid back type', the 'fighter's' emotions are deeply involved in coming to grips with his or her situation. The 'fighters' take problems of assimilation very seriously. Generalized negative statements about failure are frequent, and responsibility for this failure is usually attributed to the west. On the other hand, these informants desperately try to change their situation although they do not often succeed in doing so. For example:

Meine Kollegen reden immer schlecht über die DDR und so reden sie auch schlecht über mich. Mehr als einmal habe ich schon gehört, dass die Mauer wieder aufgebaut werden soll. (K21, VII)
(My colleagues are always saying bad things about the GDR, and so they say bad things about me, too. More than once I've heard people saying that the wall should be rebuilt.)

Looking at the different attitudes towards the varieties of German in combination with loyalty to the region and the individual perception of migration, it is the 'fighter' for whom the use of a special variety is most important. On the one hand, a 'fighter' with loyalty towards the receiving region strongly prefers the dialect of the new region or the standard variety and does not want to speak USV any more. This is evident from remarks such as the following:

> Ich spreche nicht gerne Sächsisch, ich bevorzuge Standard oder den regionalen Dialekt hier in der Umgebung, sonst denken die Leute womöglich noch, dass ich ein bisschen blöd bin.   (K15, VII)
> (I don't like to speak Saxon dialect, I prefer standard or the dialect of this region here. Otherwise people might think I'm a bit stupid.)

> Ich habe den sächsischen Dialekt noch nie gemocht, nie. Ich kann es nicht mehr hören.   (K21, V)
> (I've never liked the Saxon dialect, never. I can't listen to it any more.)

On the other hand, a 'fighter' with loyalty towards the old region rejects both the standard variety and the variety of the new region: such individuals see no reason to change their speech. They know the low prestige of USV but are nevertheless proud to be Saxon and to speak USV:

> Ich bin stolz, Sachse zu sein, und ich bin stolz, Sächsisch zu reden. Ich bin Sachse, und ich rede so, wie ich rede.   (S23, VII)
> (I am proud to be a Saxon, and I'm proud to speak Saxon dialect. I am a Saxon and speak the way I speak.)

Up to this point, we have looked separately at the general linguistic results, social networks, and attitudes. We can now go on to explore the interdependence of linguistic and social integration. Linguistic data, social networks, and attitudes are combined with each other and result in six integration types: four main ones (A, B, C, D) and two intermediate ones (AB, BC). The intermediate types are mixtures of two main ones. The type AB represents some features of type A and some of type B; type BC represents some of type B, and some of type C. The general results are summarized in Table 13.2.

For a comparison of the data on the types of integration, we differentiated between a value for absolute language change and a value for relative language change listed in Table 13.2 under the heading 'linguistic accommodation to the standard variety'. These values refer to all non-standard realizations. The absolute value means the real difference in the number of realizations; the relative value means the relative reduction of the non-standard forms in comparison to the Saxon dialect level in the first interview. Generally, it can be seen that all types of integration except type C reduce USV. Type D (–45 per cent) reduces Saxon realizations the most followed by type A

Table 13.2 Type of integration and type of linguistic accommodation in the study as a whole

	Type A (15)	Type AB (6)	Type B (10)	Type BC (5)	Type C (2)	Type D (10)	Total
Network							
density	+	+	–	–	–	–	
satisfaction	+	+	+	+	–	–	
contacts with Saxons	–	–	–	+	+	–	
Attitudes							
Regional affiliation							
with new region	+	+	–	–	–	+	
'cosmopolitan'	+	–	+	–	–	+	
with Saxony	–	–	–	+	+	–	
Perception of migration							
'the cheerful soul'	+	–	–	–	–	–	
'the laid back type'	–	+	+	+	–	–	
'the fighter'	–	–	–	–	+	+	
Linguistic accommodation							
To the standard variety							
(absolute change over two years)	–16%	–10%	–11%	–5%	13%	–24%	–11%
(relative change over two years)	–38%	–15%	–27%	–9%	29%	–45%	–29%
To the local dialect (over two years)	yes	yes	no	no	no	yes	yes

(–38 per cent), type B (–27 per cent), type AB (–15 per cent), and type BC (–9 per cent). Moreover, some of the network parameters and some of the attitudinal ones are interrelated: if a person has a strong regional affiliation with Saxony on the attitudinal level, contacts with Saxons in the network are also important (types BC and C), while a person who feels a stronger affiliation with the receiving region will not seek such contacts (types A, D and AB). Furthermore, 'fighters' are always dissatisfied with their social networks (types C and D), while 'cheerful souls' or 'laid back types' are always satisfied with them.

As regards which type accommodates the most to standard German and to the dialect of the receiving area, type D (–45 per cent relative loss of USV) accommodate most followed by type A (–38 per cent relative loss of USV). In both types, either regional affiliation is connected with the west German area of residence, or they are 'cosmopolitans'. Moreover, only type AB shows exclusively a regional affiliation with the new region and also accommodates to the dialect of the region. A further related point is that contacts with Saxons are not relevant for these types. But apart from that, A and D represent very different developments. For a person of type A, the new network is densely structured, and satisfaction with the kind of social contacts is high. These informants have a positive view of their migration and represent the attitudinal type of the 'cheerful soul'. On the contrary, informants of type D are characterized by a loosely structured network, and they are not satisfied with their social network. Their attitudinal stance is that of a 'fighter'. We regard this result as evidence that very different social conditions can lead to linguistic accommodation in a new area. In the one case (type A), informants are regularly confronted with the standard variety or the local vernacular in face-to-face interactions in their dense networks. Because of the network density and the satisfaction with their social contacts, it is very likely that they will accommodate to the language of their interlocutors. In type D, the language of the new area is not so present in face-to-face interaction because of the loose network. Adopting features of this area and getting rid of USV features can be seen as an attempt (an 'act of identity': Le Page and Tabouret-Keller 1985) by these speakers to adapt themselves to the social milieu in which they want to be accepted. These people try to make stable and satisfactory contacts with members of the new region, but mostly they fail. Therefore, type D is evidence of Granovetter's (1973, 1982) thesis (taken up in sociolinguistics by Milroy and Milroy 1992) that dense networks are not necessarily a precondition of rapid change; rather open (loose) networks seem to do the same, particularly when they are not considered as satisfactory by the speaker.

Types D and C are both representative of the 'fighter': they both have loose networks and are not satisfied with their social network. But in contrast to type D, type C informants seek Saxon contacts, and their regional affiliation is connected with Saxony. As a consequence, the linguistic development of these speakers is the opposite of type D. Compared to their initial level of USV usage, they even increase the USV features in their speech: that is, there is divergence from the local speech of the receiving area. This linguistic development clearly indicates withdrawal from the west.

Finally, migrants of type B belong to the group of the 'laid back types', an attitudinal stance they share with the intermediate types AB and BC. Type B differs from AB only insofar as networks are loosely structured, and from BC only in that network contacts with Saxons are irrelevant. The general orientation of type B informants is cosmopolitan; their satisfaction with their network contacts is high. Reflecting this intermediate position between types A and C, speakers of this type do not accommodate to the local dialect, and their accommodation to the standard variety corresponds to the average of the total group (type B relative loss of 27 per cent, total group of 29 per cent).

A special case: Mr V

For most of our informants, there was some kind of linear development in the change in their language and in their adaptation to the new surroundings. But there are a few, the type C informants and two other individuals, who are not typical representatives of our group of Saxon informants as a whole. One of these informants, Mr V, will be discussed here to demonstrate how changes in social network and attitudes can influence linguistic accommodation. His speech change during the two years of our investigation is unique in several respects. None the less, we shall see that looking at this particular, exceptional case can be helpful in identifying and analysing the general social forces behind the linguistic accommodation of Saxon migrants in west Germany.

At first glance, the exceptional case of Mr V can be demonstrated by a comparison of his linguistic behaviour with that of the average speaker on a cumulative index for all variables investigated. On average, every speaker in our group reduces his or her USV value from 40 per cent to 29 per cent (see Figure 13.4) during the period of investigation, which corresponds to a relative loss of 28 per cent USV realizations. However, for Mr V, who used a comparatively high level of USV forms in the first interview (62 per cent), no such tendency is observed.

On the contrary, he used slightly more USV forms (the relative increase is 5 per cent) in the last interview. The strong realizations show a similar pattern: the value in the group as a whole is considerably diminished over the two years (relative loss of USV realizations = 38 per cent), while Mr V's strong Saxon forms slightly increased by 3 per cent. So, all in all, Mr V seems to have increased his usage of both intermediate non-standard forms and, to a lesser extent, strong Saxon realizations during the two years.

These details make Mr V a non-typical representative of our group as a whole, but in terms of the integration types, he may correspond with type C. However, the very special nature of Mr V's accommodation pattern does not become clear if it is investigated only over the two-year period as a whole. Here the relevance of a longitudinal study is obvious. Because interviews were conducted every three months, we are able to observe the social and linguistic development of Mr V at smaller intervals and to locate the points of changes. So looking at the interviews at six-monthly intervals we get a different picture (Figure 13.5): Mr V does not exhibit a linear pattern of change, but rather a zigzag-type curve. While he abandoned USV forms significantly in the first year (63 per cent in the first interview, 58 per

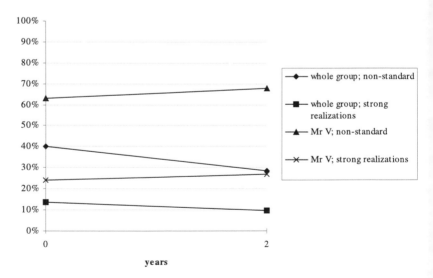

Figure 13.4 Whole group and Mr V: mean values of non-standard and strong realizations for all variables

cent in the third interview, 45 per cent in the fifth interview), this pattern changed in the second year. He returned to his old way of speaking and, in some ways, even surpassed it in USV realizations (45 per cent in the fifth interview, 61 per cent in the seventh interview, 69 per cent in the eighth interview).

Although it seems that Mr V's linguistic behaviour is strange and exceptional, the analyses of his kind of changes can be especially used to show whether and how linguistic and social behaviour are inter-related. If there is indeed a close relationship between social integration and linguistic accommodation, Mr V should exhibit a radical change in the social parameters accompanying and explaining linguistic orientation.

In the following, we will focus on Mr V's network contacts and on his attitudes, and on whether there are some radical changes which can explain his linguistic behaviour. For this reason, some general information about Mr V and his migration to west Germany are essential. Mr V was 26 years old when we started our investigation; he left the GDR shortly before the fall of the wall, and moved directly to Saarbrücken. His wife (represented by the large white network point close to Mr V's *ego* point in Figure 13.6) joined him in early 1990.

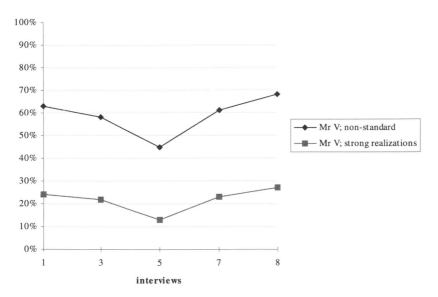

Figure 13.5   Mr V: mean values of non-standard and strong realizations for all variables

Mr V described his first experiences in Saarbrücken as positive ones. He quickly got to know some elderly people, who helped him to find a flat and a job in his old trade as a bricklayer. This job was very important for him because he wanted to improve his financial and occupational situation as soon as possible. For that purpose, he spent a lot of time on the job, and after only three months he was promoted to a higher position. This success in the job was highly satisfactory for him, and he did not care that he made only a few new social contacts. Apart from his family (wife, child, parents, and a brother and sister-in-law, all living in Saarbrücken), his network included only some locals of Saarbrücken: his colleagues, a former colleague of his wife's, and, particularly important, a female friend of about the same age (acquaintance A) ('Wir können über alles miteinander reden' W2, IV) (We can talk to each other about everything).

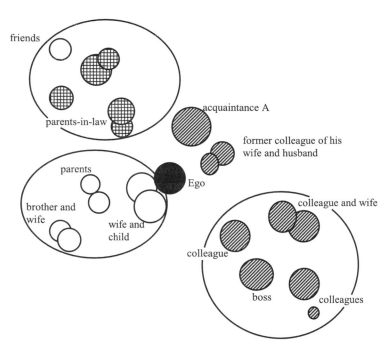

Figure 13.6   Social network of Mr V after one year network type 7

His wife still cultivated their social ties in Saxony, and they often went to Saxony to visit friends and family. However, Mr V did not really care about these contacts in Saxony, and they did not play an important role in his life. If we compare Mr V's social contacts with the network types mentioned above, we can conclude the following: until the fifth interview (the first year of investigation), Mr V was a representative of network type 7. His network was open and rather loose, and contacts with other Saxons either in Leipzig or in Saarbrücken were not of great importance to him. At the same time, he claimed to be satisfied with his network, both with the number and the emotional status of the contacts in his network. The social contacts he demonstrated to us in the fifth interview are shown in Figure 13.6.

If our attitude criteria are applied to Mr V such as he presented himself in the first year of our study, he is closest to the prototype called the 'laid back type' with his clear affiliation with and loyalty to Saarbrücken. In contrast, he views Leipzig as no more than an alternative place to live; he really feels settled in Saarbrücken:

> Mich zieht dort nichts hin. Wenn ich jetzt das Chaos sehe, bin ich zufrieden, dass ich den Schritt gemacht haben. (W2, II)
> (There is no reason to go back. When I see the chaos there I am really happy that I decided to make the step [that is the move to Saarbrücken].)

This is reflected in his attitude towards the varieties of Saxony and Saarbrücken: he accepts the Rheinpfälzisch/Moselle-Franconian variety, and he has begun to understand the dialect. He makes a lot of jokes about his experiences with his own dialect, even when he has problems being understood. On the other hand, he distances himself from USV:

> Also, welche, die schwer sächseln, das klingt dann manchmal schon ein bisschen gemein. (W2, IV)
> (People who speak strong Saxon dialect, they sometimes sound a bit vulgar.)

Now we can compare Mr V with the integration types developed for the group as a whole (see Table 13.2). In terms of integration types, he is close to type B (open network, contacts with Saxons not important, 'laid back type', satisfied with social integration); only his affiliation with Saarbrücken moves him slightly in the direction of AB. In accordance with this classification, his use of USV features is reduced by some

30 per cent in the first year, which is slightly above the average found for the group as a whole and for type B (see Table 13.3).

Until this point, Mr V fits into one of our integration types and behaves linguistically and socially like a type B. Now the question is whether we can explain the changes which occurred in the second year. Around the time of the fifth interview (after one year of investigation), Mr V had to undergo an operation. This operation, which finally left him severely handicapped, changed his life dramatically. After six months of medical treatment, he had to accept the fact that he would never be able to return to his job but had to retire instead. Besides the substantial financial losses, his network structure was marked by a fundamental shift (see Figure 13.7).

Since he could not go out by himself in the first weeks after the operation, he had to rely on the visits of friends and colleagues, and he was very dejected. Most of his Saarland contacts were lost, as they had been only somewhat superficial uniplex contacts with colleagues. His female friend (acquaintance A) completely disappeared from his network: 'Sie sagte, sie würde mal vorbeischauen, aber sie hat's nie getan' (W2, VIII) (She said she would drop in but she never did). Instead of her, a second acquaintance (B) became more important, but he met her only by chance from time to time on a playground where they both went to play with their children. So he did not feel satisfied with his local contacts and reactivated his old contacts with friends and relatives in Saxony. His wife had maintained these contacts all the time, but until this point, he did not really bother about them. Moreover, his parents had remigrated back to Saxony at that time. Mr V and his wife often returned to Leipzig for a holiday, and these contacts in Saxony became more and more important.

These bad experiences with locals in Saarbrücken reflect not only the social network but also attitudes. Mr V's view of Saarbrücken and the people there, which had formerly been positive, radically changed as a consequence of his negative experiences with insurance and bureaucratic officials. These negative experiences made him change from a 'laid back type' to a 'fighter'. He distanced himself from the 'mentality of the Saarländer', whom he accused of being unreliable, and felt closer to Leipzig again. So his local loyalty changed from an affiliation to Saarbrücken to an affiliation to Leipzig. This change of loyalty went so far that in the last interview Mr V's plans to return to east Germany had already become very concrete, although he had claimed in one of the first interviews that he would go to Leipzig only as a visitor:

Table 13.3   Mr V (first year) and Mr V (second year) compared with type B and type C

	Type B	Mr V/1st year	Type C	Mr V/2nd year
Network				
density	–	–	–	–
satisfaction	+	+	–	–
contacts with Saxons	–	–	+	+
Attitudes				
Regional affiliation				
with new region	–	+	–	–
'cosmopolitan'	+	–	–	–
with Saxony	–	–	+	+
Perception of migration				
'the cheerful soul'	–	–	–	–
'the laid back type'	+	+	–	–
'the fighter'	–	–	+	+
Linguistic accommodation				
To the standard variety				
(absolute change)	–11%	–18%	13%	23%
(relative change)	–27%	–30%	29%	47%
To the local dialect				
(over two years)	no	no	no	no

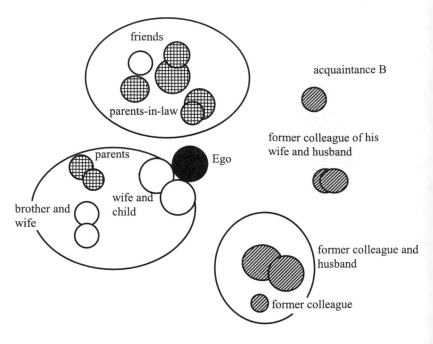

Figure 13.7   Social network of Mr V after two years: network type 6

Nun, wir werden's wohl machen [that is return to Leipzig] sobald sich hier all meine Sachen erledigt haben, obwohl ich am Anfang jedem gesagt habe, dass ich nicht für hunderttausend Mark zurück-geh.   (W2, VII.)
(Well, we'll do it [that is return to Leipzig] as soon as all my things have been settled here. Although at the beginning, I told everybody I wouldn't go back for a hundred thousand marks.)

Finally, we can compare the behaviour of Mr V with the group as a whole, and it is obvious that Mr V had changed from type B to type C (see Table 13.3). For this type (contacts with Saxons are important, 'fighter', regional affiliation with Saxony), divergence from the receiving area of migration is typical, and this was the case with Mr V. So again Mr V behaves just as we would expect him to on the basis of our general results.

Conclusion

The aim of this chapter was to show that the combination of language and more complex social features are very helpful in explaining processes of accommodation in post-unification Germany. During and after unification, extreme changes in every part of the life of east Germans suddenly began, and they could decide either to stay at their old place of residence or to move to the west. Those who moved to the west were motivated by different reasons, and the success of migrants' integration into the new environment varies from person to person. The degree of success depends on how migrants manage the tasks of settling in the new area and on their perception of how they do this. Besides the tasks of finding a flat and a job, there are many social and personal ones, such as finding new friends and establishing an attitude towards the new and old living conditions. Generally these are processes which are motivated by the desire to be a member of a particular, new society. One way of becoming a member is not only to adapt socially but also to accommodate linguistically. People from the new federal state of Saxony might feel a great deal of pressure to accommodate: they were easily recognized as coming from the east because of their dialect, which has a very low prestige. After the first euphoria of reunification had diminished, being recognized as an '*Ossi*' was not very positive for many of the east Germans.

By using the concepts of social networks and attitudes, combined with each other and with linguistic variables, we have been able to investigate the process and the perception of integration. The general survey shows that special integration types exist, some of them easily managing to be integrated (type A and B), some of them struggling to do so (type D), while others retain their 'loyalty' to their previous place of residence (type C). Finally, the case study of Mr V demonstrates in a more detailed way the general regularities and forces, both on the linguistic level and on the sociolinguistic level, that are exemplary characteristics of long-term dialect accommodation.

Notes

1 This chapter reports on some findings of a research project on long-term linguistic accommodation sponsored by the Fritz Thyssen Stiftung from 1990 to 1993 that I worked on together with Peter Auer and Beate Großkopf. For more details, see Großkopf, Barden and Auer (1997), Auer, Barden and Großkopf (1998), and Barden and Großkopf (1998).

2 In this chapter, only accommodation of this latter type (that is loss of USV features in favour of standard features) will be discussed, whereas dialect acquisition, which was also observed through the two-year period, will be disregarded.

3   For more information on these topics see, for example, Milroy (1980/1987), Bortoni-Ricardo (1985), and Barden and Großkopf (1998) for social networks, and Besch et al. (1981), Dittmar, Schlobinski and Wachs (1986), Mihm (1985a), and Barden and Großkopf (1998) for attitudes.

4   Normally density refers to the actually realized contacts in proportion to possible contacts as a whole within a network. This kind of definition follows a quantitative evaluation of the contacts with the help of a formula. We subsumed more aspects under the notion of density because we were interested in a qualitative evaluation and the three aspects named seem to represent the subjective feeling of density from the view of the informants.

References

Allensbacher Berichte (1998) *Bayrisch hören viele gern* (Allensbach: Institut für Demoskopie), No. 22.

Auer, Peter, Birgit Barden and Beate Großkopf (1998) 'Subjective and objective parameters determining "salience" in long-term dialect accommodation', in *Journal of Sociolinguistics* 2/2, 163–87.

Barden, Birgit and Beate Großkopf (1998) *Sprachliche Akkommodation und soziale Integration. Sächsische Übersiedler und Übersiedlerinnen im rhein-/moselfränkischen und alemannischen Sprachraum* (PHONAI No. 43) (Tübingen: Niemeyer).

Bausinger, Hermann (1972) *Deutsch für Deutsche. Dialekte, Sprachbarrieren, Sondersprachen* (Frankfurt/Main: Fischer).

Becker, Horst and Gunther Bergmann (1969) *Sächsische Mundartenkunde. Entstehung, Geschichte und Lautstand der Mundarten des obersächsischen Gebietes* (Halle/Saale: Niemeyer).

Besch, Werner, Jochen Hufschmidt, Angelika Kall-Holland, Eva Klein and Klaus J. Mattheier (1981) *Sprachverhalten in ländlichen Gemeinden. Ansätze zu Theorie und Methode. Forschungsbericht Erp-Projekt*, Vol. 1 (Berlin: Schmidt).

Bortoni-Ricardo, Stella Maris (1985) *The Urbanization of Rural Dialect Speakers* (Cambridge: Cambridge University Press).

Dittmar, Norbert, Peter Schlobinski and Inge Wachs (1986) *Berlinisch. Studien zum Lexikon, zur Spracheinstellung und zum Stilrepertoire* (Berlin: Spitz).

Granovetter, Mark (1973) 'The strength of weak ties', in *American Journal of Sociology* 78, 1360–80.

Granovetter, Mark (1982) 'The strength of weak ties', in Marsden and Lin (1982), 105–30.

Großkopf, Beate, Birgit Barden and Peter Auer (1997) 'Sprachliche Anpassung und soziale Haltung: zur verstehenden Soziolinguistik der innerdeutschen Migration', in Kotthoff (1997), 359–84.

Kotthoff, Helga (ed.) (1997) *Interactional Sociolinguistics* (= Folia Linguistica XXX/3–4) (Berlin, New York: de Gruyter).

Le Page, Robert B. and Andrée Tabouret-Keller (1985) *Acts of Identity: Creole-based Approaches to Language and Ethnicity* (Cambridge: Cambridge University Press).

Marsden, Peter V. and Nan Lin (eds) (1982) *Social Structure and Network Analysis* (London: Sage).

Mihm, Arend (1985a) 'Prestige und Stigma des Substandards. Zur Bewertung des Ruhrdeutschen im Ruhrgebiet', in Mihm (1985b), 163–93.

Mihm, Arend (ed.)(1985b) *Sprache an Rhein und Ruhr. Dialektologische und soziolinguistische Studien zur sprachlichen Situation im Rhein-Ruhr-Gebiet und ihrer Geschichte* (Stuttgart: Steiner).

Milroy, Lesley (1980/1987) *Language and Social Networks* (Oxford: Blackwell).

Milroy, Lesley and James Milroy (1992) 'Social network and social class. Towards an integrated sociolinguistic model', in *Language in Society* 21, 1–26.

Sauerborn, Heinrich and Gerhard Baur (1975) 'Freiwillige Befragung über das Verhältnis des Lehrers zum Dialekt' Dissertation, Pädagogische Hochschule Freiburg.

'Wiener' (1991) *Visionen. Lebenswelten der 19- bis 29jährigen* (Leonberg).

14
Competing Language Ideologies in Germany: When East Meets West
Jennifer Dailey-O'Cain

Language ideology and language attitudes in Germany

The woman is 50 years old, born in Berlin, but she has been living for years in a little town in southwestern Germany where she feels very much at home. She is a housewife by profession, which she calls 'der undankbarste Beruf der Welt' or 'the most thankless job in the world,'[1] only half-jokingly. 'Auf Ihrem Fragebogen,' she says to me:

> da konnte man auch ankreuzen: die neuen Bundesbürger werden behandelt wie Menschen zweiter Klasse. Also das kann man nun wirklich nicht sagen. Die hundertzehn Milliarden Mark, die da hineinfließen, die wachsen nicht auf Bäumen. Es sind verschiedene Dinge, die in jeder Gemeinde, in jeder Stadt, zurückgestellt werden, weil das vorhandene Geld in die DDR – in die ehemalige DDR – gepumpt wird. Wir sind uns auch darüber im klaren, daß die erst mal erwirtschaftet werden müssen. Aber sind sie dankbar? Nein, sie fühlen sich, wie gesagt, als Deutsche zweiter Klasse.
> (In your questionnaire you could circle 'the eastern Germans are being treated like second-class people.' Well, you really can't say that at all. The hundred and ten billion marks that are flowing into the east, that doesn't grow on trees. There are projects that are being abandoned in every [western] town, in every [western] city, because the available money is being pumped into East Germany – I mean former East Germany. We *are* aware that they have to be financed for a while at first. But are they thankful? No, they feel, as you say, like second-class citizens.)

There is another woman, 56 years old and no more than 500 miles away, in central eastern Germany. For years she was a highly-respected teacher in an East German, then, after unification, in an 'eastern' German elementary school. She always loved teaching, but since unification she has been depressed and feels she's just been going through the motions. She is concerned for her job, as well, because she knows that the birth rate has sunk drastically in eastern Germany since unification, and she realizes that in a matter of just a few years, there will not be the need for so many teachers. She says she *liked* living in her country, East Germany, and goes on:

> Es war nicht alles schlecht in der DDR. Die westdeutschen Politiker haben uns mit dieser Wiedervereinigung unsere Würde genommen. Und das betrifft auch die Sprache. Wissen Sie, was mich aufgeregt hat? Vor der Wende hatten wir immer unsere 'Fleischerei'; das war doch normal. Aber ich gehe dorthin, und es steht auf einmal 'Metzgerei'! Noch nie in meinem Leben hab' ich hier früher 'Metzgerei' gesehen. Warum nehmen sie uns auch unsere Sprache weg, können Sie mir das sagen?
> (Not everything was bad in East Germany. The western German politicians took away our self-worth. And that affects the language, too. Do you know what made me angry? Before the *Wende*, we always had our 'Fleischerei' ('meat shop'); that was normal. But now I go there, and suddenly it says 'Metzgerei' ('butcher shop')![2] Before that, I'd never seen 'Metzgerei' here in my whole life. Why are they taking our language away, too, can you tell me that?')

These two women are not alone in their reactions (see also Linklater, Chapter 9, this volume). The years since the official unification of Germany on 3 October 1990 have shown that unification must be seen as a process rather than an event. It is also clear that this process is by no means complete. Relations between eastern and western Germans have become increasingly strained in recent years. Many eastern Germans, who grew up believing West Germany was a land where everyone was happy and wealthy, are now faced with the realities of unemployment and a 'buyer beware' market economy. Many western Germans who grew up feeling sorry for the easterners because they could not buy videotape recorders or spend holidays in Italy now show little sympathy for their plight, and are more worried about rising taxes and their own jobs.

This situation has many implications for the study of linguistics and language in Germany. Sociolinguists and linguistic anthropologists have often discussed the conflict between the prescriptive assumption made by non-linguists that some varieties of a language are 'good language', while others are 'bad language', and one of the basic tenets of linguistics, which states that there is no such thing as 'good' and 'bad' language. Milroy and Milroy (1985:1–28) formalized this basic concept in linguistics by noting that a fully standardized language with native speakers is a linguistic impossibility, since living languages are constantly changing. While different varieties can and do certainly gain different levels of status within a society due to social and political factors, there is a great deal of evidence that language varieties which are *viewed* as inferior actually are *not* less logical, less complex, or less effective tools of communication (Labov 1969).

Sometimes the perception of 'good language' focuses on a particular geographical centre, and in Germany one often hears people say that 'the best German' is spoken in Hanover, a town in the northwestern part of the country. These Germans use Hanover to represent a geographical manifestation of their *standard language ideology,* which Lippi-Green (1997:64) defines as 'a bias toward an abstracted, idealized, homogeneous spoken language which is imposed and maintained by the dominant bloc institutions, and which names as its model the written language, but which is drawn primarily from the spoken language of the upper middle class'. The fact that a language ideology is not based on the linguistic reality of a language does not, however, mean that it is an area unworthy of investigation. Although the notions behind non-linguists' assumptions are often incorrect, an investigation into different societies' language ideologies can provide a great deal of information about the relationship between language and society which sociolinguists seek to reveal. Indeed, there is a large area of very careful theoretical research investigating the nature of language ideology (for example, Silverstein 1992, Woolard 1992, Woolard and Schieffelin 1994).

If one wishes to study the components of a language ideology empirically, however, one needs to study non-linguists' *attitudes* towards language. Such language attitude studies are particularly important because sociolinguists have demonstrated that language use is a key tool in the establishment of social identity, both in terms of language choice (Pool 1979) and in terms of variation within a language (Milroy 1980:139–76, Chambers 1995:250–3). Post-unification Germany is an ideal 'laboratory' in which to study language attitude phenomena precisely because of this link between social identity and language. The euphoria the world witnessed at the end of 1989 when the Berlin Wall fell has long since disappeared, and in its place many difficult questions involving identity have emerged. In a study under- taken by the Friedrich-Ebert-Stiftung in connection with the *polis* and *Sinus* institutes for social research in 1991, 65 per cent of easterners and 68 per cent of westerners stated that they did not trust the other group of Germans (Becker, Becker and Ruhland 1992). In a more recent empirical study undertaken in eastern Germany by the Emnid Institut and reported in the news weekly *Der Spiegel,* 67 per cent of those surveyed stated that they thought the proverbial 'wall in the mind' was growing rather than shrinking (Emnid-Institut 1995). And perhaps most revealing is a study conducted in the eastern German city of Jena (Kanning and Mummendey 1993), which stated that with respect to areas such as their financial situation, political influence, and to some extent, social behaviour, eastern Germans felt they experienced 'negative social identity' in comparison with western Germans, meaning that they saw their own identity as devalued. Based on such indications, it seems realistic to hypothesize that attitudes towards language variation will be strongly affected by the complex socio-political situation in Germany today, and that these will in turn reveal the nature of the standard language ideology or ideologies in Germany.

While speculation about the effects of different language varieties on people's credibility can be traced all the way back to Aristotle, the first study to consider language attitudes systematically was Lambert *et al.*'s (1960) work on French and English. This was the study which pioneered the use of the matched-guise technique, which has since been used with a great deal of success by many scholars in different speech communities throughout the world. Yet as versatile and useful as the matched-guise technique can be, Preston (1989; 1999) suggests that this kind of study only provides part of the picture of a speech community's language attitudes. The matched-guise technique concentrates mainly on very specific attitudes towards very specific varieties, and neglects the big picture. A more complete description of a society's language attitudes would also have to include maps of non-linguists' perception of language distribution, and the ratings of the 'correctness', 'pleasantness' and 'similarness' of different areas without a recorded stimulus. Preston's own work has centred on these, which together form the methodology he refers to as *perceptual dialectology*. This method enables the researcher to gain access to attitudes towards *geographically-based* linguistic variation on a large scale, which the matched-guise technique is much less suitable for.

Empirical data and results: the 1994 study

In 1994, I designed and carried out a study using perceptual dialectology so as to access differences in language attitudes based on perceived
geographic variation. I interviewed 200 Germans, 50 each who had
grown up in the western towns of Hanover and Munich, and 50 each
who had grown up in the eastern towns of Leipzig and Rostock, cities
chosen on the basis of geographical location. As I read aloud a list of
29 cities (27 cities in Germany plus Vienna and Zurich), informants
rated each city on a scale from one to six in terms of the 'correctness'
of the language varieties in each city, with one as most and six as least
'correct'.[3] (This scale may seem somewhat backwards, but it was chosen
to correspond to the German grading system in elementary school, in
which a one is the best grade you can get, and a six is the worst.)
Informants had only their memories and perceptions to rely on,
because no recorded stimulus was provided. For the purposes of this
chapter, I will restrict the analysis to the ratings of the nine of these
cities that are in northern Germany. (For more details, see Dailey-
O'Cain 1997, 1999.)

In order to measure the difference between attitudes towards the language of northern Germany as a whole and attitudes towards the language of Hanover, I first took a mean of all of the ratings for northern
cities to form a second variable. Then I calculated a ratio of the
Hanover variable to the general north variable. In this ratio, a mean of
less than 1 indicates that informants find Hanover to be more 'correct',
a mean of more than 1 indicates that they find the general north to be
more 'correct', and a mean of 1 indicates that they find them equally
'correct.' In Table 14.1 you can see the means for westerners and easterners separately. The mean of 0.55 for the westerners indicates that
they find that the variety of German spoken in the city of Hanover is
more 'correct' than the varieties spoken in northern Germany as a
whole. The easterners, on the other hand, have a mean rating of 0.98,
indicating that they believe the level of 'correctness' of the varieties
spoken in northern Germany is the same as the level of 'correctness' of
the variety spoken in the city of Hanover. (As Table 14.1 indicates, this
difference is significant at 0.00005 in a one-way analysis of variance,
and an eta-squared test yields a result of 0.31, indicating that 31 per
cent of the variation in the data is accounted for by this variable.)

At the time, these findings surprised me, and I expressed this to my
informants after they had given the ratings. I asked my eastern informants whether they had ever heard of the idea that the most 'correct'

Table 14.1   Analysis of the variance between westerners and easterners with respect to the difference (ratio) between 'correctness' of Hanover and 'correctness' of northern German language generally (1994 study)

	Mean
Westerners	0.55
Easterners	0.98

F-value = 0.00005; eta-squared = 0.31
(less than 1 = Hanover more 'correct'; more than 1 = general north more 'correct')

German is spoken in Hanover. No one I asked said they had heard of this. One informant, in fact, said that some northwestern German varieties were just fine, such as those around Lübeck or Hamburg, but that Hanover was simply too far south to be very 'correct'. The easterners I spoke with expressed surprise that Hanover is seen as the centre of 'correctness' in western Germany, and often voiced the question: 'Why? What's so special about Hanover?'

Empirical data and results: the 1995 study

In order to investigate this phenomenon further, I carried out a second study the following summer, in 1995. The research design was identical to that of the 1994 study, except that I interviewed people from a larger number and a wider variety of places, including 44 towns of varying sizes throughout Germany, and asked them about regions rather than just cities. As I read aloud a list of 34 regions of Germany, informants rated the 'correctness' of the varieties of German spoken in each region, which included 28 well-known regions of Germany and the cities of Berlin, Hamburg, Hanover, Cologne, Frankfurt and Munich. After this task was completed, I asked informants to provide demographic information about themselves, such as the town they grew up in, gender, age, level of education, and political affiliation. Finally, the same 218 informants conversed informally in small groups for half an hour about their attitudes towards language variation, and these conversations were recorded so that I could obtain qualitative data that would help strengthen the arguments based on the quantitative data.

As in the 1994 study, I first took a mean of all of the ratings for northern regions to form a second variable, and then calculated a ratio of the Hanover variable to the general north variable. The results from an analysis of variance can be found in Table 14.2. As was true in the

1994 study, the westerners' mean of 0.58, much less than 1, indicates that they find the Hanover variety to be much more 'correct' than northern varieties generally. On the other hand, in the 1995 study the easterners also have a mean that is less than 1, namely 0.85. Although the easterners are much closer to finding Hanover and the north generally to be equal than the westerners are, these results indicate a marked trend among easterners towards finding Hanover more 'correct' than the general north. The difference between the easterners' and westerners' ratings is still statistically significant at 0.00005, yet, as can be seen in Table 14.2, an eta-squared test yields a result of only 0.18, much lower than in 1994. This indicates that despite the statistically significant difference between westerners and easterners, only 18 per cent of the variation is accounted for by the variable of eastern versus western geographical origin. This suggests a major change in attitude in just one year. This change is illustrated more clearly on the graph in Figure 14.1, where one can see that although the solid line representing the perceptions of the westerners remains fairly constant from 1994 to 1995, the dotted line representing the perceptions of the easterners moves noticeably closer to the perceptions of the westerners from the one year to the next.

The qualitative data from the 1995 study also further serves to confirm the change suggested by the quantitative data. A 75-year-old man from Hamburg stated that:

> Ein echter Hannoveraner, der hat keinen Dialekt. Ein Eingereister, zum Beispiel von hier, der spricht Plattdeutsch, und auch Hochdeutsch. Aber der echte Hannoveraner hat keinen Dialekt.
> (A real person from Hanover doesn't have a dialect. Someone who moves there, for example from here, speaks Low German, and also standard German. But a real Hanoverian doesn't have a dialect.)

Table 14.2   Analysis of the variance between westerners and easterners with respect to the difference (ratio) between 'correctness' of Hanover and 'correctness' of northern German language generally (1995 study)

	Mean
Westerners	0.58
Easterners	0.85

F-value = 0.00005; eta-squared = 0.18
(less than 1 = Hanover more 'correct'; more than 1 = general north more 'correct')

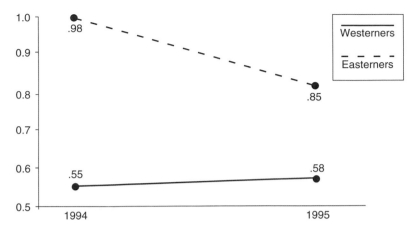

(less than 1 = Hanover more 'correct'; more than 1 = general north more 'correct')

Figure 14.1 Change in easterners' and westerners' perceptions of the difference (ratio) between 'correctness' of Hanover and 'correctness' of northern German language generally, between 1994 and 1995

A 67-year-old woman from central western Germany agreed in a separate interview, stating:

> Der einigermaßen gebildete Hannoveraner, sagt man, hat kaum Dialekt. Auch die einfachen Leute sprechen so.
> (They say that any more or less educated person from Hanover hardly has any dialect. Even ordinary people speak that way.)

The comments from easterners, however, were more mixed. Some informants clearly adhered to the older eastern language ideology that the 'most correct' German is spoken in the north generally, such as a 50-year-old man from central eastern Germany who stated:

> Ich glaub' das beste Hochdeutsch wird in der Altmark gesprochen. Und in der niedersächsischen Gegend, bis zur Küste.
> (I think the best German is spoken in the Altmark region [in northeastern Germany]. And in the area around Lower Saxony, up to the north coast.)

However, examples such as this conversation between a 40-year-old man and his 29-year-old wife, both from northeastern Germany, were also common.

Fieldworker: Wo wird Hochdeutsch gesprochen?
Woman, 29: Na, bei uns natürlich!
Man, 40: Nein, nein. Ich würde eher sagen so die Hannoversche Ecke vielleicht. Bei uns ist doch noch einiges mit ... Platt.
Woman, 29: Nee. Bei uns? So direkt Mecklenburg-Vorpommern? Wir sprechen doch Hochdeutsch!
(Field worker: 'Where is standard German spoken?'
Woman, 29: 'Well, here, of course!'
Man, 40: 'No, no, I'd say the area around Hanover. Here we speak some things in a sort of Low German way.'
Women, 29: 'No way! Here? Directly in Mecklenburg-Western Pomerania? We speak standard German!')

In the following example, a similar debate takes place between a 38-year-old woman from central eastern Germany and her 17-year-old son.

Fieldworker: Wo wird Hochdeutsch gesprochen?
Woman, 38: Im Norden.
Man, 17[son]: Nein, in Niedersachsen. Hannover, so die Ecke.
Woman, 38: Ja, genau. Hannover auf jeden Fall. Ich glaube, sie haben die sauberste Sprache.
(Fieldworker: Where is standard German spoken?
Woman, 38: In the north.
Man, 17: No, in Lower Saxony. The area around Hanover.
Woman, 38: Yes, exactly. Hanover, absolutely. I think they have the cleanest language.)

The change in the easterners' perceptions from 1994 to 1995 can also be confirmed by an analysis of the variance. Table 14.3 shows the statistical significance of the effects of whether the informants are easterners or westerners, as well as whether they participated in the 1994 study or the 1995 study. Eastern or western origin of informant is significant at 0.0005, indicating that easterners generally have different perceptions from westerners, regardless of the year. The year alone is not revealed as significant, which suggests that there is no overall difference in perception from one year to the next. The most relevant finding, though, is that the interaction between the two variables is significant at 0.005. This reveals that the easterners' change in perception of where 'correct' German is spoken is not only a noticeable trend, but a statistically significant one.

Table 14.3 Factors influencing the difference (ratio) between perceptions of the 'correctness' of Hanover language and the 'correctness' of northern German language generally

Source of variation	Significance
Geographical origin of informant (east or west)	0.0005
Year (1994 or 1995)	n.s.
Year (1994 or 1995) interacting with geographical origin of informant (east or west)	0.005
Entire statistical model	0.0005

R-squared = 0.28

When I asked easterners directly about Hanover as the most 'correct' German, much as I had the previous year, the plot thickened even more. Many of them were uncomfortable about what I was investigating, thinking that I was revealing a major ignorance on the part of the easterners about the 'truth' about standard German. They often protested, saying that they had 'no way of knowing' that the most correct German is spoken in Hanover, since they were not allowed to go there until 1989. In other words, they had accepted the idea that Hanover was the centre of spoken standard German as a 'fact' to 'know', not something that westerners believed but which they disagreed with.

As previously mentioned, I also enquired in the 1995 study about several other pieces of demographic information about the informants, and was able to examine which of these variables play a role here by means of an analysis of the variance. The results of this test are shown in Table 14.4. Probably unsurprisingly from what we already know, the greatest influence is, indeed, eastern or western origin of informant. Yet two other variables play a role as well. Although education is not significant alone, more educated easterners have a greater tendency to view the difference between the 'correctness' of Hanover and of northern Germany as small or non-existent (with a mean of 0.88 for those with a college or university education, and a mean of 0.78 for those with no higher education), yielding a significant interaction between western or eastern origin and level of education. Political party affiliation is also significant here, but only for easterners. Easterners who vote for the PDS (the new party formed from the former East German Communist Party) are much less likely to view the language of Hanover as being superior to northern Germany in general than those

Table 14.4   Additional factors influencing the difference (ratio) between perceptions of the 'correctness' of Hanover language and the 'correctness' of northern German language generally (1995 data only)

Source of variation	Significance
Geographical origin of informant (east or west)	0.0005
Level of education	n.s.
Political affiliation	n.s.
Level of education interacting with geographical origin of informant (east or west)	0.05
Political affiliation interacting with geographical origin of informant (east or west)	0.05
Entire statistical model	0.0005

R-squared = 0.36

who vote for other political parties (the PDS voters have a mean of 1.10, while the others have a mean of 0.84), which causes a significant interaction between western or eastern origin and political party affiliation as well.

Summary of findings

What is it, then, that we know about attitudes towards language variation in post-unification Germany? In the 1994 study, easterners and westerners clearly had two competing standard language ideologies, with westerners contending that the most 'correct' German is spoken in Hanover and easterners contending that it is spoken in the whole of northern Germany. One year later, in the present study, there is a strong new tendency for easterners to adopt the western ideology that the most 'correct' German is spoken in Hanover. Yet this tendency is mitigated or blocked in easterners with certain characteristics: a high level of education and political affiliation with the PDS.

This is almost certainly not a single event that began in 1994 and ended in 1995, but a glimpse at a process which began with the fall of the Berlin Wall in 1989 and is still ongoing. Although the process may be quite a fight, as a significant minority of easterners seem reluctant to agree that the only truly 'correct' German is spoken in the west, it seems likely that the western German standard language ideology that the most 'correct' German is spoken in Hanover will prevail, and that the eastern German language ideology will take the path of the East German car, the 'Trabant', and so many former East German laws.

It is the case that in the more recent of these two studies, easterners and westerners largely agree on the 'correctness' of western language. Yet while easterners tend to believe the language of the east is no better and no worse than that of the west, westerners rate the language of the east as consistently less 'correct' than that of the west. This indicates, perhaps, that while easterners want linguistic acceptance from westerners, westerners want linguistic distance from easterners. It is important to mention, however, that these findings only reflect a change in language *attitudes*, not a change in language *use*. There is no evidence in this study that eastern Germans are suddenly attempting to emulate the variety spoken in Hanover, but simply that they are coming to believe that the Hanover variety is the variety closest to a spoken standard language (though other studies, such as Barden, Chapter 13, this volume, have indicated that there may be some accommodation in language itself as well, at least among those easterners who move to the west).

Possible consequences of standard language ideology

Labov (1991:121) refers to a speech community as being defined by 'participation in a shared set of norms', and on one hand it seems natural that if the two Germanies are now one country, they will also eventually become a single speech community. Yet it is not a coincidence that it is the western German language ideology and not the eastern one that is becoming the sole language ideology in a unified Germany. Lippi-Green (1997:173) writes that 'standard language ideology is concerned not so much with the choice of one possible variant, but with the elimination of *socially unacceptable* difference. This is externalized in the targeting of particular variants linked to specific social identities.' What is being 'targeted' here, whether consciously or subconsciously, is an East German or eastern German social identity. Post-unification Germany is a place where two countries have become • one country, not by force, but by popular opinion on the part of a majority of eastern Germans, who voluntarily voted their country out of existence. It is a place where two countries came together which were *not* seen as equals: West Germany had the greater economic power, greater population, greater land mass, and its political system was regarded as the one which had succeeded while the other had failed. It is a place which, after unification, took on the name of former West Germany, the constitution of former West Germany, and the laws of former West Germany. Maintaining an eastern identity in post-unification Germany means being accused of being nostalgic for an old way of life which did not work. Adopting a western German language ideology, therefore, like buying western German cars and participating in a new western German political system, is a way of showing that one has moved forward.

Although studies such as this one could be replicated in most any other society, this kind of study is essential in situations such as post-unification Germany, because standard language ideology is one of the most important tools a society uses to help determine official language policy in arenas such as education (Williams *et al.* 1976), the media (Lippi-Green 1997:133–51), the courts (Lippi-Green 1994), as well as something as simple as whether or not a certain person is hired for a certain job (Rey 1977). While language attitudes and language ideology are arguably inevitable phenomena arising from society as a whole, if they are allowed to influence behaviour and official policy to any great degree, difficult consequences can occur for speakers of stigmatized varieties.

That can be a rather frightening idea if we take that into account while looking at some of the commentary that has been made about these issues. An 18-year-old man from central western Germany summed up one potential problem by saying:

> Also wenn ich zum Beispiel beim Kundendienst anrufe, ist es ganz angenehm, daß derjenige jetzt normal spricht, und nicht wenn dir da ein Sachse so entgegenhaut, der so richtig so: 'Wömit gann isch Ihnen helfen' sagt.
> (Well, when I call customer service, it's really nice if the person I'm talking to speaks normally, and not if some Saxon starts in, pronouncing 'Womit kann ich Ihnen helfen'[how can I help you] as: 'Wömit gann isch Ihnen helfen'.)

This is expressed even more clearly by a 32-year-old man from the southern part of western Germany. When I asked him whether speakers who spoke a variety viewed as non-standard would have trouble getting a job in a bank where he lives, he had this to say:

> Man, 32: Ein Bayer hätte kein Problem, diesen Job zu bekommen.
> Fieldworker: Aber wenn's ein Hesse ist, und man weiß sofort, wo er herkommt?
> Man, 32: Nein, ich glaub' der hätte auch kein Problem. Glaub' ich überhaupt nicht.
> Fieldworker: Und wenn's ein Sachse ist?

Man, 32: Na gut, also ... das ist etwas anderes ... du mußt verstehen, wir haben diese Sprache vierzig Jahr' nit gehört. Und die ist vollkommen andersartig. Sicherlich gibt es angenehme Leut', auch gute Leut', aber von dem, was ich bisher gesehen hab', naja ... Sächsisch, des is' so ne Sprach', als würde man alle fünfzig Sekunden zu kotzen anfangen, so [vomiting noise].
(Man, 32: A Bavarian [the region in south western Germany where the informant is from]) would have no trouble getting this job.'
Fieldworker: 'But what if it's a Hessian [a region in central western Germany], and it's really obvious where he's from?'
Man, 32: 'No, I don't think he would have a problem either. I don't believe that at all.'
Fieldworker: 'And if it's a Saxon? [a region in central eastern Germany].
Man, 32: Okay, well, um that's different ... you have to understand, we didn't hear that language for forty years. And it's totally different [from anything we'd heard before]. I'm sure there are nice people, good people over there too, but from what I've seen so far, well ... Saxon German is a language that sounds like they're starting to puke every fifty seconds, like this: [vomiting noise].)

Finally, an advertisement for an accent-reduction school found in a newspaper in one of Saxony's largest cities indicated very succinctly just how connected Saxon German has become with all things eastern:

Sächsischer Dialekt in der freien Marktwirtschaft? Undenkbar! Nehmen Sie Sprechunterricht!
(Saxon dialect in a free market economy? Unthinkable! Take accent-reduction courses.)

These are, of course, only isolated examples of how language attitudes affect life in Germany, and whether discrimination based on accent or dialect actually occurs in a widespread way is an open question. But it is not at all unlikely, despite laws forbidding it. Article 3,3 of the Basic Law of the Federal Republic of Germany clearly reads (italics mine):

Niemand darf wegen seines Geschlechts, seiner Abstammung, seiner Rasse, *seiner Sprache,* seiner Heimat und Herkunft, seines Glaubens, seiner religiösen oder politischen Anschauungen benachteiligt oder bevorzugt werden.

● (No one may be disadvantaged or advantaged because of his or her sex, ancestry, race, *language*, national origin, faith, or religious or political beliefs.)

Yet despite this, the vast majority of the cases prosecuted under that law thus far have been cases involving people whose native language is not German, and the vast majority of the legal commentary on this article has centred on the rights of the Danish-speaking minority in northern Germany and of foreign workers (von Münch 1981:206, Hamann, Hamann and Lenz 1970:171–172; Hoffmann 1970:23–72). In other words, nearly all of the cases which people have thought to try have been cases involving actual *other languages* rather than variation within German.[4]

In fact, the only legal commentary which mentions the possibility of this article applying to speakers of stigmatized German varieties (Maunz, Dürig and Herzog 1984:316) takes a distressing stance, at least with respect to education, by saying:

Die Mundart schafft allenfalls für den ersten Kontakt Nähe und Gleichheit für die, die sie kennen. Für jeden neuzuziehenden Schüler wirkt sie als Sperre (vor allem, wenn wie z.B. in Schwaben nochmals von Ort zu Ort Dialekte variieren). Insgesamt erschwert sie in einer mobilen Gesellschaft die Gleichheit der Startchancen (anderwärts) und vermindert sie allen gleich zustehenden Informations- und Kommunikationsmöglichkeiten im Gesamtstaat. ... Daß geringer Wortschatz, grammatische Ungewandtheit, auf einen Dialekt verengter Sondersprachgebrauch usw. als Bildungssperren wirken können, leugnet kein Mensch ... Kompensation, Hilfen für 'unterprivilegierte' Eltern und Kinder, Anheben auf das Niveau der Hochsprache, sind zweifelsfrei verfassungsrechtliches Gleichheitsgebot.
(The dialect certainly creates closeness and equality when meeting someone new, for those who speak it. Yet for every student who moves in later it serves as a barrier (most of all when, as for example in Swabia, the dialects vary even from town to town). Generally, [speaking a dialect] makes it difficult to have equal opportunities for upward mobility in a society in which people move from place to place, and diminishes ways to access information and communicate within the federal state, ways that belong to everyone equally. ... No one contests the fact that a small vocabulary, lack of grammatical skill, unusual language usage that can be traced back to a dialect, etc., can serve as educational barriers ... Compensation, help for

'underprivileged' parents and children, raising [the dialect speaker] up to the level of the standard language, these are undoubtedly ways to promote equality guaranteed under constitutional law.)

The author first recognizes what he sees as the benefits of speaking a stigmatized variety: it creates closeness and equality among those who speak it. However, the disadvantages seem to outweigh the advantages, since speaking a stigmatized variety is said to lower your chances of getting anywhere in life. Worse still, this author associates the speaking of a stigmatized variety with a small vocabulary and a lack of grammatical skill, both of which would be considered completely false claims by linguists. He then proposes a solution to this 'problem': since the German basic law guarantees that no one should be discriminated against based on language, compensatory education aimed at 'raising the child up to the level of the standard language' is suggested as a way of coping with this situation legally.

The issue of education and language variation is certainly a thorny one, and it certainly makes sense to take practical considerations very seriously. After all, the children this author is writing about may one day wish to function in a society that does *not* regard their language as equal to all others. Yet couching one's arguments in a 'common-sense' language ideology framework and referring to stigmatized language varieties as inherently inadequate indirectly attacks their identity through their language. In doing so, the author also reveals a double standard: the notion that people suffering ethnic discrimination should change other manifestations of their identity (such as religious holiday observances and particular kinds of clothing) would be considered still more discrimination, yet when it comes to language the standard language ideology is so pervasive that these proposed solutions are considered appropriate. Although practical considerations certainly cannot be completely disregarded, it is interesting that so far no one in the German courts has thought to challenge this view, despite an article in the constitution explicitly banning discrimination based on language.

This brings us to the central question this study raises: why are eastern Germans, who are at a disadvantage under the western language ideology, so quick to give up their own language ideology, an ideology which excluded everything outside northern Germany but did not state that there were no varieties in the east as good as a particular western one? Why are eastern Germans changing their beliefs from the notion that 'standard German' is spoken all over the north (including the northeast) to believing that it is spoken only in a city in the northwest? One possible answer may be found in one of the studies mentioned at the beginning of this chapter, a study carried out in the eastern German city of Jena (Kanning and Mummendey 1993). They find that there are many strategies which are used to compensate for eastern Germans' 'negative social identity', but by far the most common one *is the assimilation to the western German norm.* In this study the very same thing is true. Many easterners in this study have very negative associations with their own and other eastern varieties, and feel they must find a way to compensate for this. In the 1994 study, the eastern and western language ideologies were much clearer and more distinct, yet this study indicates that eastern Germans feel that they have a 'negative social identity' not only with respect to financial matters, political influence and social behaviour, but also with respect to language, and easterners have therefore begun assimilating to the western German norm.

Of course, the data for this study was gathered in 1994 and 1995, and one could argue that in a rapidly changing process such as the one in post-unification Germany, the tendencies seen here may since have stopped or even reversed. Indeed, it is the case that recent years have seen many examples of eastern Germans reclaiming an eastern identity as a positive thing, as levels of eastern dissatisfaction with the current socio-political situation have increased and Germans have begun to speak more openly about this. Dance clubs in Berlin hold special evenings where they reinstate the old quota system for East German rock. A campaign was begun to preserve the 'Ampelmännchen', the uniquely eastern characters who appear on traffic lights. Certain eastern German bakeries have gone back to old pre-unification materials and recipes, and even advertise that they bake bread the way they used to (see also Kelly-Holmes, Chapter 6, this volume). Jokes about 'stupid easterners' in the west are now considered too politically incorrect for many circles. Yet all of these examples are very overt and deliberate changes. A standard language ideology is far more insidious. Beliefs about 'good' and 'bad' language are so often seen as unchangeable facts that people simply do not think of looking at things in another way. While it is not *impossible* that many eastern Germans have since reclaimed their former standard language ideology along with the bread and the 'Ampelmännchen', it seems more likely that the process has stopped short of encompassing beliefs about language, and that easterners have simply accepted the western standard language ideology as a fact that they could not possibly have been aware of before the fall of the Berlin Wall. And that standard language ideology provides a 'back door' opportunity for discrimination which, despite prescriptions of 'political correctness' in other areas of life, can be considered completely appropriate.

Eagleton, who refers to the study of ideology as the study of 'ways in which people may come to invest in their own unhappiness' (1991:xiii), states that 'it is because being oppressed sometimes brings with it some slim bonuses that we are occasionally prepared to put up with it' (1991:xiv). Eastern Germans, and particularly central eastern Germans, are not only told that their way of speaking is wrong, but that there is a particular right way of doing so *in the west*, and that they must change their language in order to overcome an inferior social position. Perhaps it is easier simply to comply with this and reap the slim bonuses promised than to fight it. This is disconcerting, because language attitudes and language ideology have been demonstrated to affect official language policy. If easterners are beginning to hear – and believe – that the only truly 'correct' variety of German is spoken in a city in northwestern Germany, eastern Germans might very well find themselves at a linguistic disadvantage in a unified Germany.

Notes

1 All quotations from informants were originally in German, and all translations are my own.
2 'Fleischer' is the term for 'butcher' normally used in eastern Germany, while 'Metzger' is normally used in south and central western Germany (Clyne 1995:89).
3 I did not define for my informants what criteria they should use to measure 'correctness'. In the qualitative data, however, whenever informants commented on particular linguistic features it became clear that their judgements were based on a combination of phonological and grammatical features of the varieties they were commenting on.
4 The one exception to this was the 1998 case of a Saxon German-speaking salesman who was told by his western German employer that no one in the west would be willing to buy products from someone with such a strong accent, and subsequently fired. He won his case, but the situation was subsequently made fun of at great length in the *Tagesspiegel* and in the *tageszeitung*.

References

Becker, Ulrich, Horst Becker and Walter Ruhland (1992) *Zwichen Angst und Aufbruch: das Lebensgefühl der Deutschen in Ost und West nach der Wiedervereinigung* (Düsseldorf, Vienna, New York, Moscow: ECON Verlag).
Chambers, J. K. (1995) *Sociolinguistic Theory: Linguistic Variation and its Social Significance* (Oxford: Blackwell).
Clyne, Michael (1995) *The German Language in a Changing Europe* (Cambridge: Cambridge University Press).

Dailey-O'Cain, Jennifer (1997) 'Geographic and socio-political influences on language ideology and attitudes toward language variation in post-unification Germany', PhD dissertation, University of Michigan.

Dailey-O' Cain, Jennifer (1999) 'Perceptions of post-unification German speech', in Preston (1999), 239–59.

Eagleton, Terry (1991) *Ideology: An Introduction* (London: Verso).

Emnid-Institut (1995) 'Stolz aufs eigene Leben', in *Der Spiegel* 27 (March), 40–52.

Hamann, Andreas, Andreas Hamann Jr and Helmut Lenz (1970) *Das Grundgesetz für die Bundesrepublik Deutschland vom 23. Mai 1949: Ein Kommentar für Wissenschaft und Praxis*, 3rd edn (Neuwied, Berlin: Luchterhand).

Hoffmann, Rudolf (1970) 'Das Diskriminierungsverbot bei der Beschäftigung ausländischer Arbeitnehmer in Deutschland', PhD dissertation.

Kanning, Uwe Peter and Amélie Mummendey (1993) 'Soziale Vergleichsprozesse und die Bewältigung "negativer sozialer Identität": eine Feldstudie in Ostdeutschland', in *Zeitschrift für Sozialpsychologie* 24/3, 211–17.

Labov, William (1969) 'The logic of non-standard English', in *Georgetown Monographs on Language and Linguistics* 22, 1–31.

Labov, William (1991) *Sociolinguistic Patterns*, originally printed 1969 (Philadelphia: University of Pennsylvania Press).

Lambert, Wallace, R. Hodgson, R. Gardner and S. Fillenbaum (1960) 'Evaluational reactions to spoken language', in *Journal of Abnormal and Social Psychology* 60, 44–51.

Lippi-Green, Rosina (1994) 'Accent, standard language ideology, and discriminatory pretext in the courts', in *Language in Society* 23, 163–98.

Lippi-Green, Rosina (1997) *English with an Accent: Language and Discrimination in the United States* (London: Routledge).

Maunz, Theodor, Günter Dürig and Roman Herzog (eds) (1984) *Grundgesetz Kommentar* 1 (articles 1–37) (Munich: C. H. Beck'sche Verlagsbuchhandlung).

Milroy, Lesley (1980) *Language and Social Networks* (Oxford: Blackwell).

Milroy, James and Lesley Milroy (1985) *Authority in Language: Investigating Language Prescription and Standardisation* (London, New York: Routledge).

Münch, Ingo von (ed.) (1981)*Grundgesetz Kommentar* 1 (preamble to article 20), 2nd edn (Munich: C. H. Beck'sche Verlagsbuchhandlung).

Pool, Jonathan (1979) 'Language planning and identity planning', in *International Journal of the Sociology of Language* 20, 5–21.

Preston, Dennis (1989) *Perceptual Dialectology* (Dordrecht: Foris).

Preston, Dennis (ed.) (1999) *Handbook of Perceptual Dialectology*, Vol. 1 (Amsterdam/Philadelphia: Benjamins).

Rey, Alberto (1977) 'Accent and employability', in *Language Sciences* 47, 7–12.

Silverstein, Michael (1992) 'The uses and utility of ideology: some reflections', in *Pragmatics* 2/3, 311–24.

Williams, Frederick, Nancy Hewitt, Robert Hopper, Leslie M. Miller, Rita C. Naremore, and Jack L. Whitehead (1976) *Explorations of the Linguistic Attitudes of Teachers* (Rowley, MA: Newbury House).

Woolard, Kathryn A. (1992) 'Language ideology: issues and approaches' in *Pragmatics* 2/3, 235–50.

Woolard, Kathryn A. and Bambi Schieffelin (1994) 'Language ideology', in *Annual Review of Anthropology* 23, 55–82.

15
Conclusions

Patrick Stevenson and John Theobald

Studies of *Wende*-discourses have shown how the GDR was talked out of existence. In this book, authors from different disciplines explore the failure to date to talk a new united Germany into existence. Collectively, they show some of the ways in which the struggle to achieve (or resist) this goal has been enacted both discursively and interactionally. The aim of the book has been to show how and why, after ten years of political and economic unification, social and cultural disunity persists, for reasons which go beyond those normally cited, such as differences in economic development, in levels of (un)employment and pay, and in material prosperity. In exploring this question from a linguistic perspective, we can see how the effects of discourses and communicative practices depend on each other, and how, in order to understand continuing cultural differences between east and west, we need to investigate both discourses *of* and *about* Germanness on the one hand, and language use *by*, and interaction *between*, Germans on the other.

In the course of the book, it becomes clear that reductive *Wende*-discourses which centred on seductive dichotomies, such as freedom versus repression, and the simplified symbolism of media images disguised the fact that the 40 years of division had seen the complex development of profoundly different social cultures. These cultures had become firmly rooted in the traditions of life in all the social units in which the respective societies were organized: families, youth organizations, political parties, places of employment, and so on. Furthermore, they were all associated with forms of talk, both in the sense of discourses (of education, socialization, political, media, cultural and historiographical representations, and so forth), and in the sense of communicative practices (address patterns, interaction in institutional settings such as classroom or courtroom, workplace or Parliament, the rituals of formalized speech events as diverse as the *Jugendweihe*, television or job interviews, buying or selling). However, it has emerged that while the social and economic infrastructure of the GDR, from its currency to its education system and even its place and street names, was replaced with great alacrity by the west German model, it was simply impossible for one set of forms of talk to be abandoned overnight. Moreover, it was to misread the complex needs, desires and aspirations of the east German population to imagine that they would necessarily want to do so. In many significant areas, long-standing 'communities of practice' (Eckert and McConnell-Ginet 1998) seem to be offering a tangible source of continuity and security in a rapidly changing social environment.

The dominant common thread which runs through the contributions, and which confirms both methodological approaches, is the constant reiteration, in multiple forms, of discursive denigration of east Germans, and their corresponding adoption of communicative strategies manifesting or reacting to inferior status, be it through selective amnesia, accommodation, humour, self-justification or protest. There is a great deal of further work to be done which will deepen and possibly contest the work published here, but the contributions in this volume, taken in the context of other ongoing work, may be seen as evidence of a developing critical mass, on the basis of which cultural needs and actions may be defined. We are now at a point where, in the post-Kohl era, the phase of eastern reactive criticism may start to blend with credible attempts at tactful assertion of more positive eastern memories, traditions and perspectives, compensating the asymmetries that Habermas rightly observed and bemoaned, not by rebounding off western clumsiness, but rather by adding authentically voiced eastern discourses which will resonate in western as well as eastern consciousness. This could eventually have the function of letting more confident easterners and somewhat chastened westerners speak to each other as equals. Should it start to come about, this will not be a straightforward or complete process, where respect is gained and given across German society and culture from one moment to the next. The false compensation of *Ostalgie* has already made its appearance, and there is, for example, an evident possibility that one reified myth of the GDR and those associated with it, past and present, will simply be replaced by another without working through the intrinsic human level complexities and pluralities, and the extrinsic relationship with equally problematized western identities. However, if reliable and mutually reinforcing diagnoses of the nature and causes of diverging discourses and communicative dissonance are emerging, and if (with the help of these diagnoses) ways can be envisaged of turning east-west German discord into counterpoint, then those pursuing research of the kind exemplified in this book will have contributed their grain of influence to positive cultural change.

References

Coates, Jennifer (ed.) (1998) *Language and Gender: A Reader* (Oxford: Blackwell).

Eckert, Penelope and Sally McConnell-Ginet (1998) 'Communities of practice: Where language, gender, and power all live', in Coates (1998), 484–94.

Index